Alister Ross.
April 1959.

OXFORD LECTURES ON POETRY

OXFORD LECTURES ON POETRY

BY

A. C. BRADLEY

LL.D., LITT.D.

FORMERLY PROFESSOR OF POETRY IN THE UNIVERSITY OF OXFORD
AND FELLOW OF BALLIOL COLLEGE

LONDON
MACMILLAN & CO LTD
NEW YORK · ST MARTIN'S PRESS
1955

MACMILLAN AND COMPANY LIMITED
London Bombay Calcutta Madras Melbourne

THE MACMILLAN COMPANY OF CANADA LIMITED
Toronto

ST MARTIN'S PRESS INC
New York

First Edition, May 1909. Second Edition, November 1909
Reprinted 1911, 1914, 1917, 1919, 1920, 1923, 1926, 1934,
1941, 1950, 1955

PRINTED IN GREAT BRITAIN

PREFACE

THIS volume consists of lectures delivered during my tenure of the Chair of Poetry at Oxford and not included in *Shakespearean Tragedy*. Most of them have been enlarged, and all have been revised. As they were given at intervals, and the majority before the publication of that book, they contained repetitions which I have not found it possible wholly to remove. Readers of a lecture published by the University of Manchester on *English Poetry and German Philosophy in the Age of Wordsworth* will pardon also the restatement of some ideas expressed in it.

The several lectures are dated, as I have been unable to take account of most of the literature on their subjects published since they were delivered.

They are arranged in the order that seems best to me, but it is of importance only in the case of the four which deal with the poets of Wordsworth's time.

I am indebted to the Delegates of the University Press, and to the proprietors and editors of the *Hibbert Journal* and the *Albany, Fortnightly*, and *Quarterly Reviews*, respectively, for permission to republish the first, third, fifth, eighth, and ninth lectures. A like acknowledgment is due for leave to use some sentences of an article on Keats contributed to *Chambers's Cyclopaedia of English Literature* (1903).

In the revision of the proof-sheets I owed much help to a sister who has shared many of my Oxford friendships.

NOTE TO THE SECOND EDITION

THIS edition is substantially identical with the first; but it and its later impressions contain a few improvements in points of detail, and, thanks to criticisms by my brother, F. H. Bradley, I hope to have made my meaning clearer in some pages of the second lecture.

There was an oversight in the first edition which I regret. In adding the note on p. 247 I forgot that I had not referred to Professor Dowden in the lecture on " Shakespeare the Man." In everything that I have written on Shakespeare I am indebted to Professor Dowden, and certainly not least in that lecture.

PREFACE

THIS volume consists of lectures delivered during my tenure of the Chair of Poetry at Oxford and not included in *Shakespearean Tragedy*. Most of them have been enlarged, and all have been revised. As they were given at intervals, and the majority before the publication of that book, they contained repetitions which I have not found it possible wholly to remove. Readers of a lecture published by the University of Manchester on *English Poetry and German Philosophy in the Age of Wordsworth* will pardon also the restatement of some ideas expressed in it.

The several lectures are dated, as I have been unable to take account of most of the literature on their subjects published since they were delivered.

They are arranged in the order that seems best to me, but it is of importance only in the case of the four which deal with the poets of Wordsworth's time.

I am indebted to the Delegates of the University Press, and to the proprietors and editors of the *Hibbert Journal* and the *Albany*, *Fortnightly*, and *Quarterly Reviews*, respectively, for permission to republish the first, third, fifth, eighth, and ninth lectures. A like acknowledgment is due for leave to use some sentences of an article on Keats contributed to *Chambers's Cyclopaedia of English Literature* (1903).

In the revision of the proof-sheets I owed much help to a sister who has shared many of my Oxford friendships.

NOTE TO THE SECOND EDITION

THIS edition is substantially identical with the first; but it and its later impressions contain a few improvements in points of detail, and, thanks to criticisms by my brother, F. H. Bradley, I hope to have made my meaning clearer in some pages of the second lecture.

There was an oversight in the first edition which I regret. In adding the note on p. 247 I forgot that I had not referred to Professor Dowden in the lecture on "Shakespeare the Man." In everything that I have written on Shakespeare I am indebted to Professor Dowden, and certainly not least in that lecture.

CONTENTS

		PAGE
Poetry for Poetry's Sake		3
The Sublime		37
Hegel's Theory of Tragedy		69
Wordsworth		99
Shelley's View of Poetry		151
The Long Poem in the Age of Wordsworth		177
The Letters of Keats		209
The Rejection of Falstaff		247
Shakespeare's Antony and Cleopatra		279
Shakespeare the Man		311
Shakespeare's Theatre and Audience		361

POETRY FOR POETRY'S SAKE

POETRY FOR POETRY'S SAKE[1]

(INAUGURAL LECTURE)

ONE who, after twenty years, is restored to the University where he was taught and first tried to teach, and who has received at the hands of his Alma Mater an honour of which he never dreamed, is tempted to speak both of himself and of her. But I remember that you have come to listen to my thoughts about a great subject, and not to my feelings about myself; and of Oxford who that holds this Professorship could dare to speak, when he recalls the exquisite verse in which one of his predecessors described her beauty, and the prose in which he gently touched on her illusions and protested that they were as nothing when set against her age-long warfare with the Philistine? How, again, remembering him and others, should I venture to praise my predecessors? It would be pleasant to do so, and even pleasanter to me and you if, instead of lecturing, I quoted to you some of their best passages. But I could not do this for five years. Sooner or later, my own words would have

[1] The lecture, as printed in 1901, was preceded by the following note: "This Lecture is printed almost as it was delivered. I am aware that, especially in the earlier pages, difficult subjects are treated in a manner far too summary, but they require an exposition so full that it would destroy the original form of the Lecture, while a slight expansion would do little to provide against misunderstandings." A few verbal changes have now been made, some notes have been added, and some of the introductory remarks omitted.

to come, and the inevitable contrast. Not to sharpen
it now, I will be silent concerning them also; and
will only assure you that I do not forget them, or
the greatness of the honour of succeeding them,
or the responsibility which it entails.

The words 'Poetry for poetry's sake' recall the
famous phrase 'Art for Art.' It is far from my
purpose to examine the possible meanings of that
phrase, or all the questions it involves. I propose
to state briefly what I understand by 'Poetry for
poetry's sake,' and then, after guarding against one
or two misapprehensions of the formula, to consider
more fully a single problem connected with it. And
I must premise, without attempting to justify them,
certain explanations. We are to consider poetry in
its essence, and apart from the flaws which in most
poems accompany their poetry. We are to include
in the idea of poetry the metrical form, and not to
regard this as a mere accident or a mere vehicle.
And, finally, poetry being poems, we are to think of
a poem as it actually exists; and, without aiming
here at accuracy, we may say that an actual poem
is the succession of experiences—sounds, images,
thoughts, emotions—through which we pass when
we are reading as poetically as we can.[1] Of course
this imaginative experience—if I may use the phrase
for brevity—differs with every reader and every
time of reading: a poem exists in innumerable
degrees. But that insurmountable fact lies in the
nature of things and does not concern us now.

What then does the formula 'Poetry for poetry's
sake' tell us about this experience? It says, as I
understand it, these things. First, this experience
is an end in itself, is worth having on its own
account, has an intrinsic value. Next, its *poetic*
value is this intrinsic worth alone. Poetry may
have also an ulterior value as a means to culture or

[1] Note A.

religion; because it conveys instruction, or softens the passions, or furthers a good cause; because it brings the poet fame or money or a quiet conscience. So much the better: let it be valued for these reasons too. But its ulterior worth neither is nor can directly determine its poetic worth as a satisfying imaginative experience; and this is to be judged entirely from within. And to these two positions the formula would add, though not of necessity, a third. The consideration of ulterior ends, whether by the poet in the act of composing or by the reader in the act of experiencing, tends to lower poetic value. It does so because it tends to change the nature of poetry by taking it out of its own atmosphere. For its nature is to be not a part, nor yet a copy, of the real world (as we commonly understand that phrase), but to be a world by itself, independent, complete, autonomous; and to possess it fully you must enter that world, conform to its laws, and ignore for the time the beliefs, aims, and particular conditions which belong to you in the other world of reality.

Of the more serious misapprehensions to which these statements may give rise I will glance only at one or two. The offensive consequences often drawn from the formula 'Art for Art' will be found to attach not to the doctrine that Art is an end in itself, but to the doctrine that Art is the whole or supreme end of human life. And as this latter doctrine, which seems to me absurd, is in any case quite different from the former, its consequences fall outside my subject. The formula ' Poetry is an end in itself' has nothing to say on the various questions of moral judgment which arise from the fact that poetry has its place in a many-sided life. For anything it says, the intrinsic value of poetry might be so small, and its ulterior effects so mischievous, that it had better not exist. The formula only tells us that we must not place in antithesis poetry and

human good, for poetry is one kind of human good;
and that we must not determine the intrinsic value
of this kind of good by direct reference to another.
If we do, we shall find ourselves maintaining what
we did not expect. If poetic value lies in the stimulation of religious feelings, *Lead, kindly Light* is no
better a poem than many a tasteless version of a
Psalm : if in the excitement of patriotism, why is
Scots, wha hae superior to *We don't want to fight*?
if in the mitigation of the passions, the Odes of
Sappho will win but little praise : if in instruction,
Armstrong's *Art of preserving Health* should win
much.

Again, our formula may be accused of cutting
poetry away from its connection with life. And this
accusation raises so huge a problem that I must ask
leave to be dogmatic as well as brief. There is
plenty of connection between life and poetry, but it
is, so to say, a connection underground. The two
may be called different forms of the same thing: one
of them having (in the usual sense) reality, but
seldom fully satisfying imagination ; while the other
offers something which satisfies imagination but has
not full 'reality.' They are parallel developments
which nowhere meet, or, if I may use loosely a word
which will be serviceable later, they are analogues.
Hence we understand one by help of the other, and
even, in a sense, care for one because of the other ;
but hence also, poetry neither is life, nor, strictly
speaking, a copy of it. They differ not only because
one has more mass and the other a more perfect
shape, but because they have different *kinds* of
existence. The one touches us as beings occupying
a given position in space and time, and having
feelings, desires, and purposes due to that position :
it appeals to imagination, but appeals to much
besides. What meets us in poetry has not a position in the same series of time and space, or, if it has
or had such a position, it is taken apart from much

that belonged to it there;[1] and therefore it makes
no direct appeal to those feelings, desires, and purposes, but speaks only to contemplative imagination
—imagination the reverse of empty or emotionless,
imagination saturated with the results of 'real'
experience, but still contemplative.   Thus, no doubt,
one main reason why poetry has poetic value for us
is that it presents to us in its own way something
which we meet in another form in nature or life; and
yet the test of its poetic value for us lies simply in
the question whether it satisfies our imagination; the
rest of us, our knowledge or conscience, for example,
judging it only so far as they appear transmuted in
our imagination.   So also Shakespeare's knowledge
or his moral insight, Milton's greatness of soul,
Shelley's 'hate of hate' and 'love of love,' and that
desire to help men or make them happier which may
have influenced a poet in hours of meditation—all
these have, as such, no poetical worth: they have
that worth only when, passing through the unity
of the poet's being, they reappear as qualities of
imagination, and then are indeed mighty powers
in the world of poetry.

I come to a third misapprehension, and so to my
main subject.   This formula, it is said, empties
poetry of its meaning: it is really a doctrine of form
for form's sake.   'It is of no consequence what a
poet says, so long as he says the thing well.   The
what is poetically indifferent: it is the *how* that
counts.   Matter, subject, content, substance, deter-
mines nothing; there is no subject with which
poetry may not deal: the form, the treatment, is
everything.   Nay, more: not only is the matter
indifferent, but it is the secret of Art to "eradicate
the matter by means of the form,"'—phrases and
statements like these meet us everywhere in current
criticism of literature and the other arts.   They

[1] Note B.

are the stock-in-trade of writers who understand of them little more than the fact that somehow or other they are not 'bourgeois.' But we find them also seriously used by writers whom we must respect, whether they are anonymous or not; something like one or another of them might be quoted, for example, from Professor Saintsbury, the late R. A. M. Stevenson, Schiller, Goethe himself; and they are the watchwords of a school in the one country where Aesthetics has flourished. They come, as a rule, from men who either practise one of the arts, or, from study of it, are interested in its methods. The general reader—a being so general that I may say what I will of him—is outraged by them. He feels that he is being robbed of almost all that he cares for in a work of art. 'You are asking me,' he says, 'to look at the Dresden Madonna as if it were a Persian rug. You are telling me that the poetic value of *Hamlet* lies solely in its style and versification, and that my interest in the man and his fate is only an intellectual or moral interest. You allege that, if I want to enjoy the poetry of *Crossing the Bar*, I must not mind what Tennyson says there, but must consider solely his way of saying it. But in that case I can care no more for a poem than I do for a set of nonsense verses; and I do not believe that the authors of *Hamlet* and *Crossing the Bar* regarded their poems thus.'

These antitheses of subject, matter, substance on the one side, form, treatment, handling on the other, are the field through which I especially want, in this lecture, to indicate a way. It is a field of battle; and the battle is waged for no trivial cause; but the cries of the combatants are terribly ambiguous. Those phrases of the so-called formalist may each mean five or six different things. Taken in one sense they seem to me chiefly true; taken as the general reader not unnaturally takes them, they seem to me false and mischievous. It would be absurd to pre-

tend that I can end in a few minutes a controversy
which concerns the ultimate nature of Art, and leads
perhaps to problems not yet soluble; but we can at
least draw some plain distinctions which, in this
controversy, are too often confused.

In the first place, then, let us take 'subject' in
one particular sense; let us understand by it that
which we have in view when, looking at the title of
an un-read poem, we say that the poet has chosen
this or that for his subject. The subject, in this
sense, so far as I can discover, is generally something, real or imaginary, as it exists in the minds of
fairly cultivated people. The subject of *Paradise
Lost* would be the story of the Fall as that story
exists in the general imagination of a Bible-reading
people. The subject of Shelley's stanzas *To a Skylark* would be the ideas which arise in the mind
of an educated person when, without knowing the
poem, he hears the word 'skylark.' If the title of a
poem conveys little or nothing to us, the 'subject'
appears to be either what we should gather by
investigating the title in a dictionary or other book
of the kind, or else such a brief suggestion as might
be offered by a person who had read the poem, and
who said, for example, that the subject of *The
Ancient Mariner* was a sailor who killed an alba-
tross and suffered for his deed.

Now the subject, in this sense (and I intend to
use the word in no other), is not, as such, inside the
poem, but outside it. The contents of the stanzas
To a Skylark are not the ideas suggested by the
work 'skylark' to the average man; they belong to
Shelley just as much as the language does. The
subject, therefore, is not the matter *of* the poem at
all; and its opposite is not the *form* of the poem,
but the whole poem. The subject is one thing;
the poem, matter and form alike, another thing.
This being so, it is surely obvious that the poetic
value cannot lie in the subject, but lies entirely in

its opposite, the poem. How can the subject determine the value when on one and the same subject
poems may be written of all degrees of merit and
demerit; or when a perfect poem may be composed
on a subject so slight as a pet sparrow, and, if
Macaulay may be trusted, a nearly worthless poem
on a subject so stupendous as the omnipresence of
the Deity? The 'formalist' is here perfectly right.
Nor is he insisting on something unimportant. He
is fighting against our tendency to take the work of
art as a mere copy or reminder of something already
in our heads, or at the best as a suggestion of some
idea as little removed as possible from the familiar.
The sightseer who promenades a picture-gallery,
remarking that this portrait is so like his cousin, or
that landscape the very image of his birthplace, or
who, after satisfying himself that one picture is about
Elijah, passes on rejoicing to discover the subject,
and nothing but the subject, of the next—what
is he but an extreme example of this tendency?
Well, but the very same tendency vitiates much
of our criticism, much criticism of Shakespeare, for
example, which, with all its cleverness and partial
truth, still shows that the critic never passed from
his own mind into Shakespeare's; and it may be
traced even in so fine a critic as Coleridge, as when
he dwarfs the sublime struggle of Hamlet into the
image of his own unhappy weakness. Hazlitt by
no means escaped its influence. Only the third of
that great trio, Lamb, appears almost always to
have rendered the conception of the composer.

Again, it is surely true that we cannot determine
beforehand what subjects are fit for Art, or name
any subject on which a good poem might not
possibly be written. To divide subjects into two
groups, the beautiful or elevating, and the ugly or
vicious, and to judge poems according as their
subjects belong to one of these groups or the other,
is to fall into the same pit, to confuse with our

pre-conceptions the meaning of the poet. What the thing is in the poem he is to be judged by, not by the thing as it was before he touched it ; and how can we venture to say beforehand that he cannot make a true poem out of something which to us was merely alluring or dull or revolting ? The question whether, having done so, he ought to publish his poem ; whether the thing in the poet's work will not be still confused by the incompetent Puritan or the incompetent sensualist with the thing in *his* mind, does not touch this point : it is a further question, one of ethics, not of art. No doubt the upholders of ' Art for art's sake ' will generally be in favour of the courageous course, of refusing to sacrifice the better or stronger part of the public to the weaker or worse ; but their maxim in no way binds them to this view. Rossetti suppressed one of the best of his sonnets, a sonnet chosen for admiration by Tennyson, himself extremely sensitive about the moral effect of poetry ; suppressed it, I believe, because it was called fleshly. One may regret Rossetti's judgment and at the same time respect his scrupulousness ; but in any case he judged in his capacity of citizen, not in his capacity of artist.

So far then the 'formalist' appears to be right. But he goes too far, I think, if he maintains that the subject is indifferent and that all subjects are the same to poetry. And he does not prove his point by observing that a good poem might be written on a pin's head, and a bad one on the Fall of Man. That truth shows that the subject *settles* nothing, but not that it counts for nothing. The Fall of Man is really a more favourable subject than a pin's head. The Fall of Man, that is to say, offers opportunities of poetic effects wider in range and more penetrating in appeal. And the fact is that such a subject, as it exists in the general imagination, has some aesthetic value before the poet touches it. It is, as you may choose to call it, an inchoate poem or the débris of a poem. It is not an abstract idea or a bare isolated fact, but an assemblage of figures, scenes, actions, and events, which already appeal to emotional imagination; and it is already in some degree organized and formed. In spite of this a bad poet would make a bad poem on it; but then we should say he was unworthy of the subject. And we should not say this if he wrote a bad poem on a pin's head. Conversely, a good poem on a pin's head would almost certainly transform its subject far more than a good poem on the Fall of Man. It might revolutionize its subject so completely that we should say, 'The subject may be a pin's head, but the substance of the poem has very little to do with it.'

This brings us to another and a different antithesis. Those figures, scenes, events, that form part of the subject called the Fall of Man, are not the substance of *Paradise Lost*; but in *Paradise Lost* there are figures, scenes, and events resembling them in some degree. These, with much more of the same kind, may be described as its substance, and may then be contrasted with the measured language of the poem, which will be called its form. Subject is the opposite not of form but of the whole poem. Substance is within the poem, and its opposite, form, is also within the poem. I am not criticizing this antithesis at present, but evidently it is quite different from the other. It is practically the distinction used in the old-fashioned criticism of epic and drama, and it flows down, not unsullied, from Aristotle. Addison, for example, in examining *Paradise Lost* considers in order the fable, the characters, and the sentiments; these will be the substance: then he considers the language, that is, the style and numbers; this will be the form. In like manner, the substance or meaning of a lyric may be distinguished from the form.

Now I believe it will be found that a large part
of the controversy we are dealing with arises from
a confusion between these two distinctions of substance and form, and of subject and poem. The
extreme formalist lays his whole weight on the form
because he thinks its opposite is the mere subject.
The general reader is angry, but makes the same
mistake, and gives to the subject praises that rightly
belong to the substance.[1]   I will read an example of
what I mean. I can only explain the following
words of a good critic by supposing that for the
moment he has fallen into this confusion : 'The
mere matter of all poetry—to wit, the appearances
of nature and the thoughts and feelings of men—
being unalterable, it follows that the difference between poet and poet will depend upon the manner
of each in applying language, metre, rhyme, cadence,
and what not, to this invariable material.' What
has become here of the substance of *Paradise Lost*—
the story, scenery, characters, sentiments, as they
are in the poem ? They have vanished clean away.
Nothing is left but the form on one side, and on the
other not even the subject, but a supposed invariable material, the appearances of nature and the
thoughts and feelings of men. Is it surprising that
the whole value should then be found in the form ?

So far we have assumed that this antithesis of
substance and form is valid, and that it always has
one meaning. In reality it has several, but we will
leave it in its present shape, and pass to the question
of its validity. And this question we are compelled
to raise, because we have to deal with the two contentions that the poetic value lies wholly or mainly

---

[1] What is here called 'substance' is what people generally mean
when they use the word 'subject' and insist on the value of the
subject. I am not arguing against this usage, or in favour of the
usage which I have adopted for the sake of clearness. It does not
matter which we employ, so long as we and others know what we
mean. (I use 'substance' and 'content' indifferently.)

in the substance, and that it lies wholly or mainly in the form. Now these contentions, whether false or true, may seem at least to be clear ; but we shall find, I think, that they are both of them false, or both of them nonsense : false if they concern anything outside the poem, nonsense if they apply to something in it. For what do they evidently imply? They imply that there are in a poem two parts, factors, or components, a substance and a form ; and that you can conceive them distinctly and separately, so that when you are speaking of the one you are not speaking of the other. Otherwise how can you ask the question, In which of them does the value lie? But really in a poem, apart from defects, there are no such factors or components ; and therefore it is strictly nonsense to ask in which of them the value lies. And on the other hand, if the substance and the form referred to are not in the poem, then both the contentions are false, for its poetic value lies in itself.

What I mean is neither new nor mysterious ; and it will be clear, I believe, to any one who reads poetry poetically and who closely examines his experience. When you are reading a poem, I would ask—not analysing it, and much less criticizing it, but allowing it, as it proceeds, to make its full impression on you through the exertion of your re-creating imagination—do you then apprehend and enjoy as one thing a certain meaning or substance, and as another thing certain articulate sounds, and do you somehow compound these two? Surely you do not, any more than you apprehend apart, when you see some one smile, those lines in the face which express a feeling, and the feeling that the lines express. Just as there the lines and their meaning are to you one thing, not two, so in poetry the meaning and the sounds are one : there is, if I may put it so, a resonant meaning, or a meaning resonance. If you read the line, ' The sun is warm, the

sky is clear,' you do not experience separately the
image of a warm sun and clear sky, on the one side,
and certain unintelligible rhythmical sounds on the
other; nor yet do you experience them together,
side by side; but you experience the one *in* the
other. And in like manner, when you are really
reading *Hamlet*, the action and the characters are
not something which you conceive apart from the
words; you apprehend them from point to point *in*
the words, and the words as expressions of them.
Afterwards, no doubt, when you are out of the
poetic experience but remember it, you may by
analysis decompose this unity, and attend to a substance more or less isolated, and a form more or
less isolated. But these are things in your analytic
head, not in the poem, which is *poetic* experience.
And if you want to have the poem again, you cannot find it by adding together these two products of
decomposition; you can only find it by passing back
into poetic experience. And then what you recover
is no aggregate of factors, it is a unity in which you
can no more separate a substance and a form than
you can separate living blood and the life in the
blood. This unity has, if you like, various 'aspects'
or 'sides,' but they are not factors or parts; if you
try to examine one, you find it is also the other.
Call them substance and form if you please, but
these are not the reciprocally exclusive substance
and form to which the two contentions *must* refer.
They do not 'agree,' for they are not apart: they
are one thing from different points of view, and in
that sense identical. And this identity of content
and form, you will say, is no accident; it is of the
essence of poetry in so far as it is poetry, and of all
art in so far as it is art. Just as there is in music
not sound on one side and a meaning on the other,
but expressive sound, and if you ask what is the
meaning you can only answer by pointing to the
sounds; just as in painting there is not a meaning

plus paint, but a meaning *in* paint, or significant paint, and no man can really express the meaning in any other way than in paint and in *this* paint; so in a poem the true content and the true form neither exist nor can be imagined apart. When then you are asked whether the value of a poem lies in a substance got by decomposing the poem, and present, as such, only in reflective analysis, or whether the value lies in a form arrived at and existing in the same way, you will answer, ' It lies neither in one, nor in the other, nor in any addition of them, but in the poem, where they are not.'

We have then, first, an antithesis of subject and poem. This is clear and valid; and the question in which of them does the value lie is intelligible; and its answer is, In the poem. We have next a distinction of substance and form. If the substance means ideas, images, and the like taken alone, and the form means the measured language taken by itself, this is a possible distinction, but it is a distinction of things not in the poem, and the value lies in neither of them. If substance and form mean anything *in* the poem, then each is involved in the other, and the question in which of them the value lies has no sense. No doubt you may say, speaking loosely, that in this poet or poem the aspect of substance is the more noticeable, and in that the aspect of form; and you may pursue interesting discussions on this basis, though no principle or ultimate question of value is touched by them. And apart from that question, of course, I am not denying the usefulness and necessity of the distinction. We cannot dispense with it. To consider separately the action or the characters of a play, and separately its style or versification, is both legitimate and valuable, so long as we remember what we are doing. But the true critic in speaking of these apart does not really think of them apart; the whole, the poetic experience, of which they are but aspects, is always in his mind; and he is always aiming at a richer, truer, more intense repetition of that experience.   On the other hand, when the question of principle, of poetic value, is raised, these aspects *must* fall apart into components, separately conceivable; and then there arise two heresies, equally false, that the value lies in one of two things, both of which are outside the poem, and therefore where its value cannot lie.

On the heresy of the separable substance a few additional words will suffice.   This heresy is seldom formulated, but perhaps some unconscious holder of it may object : ' Surely the action and the characters of *Hamlet* are in the play; and surely I can retain these, though I have forgotten all the words.   I admit that I do not possess the whole poem, but I possess a part, and the most important part.'   And I would answer : ' If we are not concerned with any question of principle, I accept all that you say except the last words, which do raise such a question.   Speaking loosely, I agree that the action and characters, as you perhaps conceive them, together with a great deal more, are in the poem. Even then, however, you must not claim to possess all of this kind that is in the poem; for in forgetting the words you must have lost innumerable details of the action and the characters.   And, when the question of value is raised, I must insist that the action and characters, as you conceive them, are not in *Hamlet* at all.   If they are, point them out. You cannot do it.   What you find at any moment of that succession of experiences called *Hamlet* is words.   In these words, to speak loosely again, the action and characters (more of them than you can conceive apart) are focussed; but your experience is not a combination of them, as ideas, on the one side, with certain sounds on the other; it is an experience of something in which the two are indissolubly fused.   If you deny this, to be sure I can make no answer, or can only answer that I have

O.L.   B

reason to believe that you cannot read poetically, or else are misinterpreting your experience. But if you do not deny this, then you will admit that the action and characters of the poem, as you separately imagine them, are no part of it, but a product of it in your reflective imagination, a faint analogue of one aspect of it taken in detachment from the whole. Well, I do not dispute, I would even insist, that, in the case of so long a poem as *Hamlet*, it may be necessary from time to time to interrupt the poetic experience, in order to enrich it by forming such a product and dwelling on it. Nor, in a wide sense of "poetic," do I question the poetic value of this product, as you think of it apart from the poem. It resembles our recollections of the heroes of history or legend, who move about in our imaginations, "forms more real than living man," and are worth much to us though we do not remember anything they said. Our ideas and images of the "substance" of a poem have this poetic value, and more, if they are at all adequate. But they cannot determine the poetic value of the poem, for (not to speak of the competing claims of the "form") nothing that is outside the poem can do that, and they, as such, are outside it.'[1]

Let us turn to the so-called form—style and versification. There is no such thing as mere form in poetry. All form is expression. Style may have indeed a certain aesthetic worth in partial abstraction from the particular matter it conveys, as in a well-built sentence you may take pleasure in the build almost apart from the meaning. Even so, style is expressive—presents to sense, for example, the order, ease, and rapidity with which ideas move in the writer's mind—but it is not expressive of the

[1] These remarks will hold good, *mutatis mutandis*, if by 'substance' is understood the 'moral' or the 'idea' of a poem, although perhaps in one instance out of five thousand this may be found in so many words in the poem.

meaning of that particular sentence. And it is possible, interrupting poetic experience, to decompose it and abstract for comparatively separate consideration this nearly formal element of style. But the aesthetic value of style so taken is not considerable ;[1] you could not read with pleasure for an hour a composition which had no other merit. And in poetic experience you never apprehend this value by itself; the style is here expressive also of a particular meaning, or rather is one aspect of that unity whose other aspect is meaning. So that what you apprehend may be called indifferently an expressed meaning or a significant form. Perhaps on this point I may in Oxford appeal to authority, that of Matthew Arnold and Walter Pater, the latter at any rate an authority whom the formalist will not despise. What is the gist of Pater's teaching about style, if it is not that in the end the one virtue of style is truth or adequacy; that the word, phrase, sentence, should express perfectly the writer's perception, feeling, image, or thought; so that, as we read a descriptive phrase of Keats's, we exclaim, 'That is the thing itself'; so that, to quote Arnold, the words are 'symbols equivalent with the thing symbolized,' or, in our technical language, a form identical with its content? Hence in true poetry it is, in strictness, impossible to express the meaning in any but its own words, or to change the words without changing the meaning. A translation of such poetry is not really the old meaning in a fresh dress ; it is a new product, something like the poem, though, if one chooses to say so, more like it in the aspect of meaning than in the aspect of form.

No one who understands poetry, it seems to me, would dispute this, were it not that, falling away from his experience, or misled by theory, he takes

[1] On the other hand, the absence, or worse than absence, of style, in this sense, is a serious matter.

the word 'meaning' in a sense almost ludicrously
inapplicable to poetry. People say, for instance,
'steed' and 'horse' have the same meaning; and
in bad poetry they have, but not in poetry that
is poetry.

> 'Bring forth the horse!' The horse was brought:
> In truth he was a noble steed!

says Byron in *Mazeppa*. If the two words mean
the same here, transpose them:

> 'Bring forth the steed!' The steed was brought:
> In truth he was a noble horse!

and ask again if they mean the same. Or let me
take a line certainly very free from 'poetic diction':

> To be or not to be, that is the question.

You may say that this means the same as ' What is
just now occupying my attention is the comparative
disadvantages of continuing to live or putting an
end to myself.' And for practical purposes—the
purpose, for example, of a coroner—it does. But
as the second version altogether misrepresents the
speaker at that moment of his existence, while the
first does represent him, how can they for any but a
practical or logical purpose be said to have the same
sense? Hamlet was well able to 'unpack his heart
with words,' but he will not unpack it with our
paraphrases.

These considerations apply equally to versification. If I take the famous line which describes
how the souls of the dead stood waiting by the
river, imploring a passage from Charon:

> Tendebantque manus ripae ulterioris amore;

and if I translate it, 'and were stretching forth their
hands in longing for the further bank,' the charm of
the original has fled. Why has it fled? Partly
(but we have dealt with that) because I have sub-
stituted for five words, and those the words of
Virgil, twelve words, and those my own. In some

measure because I have turned into rhythmless
prose a line of verse which, as mere sound, has
unusual beauty.   But much more because in doing
so I have also changed the *meaning* of Virgil's line.
What that meaning is *I* cannot say: Virgil has said
it.   But I can see this much, that the translation
conveys a far less vivid picture of the outstretched
hands and of their remaining outstretched, and a
far less poignant sense of the distance of the shore
and the longing of the souls.   And it does so partly
because this picture and this sense are conveyed
not only by the obvious meaning of the words,
but through the long-drawn sound of 'tendebant-
que,' through the time occupied by the five syllables
and therefore by the idea of 'ulterioris,' and
through the identity of the long sound 'or' in the
penultimate syllables of 'ulterioris amore'—all this,
and much more, apprehended not in this analytical
fashion, nor as *added* to the beauty of mere sound
and to the obvious meaning, but in unity with them
and so as expressive of the poetic meaning of the
whole.

It is always so in fine poetry.   The value of
versification, when it is indissolubly fused with
meaning, can hardly be exaggerated.   The gift for
feeling it, even more perhaps than the gift for
feeling the value of style, is the *specific* gift for
poetry, as distinguished from other arts.   But versification, taken, as far as possible, all by itself, has
a very different worth.   Some aesthetic worth it
has ; how much, you may experience by reading
poetry in a language of which you do not understand a syllable.[1]   The pleasure is quite appreciable,
but it is not great ; nor in actual poetic experience
do you meet with it, as such, at all.   For, I repeat,
it is not *added* to the pleasure of the meaning
when you read poetry that you do understand : by
some mystery the music is then the music *of* the

[1] Note C.

meaning, and the two are one.   However fond of
versification you might be, you would tire very
soon of reading verses in Chinese ; and before long
of reading Virgil and Dante if you were ignorant
of their languages.   But take the music as it is *in*
the poem, and there is a marvellous change.   Now

> It gives a very echo to the seat
> Where love is throned ;

or 'carries far into your heart,' almost like music
itself, the sound

> Of old, unhappy, far-off things
> And battles long ago.

What then is to be said of the following sentence
of the critic quoted before : 'But when any one
who knows what poetry is reads—

> Our noisy years seem moments in the being
> Of the eternal silence,

he sees that, quite independently of the meaning,
. . . there is one note added to the articulate music
of the world—a note that never will leave off
resounding till the eternal silence itself gulfs it ' ?   I
must think that the writer is deceiving himself.   For
I could quite understand his enthusiasm, if it were
an enthusiasm for the music of the meaning ; but as
for the music, 'quite independently of the meaning,'
so far as I can hear it thus (and I doubt if any one
who knows English can quite do so), I find it gives
some pleasure, but only a trifling pleasure.   And
indeed I venture to doubt whether, considered as
mere sound, the words are at all exceptionally
beautiful, as Virgil's line certainly is.

When poetry answers to its idea and is purely or
almost purely poetic, we find the identity of form
and content ; and the degree of purity attained may
be tested by the degree in which we feel it hopeless
to convey the effect of a poem or passage in any
form but its own.   Where the notion of doing so is

simply ludicrous, you have quintessential poetry.
But a great part even of good poetry, especially in
long works, is of a mixed nature; and so we find in
it no more than a partial agreement of a form and
substance which remain to some extent distinct.
This is so in many passages of Shakespeare (the
greatest of poets when he chose, but not always a
conscientious poet); passages where something was
wanted for the sake of the plot, but he did not care
about it or was hurried. The conception of the
passage is then distinct from the execution, and
neither is inspired. This is so also, I think,
wherever we can truly speak of merely decorative
effect. We seem to perceive that the poet had a
truth or fact—philosophical, agricultural, social—
distinctly before him, and then, as we say, clothed
it in metrical and coloured language. Most argumentative, didactic, or satiric poems are partly of
this kind; and in imaginative poems anything which
is really a mere 'conceit' is mere decoration. We
often deceive ourselves in this matter, for what we
call decoration has often a new and genuinely poetic
content of its own; but wherever there is mere
decoration, we judge the poetry to be not wholly
poetic. And so when Wordsworth inveighed
against poetic diction, though he hurled his darts
rather wildly, what he was rightly aiming at was a
phraseology, not the living body of a new content,
but the mere worn-out body of an old one.[1]

In pure poetry it is otherwise. Pure poetry is not
the decoration of a preconceived and clearly defined
matter: it springs from the creative impulse of a
vague imaginative mass pressing for development
and definition. If the poet already knew exactly
what he meant to say, why should he write the
poem? The poem would in fact already be written.
For only its completion can reveal, even to him,
exactly what he wanted. When he began and

[1] This paragraph is criticized in Note D.

while he was at work, he did not possess his meaning ; it possessed him.   It was not a fully formed
soul asking for a body : it was an inchoate soul in
the inchoate body of perhaps two or three vague
ideas and a few scattered phrases.   The growing of
this body into its full stature and perfect shape was
the same thing as the gradual self-definition of the
meaning.[1]   And this is the reason why such poems
strike us as creations, not manufactures, and have
the magical effect which mere decoration cannot
produce.   This is also the reason why, if we insist
on asking for the meaning of such a poem, we can
only be answered ' It means itself.'

And so at last I may explain why I have troubled
myself and you with what may seem an arid controversy about mere words.   It is not so.   These
heresies which would make poetry a compound of
two factors—a matter common to it with the merest
prose, *plus* a poetic form, as the one heresy says : a
poetical substance *plus* a negligible form, as the
other says—are not only untrue, they are injurious
to the dignity of poetry.   In an age already inclined
to shrink from those higher realms where poetry
touches religion and philosophy, the formalist heresy
encourages men to taste poetry as they would a fine
wine, which has indeed an aesthetic value, but a
small one.   And then the natural man, finding an
empty form, hurls into it the matter of cheap pathos,
rancid sentiment, vulgar humour, bare lust, ravenous
vanity—everything which, in Schiller's phrase,[2] the
form should extirpate, but which no mere form can
extirpate.   And the other heresy—which is indeed
rather a practice than a creed—encourages us in the
habit so dear to us of putting our own thoughts or
fancies into the place of the poet's creation.   What
he meant by *Hamlet*, or the *Ode to a Nightingale*,
or *Abt Vogler*, we say, is this or that which we

---

[1] Note E.

[2] Not that to Schiller ' form' meant mere style and versification.

knew already ; and so we lose what he had to tell
us.   But he meant what he said, and said what he
meant.

Poetry in this matter is not, as good critics of
painting and music often affirm, different from the
other arts ; in all of them the content is one thing
with the form.   What Beethoven meant by his
symphony, or Turner by his picture, was not something which you can name, but the picture and the
symphony.   Meaning they have, but *what* meaning
can be said in no language but their own : and we
know this, though some strange delusion makes us
think the meaning has less worth because we cannot
put it into words.   Well, it is just the same with
poetry.   But because poetry is words, we vainly
fancy that some other words than its own will
express its meaning.   And they will do so no more
—or, if you like to speak loosely, only a trifle
more—than words will express the meaning of the
Dresden Madonna.[1]   Something a little like it they
may indeed express.   And we may find analogues
of the meaning of poetry outside it, which may help
us to appropriate it.   The other arts, the best ideas
of philosophy or religion, much that nature and life
offer us or force upon us, are akin to it.   But they
are only akin.   Nor is it the expression of them.
Poetry does not present to imagination our highest
knowledge or belief, and much less our dreams
and opinions ; but it, content and form in unity,
embodies in its own irreplaceable way something
which embodies itself also in other irreplaceable
ways, such as philosophy or religion.   And just
as each of these gives a satisfaction which the
other cannot possibly give, so we find in poetry,
which cannot satisfy the needs they meet, that
which by their natures they cannot afford us.
But we shall not find it fully if we look for something else.

[1] Note F.

And now, when all is said, the question will still recur, though now in quite another sense, What does poetry mean?[1] This unique expression, which cannot be replaced by any other, still seems to be trying to express something beyond itself. And this, we feel, is also what the other arts, and religion, and philosophy are trying to express: and that is what impels us to seek in vain to translate the one into the other. About the best poetry, and not only the best, there floats an atmosphere of infinite suggestion. The poet speaks to us of one thing, but in this one thing there seems to lurk the secret of all. He said what he meant, but his meaning seems to beckon away beyond itself, or rather to expand into something boundless which is only focussed in it; something also which, we feel, would satisfy not only the imagination, but the whole of us; that something within us, and without, which everywhere

> makes us seem
> To patch up fragments of a dream,
> Part of which comes true, and part
> Beats and trembles in the heart.

Those who are susceptible to this effect of poetry find it not only, perhaps not most, in the ideals which she has sometimes described, but in a child's song by Christina Rossetti about a mere crown of wind-flowers, and in tragedies like *Lear*, where the sun seems to have set for ever. They hear this spirit murmuring its undertone through the *Aeneid*, and catch its voice in the song of Keats's nightingale, and its light upon the figures on the Urn, and it pierces them no less in Shelley's hopeless lament, *O world, O life, O time*, than in the rapturous ecstasy of his *Life of Life*. This all-embracing perfection cannot be expressed in poetic words or words of any kind, nor yet in music or in colour, but the suggestion of it is in much poetry, if not all,

[1] Note G.

and poetry has in this suggestion, this 'meaning,' a great part of its value. We do it wrong, and we defeat our own purposes, when we try to bend it to them :

> We do it wrong, being so majestical,
> To offer it the show of violence ;
> For it is as the air invulnerable,
> And our vain blows malicious mockery.

It is a spirit. It comes we know not whence. It will not speak at our bidding, nor answer in our language. It is not our servant ; it is our master.

1901.

NOTE A

The purpose of this sentence was not, as has been supposed, to give a definition of poetry. To define poetry as something that goes on in us when we read poetically would be absurd indeed. My object was to suggest to my hearers in passing that it is futile to ask questions about the end, or substance, or form of poetry, if we forget that a poem is neither a mere number of black marks on a white page, nor such experience as is evoked in us when we read these marks as we read, let us say, a newspaper article; and I suppose my hearers to know, sufficiently for the purpose of the lecture, how that sort of reading differs from poetical reading.

The truths thus suggested are so obvious, when stated, that I thought a bare reminder of them would be enough. But in fact the mistakes we make about 'subject,' 'substance,' 'form,' and the like, are due not solely to misapprehension of our poetic experience, but to our examining what is not this experience. The whole lecture may be called an expansion of this statement.

The passage to which the present note refers raises difficult questions which any attempt at a 'Poetics' ought to discuss. I will mention three. (1) If the experience called a poem varies 'with every reader and every time of reading' and 'exists in innumerable degrees,' what is the poem itself, if there is such a thing? (2) How does a series of successive experiences form *one* poem? (3) If the object in the case of poetry and music ('arts of hearing') is a succession somehow and to some extent unified, how does it differ in this respect from the object in 'arts of sight'—a building, a statue, a picture?

NOTE B

A lyric, for example, may arise from 'real' emotions due to transitory conditions peculiar to the poet. But these emotions and conditions, however interesting biographically, are poetically irrelevant. The poem, what the poet *says*, is universal, and is appropriated by people who live centuries after him and perhaps know nothing of him and his life; and if it arose from mere imagination it is none the worse (or the better) for that. So far as it cannot be appropriated without a knowledge of the circumstances in which it arose, it is probably, so far, faulty (probably, because the difficulty *may* come from our distance from the whole mental world of the poet's time and country).

What is said in the text applies equally to all the arts. It applies also to such aesthetic apprehension as does not issue in a work of art. And it applies to this apprehension whether the object belongs to 'Nature' or to 'Man.' A beautiful land-scape is not a 'real' landscape. Much that belongs to the 'real' landscape is ignored when it is apprehended aesthetically; and the painter only carries this unconscious idealisation further when he deliberately alters the 'real' landscape in further ways.

All this does not in the least imply that the 'real' thing, where there is one (personal emotion, landscape, historical event, etc.), is of small importance to the aesthetic apprehension or the work of art. But it is relevant only as it appears *in* that apprehension or work.

If an artist alters a reality (*e.g.* a well-known scene or historical character) so much that his product clashes violently with our familiar ideas, he may be making a mistake: not because his product is untrue to the reality (this by itself is perfectly irrelevant), but because the 'untruth' may make it difficult or impossible for others to appropriate his product, or because this product may be aesthetically inferior to the reality even as it exists in the general imagination.

NOTE C

For the purpose of the experiment you must, of course, know the sounds denoted by the letters, and you must be able to make out the rhythmical scheme. But the experiment will be vitiated if you get some one who understands the language to read or recite to you poems written in it, for he will certainly so read or recite as to convey to you something of the meaning through the sound (I do not refer of course to the logical meaning).

Hence it is clear that, if by 'versification taken by itself' one means the versification of a *poem*, it is impossible under the requisite conditions to get at this versification by itself. The versification of a poem is always, to speak loosely, influenced by the sense. The bare metrical scheme, to go no further, is practically never followed by the poet. Suppose yourself to know no English, and to perceive merely that in its general scheme

> It gives a very echo to the seat

is an iambic line of five feet; and then read the line as you would have to read it; and then ask if *that* noise is the sound of the line *in the poem*.

In the text, therefore, more is admitted than in strictness should be admitted. For I have assumed for the moment that you can hear the sound of poetry if you read poetry which you do not in the least understand, whereas in fact that sound cannot be produced at all except by a person who knows something of the meaning.

NOTE D

This paragraph has not, to my knowledge, been adversely criticised, but it now appears to me seriously misleading. It refers to certain kinds of poetry, and again to certain passages in poems, which we feel to be less poetical than some other kinds or passages. But this difference of degree in poeticalness (if I may use the word) is put as a difference between 'mixed' and 'pure' poetry; and that distinction is, I think, unreal and mischievous. Further, it is implied that in less poetical poetry there necessarily is only a partial unity of content and form. This (unless I am now mistaken) is a mistake, and a mistake due to failure to hold fast the main idea of the lecture. Naturally it would be most agreeable to me to re-write the paragraph, but if I reprint it and expose my errors the reader will perhaps be helped to a firmer grasp of that idea.

It is true that where poetry is most poetic we feel most decidedly how impossible it is to separate content and form. But where poetry is less poetic and does not make us feel this unity so decidedly, it does not follow that the unity is imperfect. Failure or partial failure in this unity is always (as in the case of Shakespeare referred to) a failure on the part of the *poet* (though it is not always due to the same causes). It does not lie of necessity in the nature of a particular kind of poetry (*e.g.* satire) or in the nature of a particular passage. All poetry cannot be equally poetic, but *all* poetry ought to maintain the unity of content and form, and, in that sense, to be 'pure.' Only in certain kinds, and in certain passages, it is more difficult for the poet to maintain it than in others.

Let us take first the 'passages' and suppose them to occur in one of the more poetic kinds of poetry. In certain parts of any epic or tragedy matter has to be treated which, though necessary to the whole, is not in itself favourable to poetry, or would not in itself be a good 'subject.' But it is the business of the poet to do his best to make this matter poetry, and pure poetry. And, if he succeeds, the passage, though it will probably be less poetic than the bulk of the poem, will exhibit the complete unity of content and form. It will not strike us as a mere bridge between other passages; it will be enjoyable for itself; and it will not occur to us to think that the poet was dealing with an un-poetic 'matter' and found his task difficult or irksome. Shakespeare frequently does not trouble himself to face this problem and leaves an imperfect unity. The conscientious artists, like Virgil, Milton, Tennyson, habitually face it and frequently solve it.[1] And when they wholly or partially fail, the fault is still *theirs*. It is, in one sense, due to the 'matter,' which set a hard problem; but they would be the first to declare that *nothing* in the poem ought to be only mixedly poetic.

In the same way, satire is not in its nature a highly poetic kind of poetry, but it ought, in its own kind, to be poetry throughout, and therefore ought not to show a merely partial

---

[1] In Schiller's phrase, they have extirpated the mere 'matter.' We often say that they do this by dint of style. This is roughly true, but in strictness it means, as we have seen, not that they decorate the mere 'matter' with a mere 'form,' but that they produce a new content-form.

unity of content and form. If the satirist makes us exclaim 'This is sheer prose wonderfully well disguised,' that is a fault, and *his* fault (unless it happens to be ours). The idea that a tragedy or lyric could really be reproduced in a form not its own strikes us as ridiculous; the idea that a satire could so be reproduced seems much less ridiculous; but if it were true the satire would not be poetry at all.

The reader will now see where, in my judgment, the paragraph is wrong. Elsewhere it is, I think, right, though it deals with a subject far too large for a paragraph. This is also true of the next paragraph, which uses the false distinction of 'pure' and 'mixed,' and which will hold in various degrees of poetry in various degrees poetical.

It is of course possible to use a distinction of 'pure' and 'mixed' in another sense. Poetry, whatever its kind, would be pure as far as it preserved the unity of content and form; mixed, so far as it failed to do so—in other words, failed to be poetry and was partly prosaic.

NOTE E

It is possible therefore that the poem, as it existed at certain stages in its growth, may correspond roughly with the poem as it exists in the memories of various readers. A reader who is fond of the poem and often thinks of it, but remembers only half the words and perhaps fills up the gaps with his own words, may possess something like the poem as it was when half-made. There are readers again who retain only what they would call the 'idea' of the poem; and the poem *may* have begun from such an idea. Others will forget all the words, and will not profess to remember even the 'meaning,' but believe that they possess the 'spirit' of the poem. And what they possess may have, I think, an immense value. The poem, of course, it is not; but it may answer to the state of imaginative feeling or emotional imagination which was the germ of the poem. This is, in one sense, quite definite: it would not be the germ of a decidedly different poem: but in another sense it is indefinite, comparatively structureless. more a 'stimmung' than an idea.

Such correspondences, naturally, must be very rough, if only because the readers have been at one time in contact with the fully grown poem.

NOTE F

I should be sorry if what is said here and elsewhere were taken to imply depreciation of all attempts at the interpretation of works of art. As regards poetry, such attempts, though they cannot possibly express the whole meaning of a poem, may do much to facilitate the poetic apprehension of that meaning. And, although the attempt is still more hazardous in the case of music and painting, I believe it may have a similar value. That its results *may* be absurd or disgusting goes without saying, and whether they are ever of use to musicians or the musically educated I do not know. But I see no reason why an exceedingly competent person should no* try to indicate the emotional tone of a composition, movement, or passage, or the changes of feeling within it, or even, very roughly, the 'idea' he may suppose it to embody (though he need not imply that the composer had any of this before his mind). And I believe that such indications, however inadequate they must be, may greatly help the uneducated lover of music to hear more truly the music itself.

NOTE G

This new question has 'quite another sense' than that of the question, What is the meaning or content expressed by the form of a poem? The new question asks, What is it that the *poem*, the unity of this content and form, is trying to express? This 'beyond' is beyond the content as well as the form.

Of course, I should add, it is not *merely* beyond them or outside of them. If it were, they (the poem) could not 'suggest' it. They are a partial manifestation of it, and point beyond themselves to it, both because they *are* a manifestation and because this is partial.

The same thing is true, not only (as is remarked in the text) of the other arts and of religion and philosophy, but also of what is commonly called reality. This reality is a manifestation of a different order from poetry, and in certain important respects a much more imperfect manifestation. Hence, as was pointed out (pp. 6, 7, note B), poetry is not a copy of it, but in dealing with it idealises it, and in doing so produces in certain respects a fuller manifestation. On the other hand, that imperfect 'reality' has for us a character in which poetry is deficient,— the character in virtue of which we call it 'reality.' It is, we feel, thrust upon us, not made by us or by any other man. And in this respect it seems more akin than poetry to that 'beyond,' or absolute, or perfection, which we want, which partially expresses itself in both, and which could not be perfection and could not satisfy us if it were not real (though it cannot be real in the same sense as that imperfect 'reality'). This seems the ultimate ground of the requirement that poetry, though no copy of 'reality,' should not be mere 'fancy,' but should refer to, and interpret, that 'reality.' For that reality, however imperfectly it reveals perfection, is at least no mere fancy. (Not that the merest fancy can fail to reveal something of perfection.)

The lines quoted on p. 26 are from a fragment of Shelley's, beginning 'Is it that in some brighter sphere.'

THE SUBLIME

THE SUBLIME [1]

COLERIDGE used to tell a story about his visit to the Falls of Clyde; but he told it with such variations that the details are uncertain, and without regard to truth I shall change it to the shape that suits my purpose best. After gazing at the Falls for some time, he began to consider what adjective would answer most precisely to the impression he had received; and he came to the conclusion that the proper word was 'sublime.' Two other tourists arrived, and, standing by him, looked in silence at the spectacle. Then, to Coleridge's high satisfaction, the gentleman exclaimed, 'It is sublime.' To which the lady responded, 'Yes, it is the prettiest thing I ever saw.'

This poor lady's incapacity (for I assume that Coleridge and her husband were in the right) is ludicrous, but it is also a little painful. Sublimity and prettiness are qualities separated by so great a distance that our sudden attempt to unite them has a comically incongruous effect. At the same time the first of these qualities is so exalted that the exhibition of entire inability to perceive it is distressing. Astonishment, rapture, awe, even self-abasement, are among the emotions evoked by sublimity. Many would be inclined to pronounce it

---

[1] I have learned something from many discussions of this subject. In its outline the view I have taken is perhaps nearer to Hartmann's than to any other.

the very highest of all the forms assumed by beauty, whether in nature or in works of imagination.

I propose to make some remarks on this quality, and even to attempt some sort of answer to the question what sublimity is. I say 'some sort of answer,' because the question is large and difficult, and I can deal with it only in outline and by drawing artificial limits round it and refusing to discuss certain presuppositions on which the answer rests. What I mean by these last words will be evident if I begin by referring to a term which will often recur in this lecture—the term 'beauty.'

When we call sublimity a form of beauty, as I did just now, the word 'beauty' is obviously being used in the widest sense. It is the sense which the word bears when we distinguish beauty from good-ness and from truth, or when 'beautiful' is taken to signify anything and everything that gives aesthetic satisfaction, or when 'Aesthetics' and 'Philosophy of the Beautiful' are used as equivalent expressions. Of beauty, thus understood, sublimity is one par-ticular kind among a number of others, for instance prettiness. But 'beauty' and 'beautiful' have also another meaning, narrower and more specific, as when we say that a thing is pretty but not beautiful, or that it is beautiful but not sublime. The beauty we have in view here is evidently not the same as beauty in the wider sense; it is only, like sublimity or prettiness, a particular kind or mode of that beauty. This ambiguity of the words 'beauty' and 'beautiful' is a great inconvenience, and especially so in a lecture, where it forces us to add some qualification to the words whenever they occur: but it cannot be helped. (Now that the lecture is printed I am able to avoid these qualifications by printing the words in inverted commas where they bear the narrower sense.)[1]

---

[1] Popular usage coincides roughly with this sense. Indeed, it can hardly be said to recognise the wider one at all. 'Beauty' and

Now, obviously, all the particular kinds or modes
of beauty must have, up to a certain point, the same
nature. They must all possess that character in
virtue of which they are called beautiful rather than
good or true. And so a philosopher, investigating
one of these kinds, would first have to determine
this common nature or character ; and then he would
go on to ascertain what it is that distinguishes the
particular kind from its companions. But here we
cannot follow such a method. The nature of beauty
in general is so much disputed and so variously
defined that to discuss it here by way of preface
would be absurd ; and on the other hand it would
be both presumptuous and useless to assume the
truth of any one account of it. Our only plan,
therefore, must be to leave it entirely alone, and to
consider merely the distinctive character of sublimity.
Let beauty in general be what it may, what is it
that marks off *this* kind of beauty from others, and
what is there peculiar in our state of mind when we
are moved to apply to anything the specific epithet
'sublime'?—such is our question. And this plan is
not merely the only possible one, but it is, I believe,
quite justifiable, since, so far as I can see, the answer
to our particular question, unless it is pushed further
than I propose to go, is unaffected by the differences among theories of repute concerning beauty
in general. At the same time, it is essential to
realise and always to bear in mind one consequence
of this plan ; which is that our account of what is
peculiar to sublimity will not be an account of
sublimity in its full nature. For sublimity is not
those peculiar characteristics alone, it is that *beauty*
which is distinguished by them, and a large part of

'beautiful,' in that wider sense, are technical terms of Aesthetics.
It is a misfortune that the language of Aesthetics should thus differ
from the ordinary language of speech and literature ; but the misfortune seems to be unavoidable, for there is no word in the ordinary
language which means 'whatever gives aesthetic satisfaction,' and yet
that idea *must* have a name in Aesthetics.

its effect is due to that general nature of beauty which it shares with other kinds, and which we leave unexamined.

In considering the question thus defined I propose to start from our common aesthetic experience and to attempt to arrive at an answer by degrees. It will be understood, therefore, that our first results may have to be modified as we proceed. And I will venture to ask my hearers, further, to ignore for the time any doubts they may feel whether I am right in saying, by way of illustration, that this or that thing is sublime. Such differences of opinion scarcely affect our question, which is not whether in a given case the epithet is rightly applied, but what the epithet signifies. And it has to be borne in mind that, while no two kinds of beauty can be quite the same, a *thing* may very well possess beauty of two different kinds.

Let us begin by placing side by side five terms which represent five of the many modes of beauty —sublime, grand, 'beautiful,' graceful, pretty. 'Beautiful' is here placed in the middle. Before it come two terms, sublime and grand; and beyond it lie two others, graceful and pretty. Now is it not the case that the first two, though not identical, still seem to be allied in some respect; that the last two also seem to be allied in some respect; that in this respect, whatever it may be, these two pairs seem to stand apart from one another, and even to stand in contrast; that 'beauty,' in this respect, seems to hold a neutral position, though perhaps inclining rather to grace than to grandeur; and that the extreme terms, sublime and pretty, seem in this respect to be the most widely removed; so that this series of five constitutes, in a sense, a descending series,—descending not necessarily in value, but in some particular respect not yet assigned? If, for example, in the lady's answer, 'Yes, it is

the prettiest thing I ever saw,' you substitute for
'prettiest' first 'most graceful,' and then 'most
beautiful,' and then 'grandest,' you will find that
your astonishment at her diminishes at each step,
and that at the last, when she identifies sublimity
and grandeur, she is guilty no longer of an absurdity, but only of a slight anti-climax.   If, I may add,
she had said 'majestic,' the anti-climax would have
been slighter still, and, in fact, in one version of the
story Coleridge says that 'majestic' was the word
he himself chose.

What then is the 'respect' in question here,—
the something or other in regard to which sublimity
and grandeur seemed to be allied with one another,
and to differ decidedly from grace and prettiness?
It appears to be greatness.   Thousands of things
are 'beautiful,' graceful, or pretty, and yet make
no impression of greatness, nay, this impression in
many cases appears to collide with, and even to
destroy, that of grace or prettiness, so that if a
pretty thing produced it you would cease to call
it pretty.   But whatever strikes us as sublime produces an impression of greatness, and more—of
exceeding or even overwhelming greatness.   And
this greatness, further, is apparently no mere
accompaniment of sublimity, but essential to it:
remove the greatness in imagination, and the
sublimity vanishes.   Grandeur, too, seems always
to possess greatness, though not in this superlative
degree; while 'beauty' neither invariably possesses
it nor tends, like prettiness and grace, to exclude
it.   I will try, not to defend these statements by
argument, but to develop their meaning by help
of illustrations, dismissing from view the minor
differences between these modes of beauty, and,
for the most part, leaving grandeur out of account.

We need not ask here what is the exact meaning
of that 'greatness' of which I have spoken : but we
must observe at once that the greatness in question

is of more than one kind. Let us understand by
the term, to begin with, greatness of extent,—of
size, number, or duration ; and let us ask whether
sublime things are, in this sense, exceedingly great.
Some certainly are. The vault of heaven, one
expanse of blue, or dark and studded with countless
and prodigiously distant stars ; the sea that stretches
to the horizon and beyond it, a surface smooth as glass
or breaking into innumerable waves ; time, to which
we can imagine no beginning and no end,—these
furnish favourite examples of sublimity ; and to call
them great seems almost mockery, for they are
images of immeasurable magnitude. When we turn
from them to living beings, of course our standard
of greatness changes ;[1] but, using the standard
appropriate to the sphere, we find again that the
sublime things have, for the most part, great
magnitude. A graceful tree need not be a large
one ; a pretty tree is almost always small ; but a
sublime tree is almost always large. If you were
asked to mention sublime animals, you would perhaps suggest, among birds, the eagle ; among fishes,
if any, the whale ; among beasts, the lion or the
tiger, the python or the elephant. But you would
find it hard to name a sublime insect ; and indeed it
is not easy, perhaps not possible, to feel sublimity
in any animal smaller than oneself, unless one goes
beyond the special kind of greatness at present
under review. Consider again such facts as these :
that a human being of average, or even of less than
average, stature and build may be graceful and
even ' beautiful,' but can hardly, in respect of
stature and build, be grand or sublime ; that we
most commonly think of flowers as little things, and
also most commonly think of them as ' beautiful,'
graceful, pretty, but rarely as grand, and still more

[1] I do not mean to imply that in aesthetic apprehension itself we
always, or generally, make conscious use of a standard or, indeed,
think of greatness. But here we are *reflecting* on this apprehension.

rarely as sublime, and that in these latter cases we
do not think of them as small ; that a mighty river
may well be sublime, but hardly a stream ; a towering or far-stretching mountain, but hardly a low
hill ; a vast bridge, but hardly one of moderate
span ; a great cathedral, but hardly a village
church ; that a model of a sublime building is not
sublime, unless in imagination you expand it to the
dimensions of its original ; that a plain, though flat,
may be sublime if its extent is immense ; that while
we constantly say 'a pretty little thing,' or even 'a
beautiful little thing,' nobody ever says 'a sublime
little thing.' Examples like these seem to show
clearly—not that bigness is sublimity, for bigness
need have no beauty, while sublimity is a mode of
beauty—but that this particular mode of beauty
is frequently connected with, and dependent on,
exceeding greatness of extent.

Let us now take a further step. Can there be
sublimity when such greatness is absent? And, if
there can, is greatness of some other sort always
present in such cases, and essential to the sublime
effect ? The answer to the first of these questions
is beyond doubt. Children have no great extension,
and what Wordsworth calls 'a six-years' darling of
a pigmy size ' is (if a darling) generally called pretty
but not sublime ; for it *is* 'of a pigmy size.' Yet it
certainly *may* be sublime, and it is so to the poet
who addresses it thus :

> Thou whose exterior semblance doth belie
>   Thy soul's immensity . . .
> Mighty prophet ! Seer blest !
> On whom those truths do rest
> Which we are toiling all our lives to find.

A baby is still smaller, but a baby too may be
sublime. The starry sky is not more sublime than
the babe on the arm of the Madonna di San Sisto.
A sparrow is more diminutive still ; but that it is
possible for a sparrow to be sublime is not difficult

to show.   This is a translation of a prose poem by
Tourgénieff:

I was on my way home from hunting, and was walking up the
garden avenue.   My dog was running on in front of me.
Suddenly he slackened his pace, and began to steal forward as
though he scented game ahead.
I looked along the avenue; and I saw on the ground a young
sparrow, its beak edged with yellow, and its head covered with
soft down.   It had fallen from the nest (a strong wind was
blowing, and shaking the birches of the avenue); and there it
sat and never stirred, except to stretch out its little half-grown
wings in a helpless flutter.
My dog was slowly approaching it, when suddenly, darting
from the tree overhead, an old black-throated sparrow dropt like
a stone right before his nose, and, all rumpled and flustered, with
a plaintive desperate cry flung itself, once, twice, at his open jaws
with their great teeth.
It would save its young one; it screened it with its own body;
the tiny frame quivered with terror; the little cries grew wild and
hoarse; it sank and died.   It had sacrificed itself.
What a huge monster the dog must have seemed to it!   And
yet it could not stay up there on its safe bough.   A power
stronger than its own will tore it away.
My dog stood still, and then slunk back disconcerted.   Plainly
he too had to recognise that power.   I called him to me; and a
feeling of reverence came over me as I passed on.
Yes, do not laugh.   It was really reverence I felt before that
little heroic bird and the passionate outburst of its love.
Love, I thought, is verily stronger than death and the terror of
death.   By love, only by love, is life sustained and moved.

This sparrow, it will be agreed, is sublime.   What,
then, makes it so?   Not largeness of size, assuredly,
but, we answer, its love and courage.   Yes; but
what do we mean by '*its* love and courage'?   We
often meet with love and courage, and always
admire and approve them; but we do not always
find them sublime.   Why, then, are they sublime in
the sparrow?   From their extraordinary greatness.
It is not in the quality alone, but in the quantity of
the quality, that the sublimity lies.   And this may
be readily seen if we imagine the quantity to be
considerably reduced,—if we imagine the parent
bird, after its first brave effort, flinching and flying

away, or if we suppose the bird that sacrifices itself
to be no sparrow but a turkey. In either case love
and courage would remain, but sublimity would
recede or vanish, simply because the love and
courage would no longer possess the required
immensity.[1]

The sublimity of the sparrow, then, no less than
that of the sky or sea, depends on exceeding or
overwhelming greatness—a greatness, however, not
of extension but rather of strength or power, and in
this case of spiritual power. 'Love is *stronger* than
death,' quotes the poet; 'a power *stronger* than its
own tore it away.' So it is with the dog of whom
Scott and Wordsworth sang, whose master had
perished among the crags of Helvellyn, and who
was found three months after by his master's body,

> How nourished here through such long time
> He knows who gave that love sublime,
> And gave that strength of feeling, great
> Above all human estimate.[2]

And if we look further we shall find that these cases
of sublimity are, in this respect, far from being
exceptions : ' thy soul's *immensity*,' says Wordsworth
to the child ; '*mighty* prophet' he calls it. We shall
find, in fact, that in the sublime, when there is not
greatness of extent, there is another greatness, which
(without saying that the phrase is invariably the
most appropriate) we may call greatness of power
and which in these cases is essential.

We must develop this statement a little. Naturally the power, and therefore the sublimity, will
differ in its character in different instances, and
therefore will affect us variously. It may be—to
classify very roughly—physical, or vital, or (in the
old wide sense of the word) moral, like that of the
sparrow and the dog. And physical force will

---

[1] Thus, it may be noticed, the sparrow's size, which is the reverse of
sublime, is yet indirectly essential to the sublimity of the sparrow.

[2] The poet's language here has done our analysis for us

appeal to the imagination in one way, and vital in another, and moral or spiritual in another. But it is still power of some kind that makes a thing sublime rather than graceful, and immensity of power that makes it sublime rather than merely grand. For example, the lines of the water in a thin cascade may be exquisitely graceful, but such a cascade has not power enough to be sublime. Flickering fire in a grate is often ' beautiful,' but it is not sublime ; the fire of a big bonfire is on the way to be so ; a 'great fire' frequently is so, because it gives the impression of tremendous power. The ocean, in those stanzas of *Childe Harold* which no amount of familiarity or of defect can deprive of their sublimity, is the untameable monster which engulfs men as lightly as rain-drops and shatters fleets like toys. The sublimity of Behemoth and Leviathan in the *Book of Job* lies in the contrast of their enormous might with the puny power of man ; that of the horse in the fiery energy of his courage and strength. Think of sublime figures or ideas in the world of fiction or of history, and you find that, whether they are radiant or gloomy, violent or peaceful, terrible or adorable, they all impress the imagination by their immense or even irresistible might. It is so with Achilles, standing alone beyond the wall, with the light of the divine flame soaring from his head, while he sends across the trench that shout at whose far-off sound the hearts of the Trojans die within them ; or with Odysseus, when the moment of his vengeance has come, and he casts off his rags, and leaps onto the threshold with his bow, and pours his arrows down at his feet, and looks down the long hall at the doomed faces of his feasting enemies. Milton's Satan is sublime when he refuses to accept defeat from an omnipotent foe ; he ceases to be so in tempting Eve, because here he shows not power but cunning, and we feel not the strength of his

cunning but the weakness of his victim.   In the
bust of Zeus in the Vatican, in some of the figures
of the Medici Chapel, in 'The horse and his rider,'
we feel again sublimity, because we feel gigantic
power, put forth or held in reserve.   Fate or Death,
imagined as a lurking assassin, is not sublime, but
may become so when imagined as inevitable, irresistible, *ineluctabile fatum.*   The eternal laws to
which Antigone appeals, like that Duty which
preserves the strength and freshness of the most
ancient heavens, are sublime.   Prometheus, the
saviour of mankind, opposing a boundless power of
enduring pain to a boundless power of inflicting it ;
Regulus returning unmoved to his doom ; Socrates,
serene and even joyous in the presence of injury
and death and the lamentations of his friends, are
sublime.   The words ' I have overcome the world'
are among the most sublime on record, and they
are also the expression of the absolute power of
the spirit.[1]

It seems clear, then, that sublimity very often
arises from an overwhelming greatness of power.
So abundant, indeed, are the instances that one
begins to wonder whether it ever arises from any
other kind of greatness, and whether we were right
in supposing that mere magnitude of extension can
produce it.   Would such magnitude, however prodigious, seem to us sublime unless we insensibly
construed it as the sign of power ?   In the case of
living things, at any rate, this doubt seems to be
well founded.   A tree is sublime not because it

---

[1] A word may be added here on a disputed point as to 'spiritual'
sublimity. It has been held that intellect cannot be sublime ; but
surely in the teeth of facts.   Not to speak of intellect as it appears in
the sphere of practice, how can it be denied that the intellect of
Aristotle or Shakespeare or Newton may produce the impression of
sublimity?   All that is true is, first, that the intellect must be apprehended imaginatively and not thought abstractly (otherwise it can
produce *no* aesthetic impression), and, secondly, that it appears
sublime in virtue not of its quality alone but of the quantity, or force,
of that quality.

occupies a large extent of empty space or time, but
from the power in it which raises aloft and spreads
abroad a thousand branches and a million leaves, or
which has battled for centuries with buffeting storms
and has seen summers and winters arise and pass
like the hours of our day.   It is not the mere bulk
of the lion or the eagle that wins them their title as
king of beasts or of birds, but the power exhibited
in the gigantic head and arm or the stretch of wing
and the piercing eye.   And even when we pass
from the realm of life our doubt remains.   Would
a mountain, a river, or a building be sublime to us
if we did not read their masses and lines as symbols
of force?   Would even the illimitable extent of sea
or sky, the endlessness of time, or the countlessness
of stars or sands or waves, bring us anything but
fatigue or depression if we did not apprehend them,
in some way and however vaguely, as expressions
of immeasurable power—power that created them,
or lives in them, or *can* count them ; so that what
impresses us is not the mere absence of limits, but
the presence of something that overpowers any
imaginable limit?   If these doubts are justified (as
in my opinion they are), the conclusion will follow
that the exceeding greatness required for sublimity
is *always* greatness of some kind of power, though
in one class of cases the impression of this greatness can only be conveyed through immensity of
extent.

However this question may be decided, our result
so far seems to be that the peculiarity of the
sublime lies in some exceeding and overwhelming
greatness.   But before this result can be considered
safe, two obstacles must be removed.   In the first
place, are there no negative instances?   Is it impossible to find anything sublime which does *not*
show this greatness?   Naturally I can say no more
than that I have conscientiously searched for exceptions to the rule and have searched in vain.   I can

find only apparent exceptions which in reality
confirm the rule; and I will mention only those
which look the most formidable. They are cases
where at first sight there seems to be not merely
an inconsiderable amount of power or other greatness, but actually the negation of it. For example,
the silence of night, or the sudden pause in a storm
or in stormy music, or again the silence and move-
lessness of death, may undoubtedly be sublime; and
how, it may be asked, can a mere absence of sound
and motion be an exhibition of immense greatness?
It cannot, I answer; but neither can it be sublime.
If you apprehend the silence in these cases as a
mere absence, no feeling of sublimity will arise in
your mind; and if you do apprehend the silence as
sublime, it is to you the sign of immense power,
put forth or held in reserve. The 'dead pause
abrupt of mighty winds' is the pause *of* mighty
winds and not of gentle breezes; and it is not the
absence of mighty winds, but their *pause* before
they burst into renewed fury; or if their silence is
not their will, it is a silence imposed on them by
something mightier even than they. In either case
there may be sublimity, but then there is the
impression of immense power. In the same way
the silence of night, when it seems sublime, is
apprehended not as the absence but as the subdual
of sound,—the stillness wrought by a power so
mighty that at its touch all the restless noises of the
day fall dumb,—or the brooding of an omnipotent
peace over the world. And such a peace it is,
an unassailable peace, that may make the face of
death sublime, a stillness which is not moveless
but immovable.[1]

At present, then, our result seems to stand firm.
But another danger remains. Granted that in the

---

[1] The same principle applies to other cases. If, for example, the
desolation of a landscape is felt to be sublime, it is so not as the mere
negation of life, verdure, etc., but as their *active* negation.

sublime there is always some exceeding and overwhelming greatness, is that *all* there is? Is there
not in every case some further characteristic? This
question, premising that the phrase 'overwhelming
greatness' contains important implications which
have yet to be considered, I can only answer like
the last. I do not find any other peculiarity that
is *always* present. Several have been alleged, and
one or two of these will be mentioned later, but
none of them appears to show itself indubitably
wherever sublimity is found. It is easy to give a
much fuller account of the sublime if you include in
it everything that impresses you in a sublime baby
while you omit to consider Behemoth, or if you
build upon Socrates and ignore Satan, or if you
confine yourself to the sublime thunder-storm and
forget the sublime rainbow or sunrise. But then
your account will not answer to the instances you
have ignored; and when you take them in you
will have to pare it down until perhaps you end
in a result like ours. At any rate we had better
be content with it for the present, and turn to
another aspect of the matter.[1]

So far, on the whole, we have been regarding the
sublime object as if its sublimity were independent
of our state of mind in feeling and apprehending it.
Yet the adjective in the phrase 'overwhelming
greatness' should at once suggest the truth that
this state of mind is essential to sublimity. Let us
now therefore look inward, and ask how this state
differs from our state in perceiving or imagining
what is graceful or 'beautiful.' Since Kant dealt
with the subject, most writers who have thought

---

[1] The reader will remember that in one sense of the question, Is
there no more in the sublime than overwhelming greatness? this
question must of course be answered in the affirmative. Sublimity is a
mode of beauty : the sublime is not the overwhelmingly great, it is the
beautiful which has overwhelming greatness ; and it affects us through
its whole nature, not by mere greatness.

about it have agreed that there is a decided difference, which I will try to describe broadly, and without pledging myself to the entire accuracy of the description.

When, on seeing or hearing something, we exclaim, How graceful! or How lovely! or How 'beautiful'! there is in us an immediate outflow of pleasure, an unchecked expansion, a delightful sense of harmony between the thing and ourselves.

> The air
> Nimbly and sweetly recommends itself
> Unto our gentle senses. . . . The heaven's breath
> Smells wooingly here.

The thing wins us and draws us towards itself without resistance. Something in us hastens to meet it in sympathy or love. Our feeling, we may say, is entirely affirmative. For though it is not always untouched by pain (for the thing may have sadness in it),[1] this touch of pain or sadness does not mean any disharmony between the thing and us, or involve any check in our acceptance of it.

In the case of sublimity, on the other hand, this acceptance does not seem to be so simple or immediate. There seem, in fact, to be two 'aspects' or stages in it.[2] First—if only for a fraction of a second—there is a sense of being checked, or baffled, or even stupefied, or possibly even repelled or menaced, as though something were affecting us which we could not receive, or grasp, or stand up to.

[1] I am warning the reader against a mistake which may arise from the complexity of aesthetic experience. We may make a broad distinction between 'glad' and 'sad' modes of beauty; but that does not coincide with the distinction of modes with which we are concerned in this lecture. What is lovely or 'beautiful' may be glad or sad, and so may what is grand or sublime.

[2] In what follows I have spoken as if the two were always successive stages, and as if these always came in the same order. It is easier to make the matter quickly clear by taking this view, which also seemed to answer to my own experience. But I do not wish to commit myself to an opinion on the point, which is of minor importance. What is essential is to recognise the presence of the two 'aspects' or 'stages,' and to see that both are requisite to sublimity

In certain cases we appear to shrink away from it, as though it thrust upon us a sense of our own feebleness or insignificance. This we may call by the convenient but too strong name of the negative stage. It is essential to sublimity; and nothing seems to correspond to it in our perception of loveliness or grace except sometimes a sense of surprise or wonder, which is wholly pleasant, and which does not necessarily qualify the lovely or graceful thing.

But this first stage or aspect clearly does not by itself suffice for sublimity. To it there succeeds, it may be instantaneously or more gradually, another: a powerful reaction, a rush of self-expansion, or an uplifting, or a sense of being borne out of the self that was checked, or even of being carried away beyond all checks and limits. These feelings, even when the sublime thing might be called forbidding, menacing, or terrible, are always positive,—feelings of union with it; and, when its nature permits of this, they may amount to rapture or adoration. But the mark of the negation from which they have issued, the 'smell of the fire,' usually remains on them. The union, we may say perhaps, has required a self-surrender, and the rapture or adoration is often strongly tinged with awe.

Now, this peculiar doubleness in our apprehension of sublimity, this presence of two equally necessary stages or phases, a negative and a positive, seems to correspond with the peculiarity which we found in the sublime object when we were provisionally regarding it by itself. It is its overwhelming greatness which for a moment checks, baffles, subdues, even repels us or makes us feel our littleness, and which then, forcing its way into the imagination and emotions, distends or uplifts them to its own dimensions. We burst our own limits, go out to the sublime thing, identify ourselves ideally with it, and share its immense greatness. But if, and in so far as, we remain conscious of our difference from it, we still feel the insignificance of our actual selves, and our glory is mingled with awe or even with self-abasement.[1]

In writing thus I was endeavouring simply and without any *arrière pensée* to describe a mode of aesthetic experience. But it must have occurred to some of my hearers that the description recalls other kinds of experience. And if they find it accurate in the main, they will appreciate, even if they do not accept, the exalted claim which philosophers, in various forms, have made for the sublime. It awakes in us, they say, through the check or shock which it gives to our finitude, the consciousness of an infinite or absolute; and this is the reason of the kinship we feel between this particular mode of aesthetic experience on the one side, and, on the other, morality or religion. For there, by the denial of our merely finite or individual selves, we rise into union with the law which imposes on us an unconditional demand, or with the infinite source and end of our spiritual life.

These are ideas much too large to be considered now, and even later I can but touch on them. But the mere mention of them may carry us to the last enquiries with which we can deal. For it suggests this question: Supposing that high claim to be justified at all, can it really be made for *all* sublimity, or must it not be confined to the very highest forms? A similar question must be raised as to various other statements regarding the sublime; and I go on to speak of some of these.

(1) Burke asserted that the sublime is always founded on fear; indeed he considered this to be its distinguishing characteristic. Setting aside, then, the connection of this statement with Burke's

---

[1] 'Ich fühlte mich so klein, so gross,' says Faust, remembering the vision of the Erdgeist, whom he addresses as 'Erhabener Geist.' He was at once overwhelmed and uplifted.

general doctrine (a doctrine impossible to accept), we may ask, Is it true that the 'check' administered by the sublime object is always one of fear? We must answer, first, that if this check is part of an aesthetic experience and not a mere preliminary to it, it can *never* be fear in the common meaning of that word, or what may be called practical or real fear. So far as we are *practically* afraid of a storm or a mountain, afraid, for instance, for ourselves as bodily beings in this particular spatial and temporal position, the storm or mountain is not sublime to us, it is simply terrible. *That* fear must be absent, or must not engage attention, or must be changed in character, if the object is to be for us *sublimely* terrible, something with which we identify ourselves in imaginative sympathy, and which so causes a great self-expansion. But, secondly, even if 'fear' is understood rightly as indicating a feature in an aesthetic and not a practical experience, our question must obviously be answered in the negative. There is fear in the apprehension of some sublimity, but by no means in that of all. If there is a momentary check, for example, in the case of a rainbow, a glorious sunrise, the starry night, Socrates, or Tourgénieff's sparrow, 'fear,' unless the meaning of the word is unnaturally extended, is surely not the name for this check.

Burke's mistake, however, implies a recognition of the 'negative aspect' in sublimity, and it may remind us of a truth. Instances of the sublime differ greatly in regard to the prominence and tone of this aspect. It is less marked, for example, and less obvious, in the case of a sublime rainbow or sunrise than in that of a sublime and 'terrible' thunderstorm. And in general we may say that the *distinctive* nature of sublimity appears most clearly where this aspect is most prominent,—so prominent, perhaps, that we have a more or less explicit sense of the littleness and powerlessness of ourselves, and indeed of the whole world of our usual experience. It is here that the object is most decidedly more than 'glorious,' or even 'majestic,' and that sublimity appears in antithesis to grace. Only we must not give an account of the sublime which fully applies to these cases *alone*, or suppose that the negative aspect is absent in other cases. If a rainbow or sunrise is really sublime, it is overwhelming as well as uplifting. Nor must we assume that the most distinctively sublime must also be the most sublime. The sunrise witnessed from an immense snowfield in the high Alps may be as sublime as an Alpine thunderstorm, though its sublimity is different.

(2) Grace and 'beauty,' it has been said, though not of course merely sensuous, are yet friendly to sense. It is their essence, in fact, to be a harmonious unity of sense and spirit, and so to reconcile powers which in much of our experience are conflicting and dissonant. But sublimity is harsh and hostile to sense. It makes us feel in ourselves and in the world the presence of something irresistibly superior to sense. And this is the reason why it does not soothe or delight, but uplifts us.

This statement recalls some of the ideas we have been considering, but it may easily mislead. For one thing, it is impossible for any sublimity whatever to be *merely* hostile to 'sense,' since everything aesthetic must appeal to sense or sensuous imagination, so that the sublime must at least express its hostility to sense by means of sense. And if we take the phrase in another meaning, the statement may mislead still, for it attributes to sublimity in general what is a characteristic only of certain forms of the sublime. Scores of examples could easily be quoted which show no hostility to sense : *e.g.* a sublime lion, or bull, or tree. And if we think of our old examples of the rainbow and the sunrise, or, better still, of a thunderstorm, or 'The horse and his rider,' or the 'Sanctus' in Bach's Mass, we find the sublime thing actually making a powerful appeal to sense and depending for its sublimity on the vehemence or volume of this appeal. Diminish at all markedly in these cases the amount of light, colour, or sound, and the sublimity would vanish. Of course the appeal here is not merely to sense, but it *is* to sense.

But undoubtedly there is another kind of sublimity; and it is particularly interesting. Here, it is true, a sort of despite is done to the senses and what speaks to them. As we have seen, the greatness of soul in the sparrow is enhanced by contrast with the smallness and feebleness of its body, and pours contempt on the visible magnitude of the hound; and the stillness of night or death is sublime from its active negation of sound and motion. Again, there is a famous passage which depends for its effect on this, that, first, sublime things are introduced which appeal powerfully to sense, and then something else, which does not so appeal, is made to appear even more sublime and to put them to shame : first a great and strong wind, an earthquake, a fire ; and after the fire a still small voice. Sometimes, again, as Burke observed, sublimity depends on, or is increased by, darkness, obscurity, vagueness,—refusal of satisfaction to the sense of sight. Often in these cases the sublime object is terrible, and its terror is increased by inability to see or distinguish it. Examples are the image of ' the pestilence that walketh in darkness,' or Milton's description of Death, or the lines in the *Book of Job* :

> In thoughts from the visions of the night
> When deep sleep falleth on men,
> Fear came upon me and trembling,
> Which made all my bones to shake.
> Then a spirit passed before my face ;
> The hair of my flesh stood up.
> It stood still, but I could not discern the form thereof.
> An image was before mine eyes.
> There was silence, and I heard a voice.

It has been observed that attempts to illustrate such passages as these dissipate their sublimity by diminishing the obscurity of the object. Blake's illustrations of the lines in Milton and in *Job*[1] show this, while his design of the morning-stars singing together is worthy even of the words.

We may trace this severity towards sense, again, in examples already mentioned, the ideas of Fate, of the eternal laws to which Antigone appeals, of Duty in Wordsworth's ode. We imagine these powers as removed from sight, and indeed wholly immaterial, and yet as exercising sovereign dominion over the visible and material world. And their sublimity would be endangered if we tried to bring them nearer to sense by picturing the means by which they exercise their control.

I will take a last example. It has probably been mentioned in almost every account of the sublime since Longinus quoted it in his work on Elevation of Style. And it is of special interest here because it illustrates at one and the same time the two kinds of sublimity which we are engaged in distinguishing. 'God said, Let there be light, and there was light.' The idea of the first and instantaneous appearance of light, and that the whole light of the whole world, is already sublime ; and its primary appeal is to sense. The further idea that this transcendently glorious apparition is due to mere words, to a breath—our symbol of tenuity, evanescence, impotence to influence material bulk—heightens enormously the impression of absolutely immeasurable power.

To sum up, then, on this matter. It is not safe to distinguish the sublime from the 'beautiful' by its hostility to sense. The sublime may impress its overwhelming greatness in either of two ways, by

---

[1] At least if the 'Vision' is sublime its sublimity is not that of the original. We can 'discern the form thereof' distinctly enough.

an appeal to sense, or by a kind of despite done to it. Nor can we assert, if we think of the sunrise, the thunderstorm, or of sublime music, that the second of these ways is more distinctive of the sublime than the first. But perhaps we may say this. In 'beauty' that which appears in a sensuous form seems to rest in it, to be perfectly embodied in it, and to have no tendency to pass beyond it. In the sublime, even where no such tendency is felt and sublimity is nearest to 'beauty,' we still feel the presence of a power held in reserve, which could with ease exceed its present expression. In *some* forms of sublimity, again, the sensuous embodiment seems threatening to break in its effort to express what appears in it. And in others we definitely feel that the power which for a moment intimates its presence to sense is infinite and utterly uncontainable by any or all vehicles of its manifestation. Here we are furthest (in a way) from sense, and furthest also from 'beauty.'

(3) I come finally and, as it will at first seem, needlessly to an idea which has already been touched on. The words 'boundless,' 'illimitable,' 'infinite,' constantly recur in discussions of sublimity, and it cannot be denied that our experience constantly provokes them. The sublime has been said to awake in us the consciousness of our own infinity. It has been said, again, to represent in all cases the inadequacy of all finite forms to express the infinite. And so we may be told that, even if we do not adopt some such formula, but continue to speak of 'greatness,' we ought at least to go beyond the adjective 'exceeding' or 'overwhelming,' and to substitute 'immeasurable' or 'incomparable' or 'infinite.'

Now, at the point we have reached, it would seem we might at once answer that a claim is here being made for the sublime in general which really holds good only of one kind of sublimity. Some-

times the sublime object *is* apprehended as the
Infinite, or again as an expression of it.   This is,
for example, a point of view frequent in Hebrew
poetry.   Sometimes, again, the object (*e.g.* time or
the heavens) is apprehended, not indeed as *the*
Infinite, but still as infinite or immeasurable.   But
how are we to say that a sublime lion or mountain,
or Satan or Lady Macbeth, is apprehended as the
Infinite, or as infinite, or (usually) as even an
expression of the Infinite?   And how are we to
say that the greatness of most sublime objects is
apprehended as incomparable or immeasurable?
It is only failure to observe these distinctions that
leads to errors like one recorded in Coleridge's
Table-talk (July 25, 1832): 'Could you ever discover anything sublime, in our sense of the word,
in the classic Greek literature?   I never could.
Sublimity is Hebrew by birth.'

This reply, however, though sound so far as it
goes, does not settle the question raised.   It may
still be maintained that sublimity in all cases, and
even when we have no idea of infinity before us,
does represent the inadequacy of all finite forms
to express the infinite.   And it is unfortunately
impossible for us to deal fully with this contention.
It would carry us into the region of metaphysics;
and, while believing that no theory of the sublime
can be complete which stops short of that region,
I am aiming in this lecture at no such theory, but
only at a result which may hold good without
regard to further developments.   All that I can do
is to add a few words on the question whether,
going beyond the adjective 'exceeding' or 'overwhelming,' we can say that the sublime is the
beautiful which has immeasurable, incomparable, or
infinite greatness.   And the answer which I suggest
and will go on to explain may be put thus : the
greatness is only sometimes immeasurable, but it
is *always* unmeasured.

We cannot apprehend an object as sublime while we apprehend it as comparably, measurably, or finitely great. Let the thing be what it may—physical, vital, or spiritual—the moment we say to ourselves, ' It is very great, but I know *how* great,' or ' It is very great, but something else is as great or greater,' at that moment it has ceased to be sublime. Outside the consciousness of its sublimity we may be perfectly well aware that a thing is limited, measurable, equal or inferior to something else. But then we are *not* finding it sublime. And when we *are* so finding it, we are absorbed in *its* greatness, and have no thought either of the limits of that or of its equality or inferiority to anything else. The lion of whom we are thinking, ' An elephant could kill him,' is no sublime lion. The Falls of Schaffhausen are sublime when you are lost in astonishment at them, but not when you are saying to yourself ' What must Niagara be!' This seems indubitable, and hence we may say that, in one sense, all sublimity has unmeasured greatness, and that no greatness is sublime which we apprehend as finite.

But the absence of a consciousness of measure or finitude is one thing ; the presence of a consciousness of immeasurableness or infinity is another. The first belongs to all sublimity, the second only to one kind of it,—to that where we *attempt* to measure, or find limits to, the greatness of the thing. *If* we make this attempt, as when we try in imagination to numbe: the stars or to find an end to time, then it is essential to sublimity that we should fail, and so fail that the idea of immeasurability or endlessness emerges. In like manner, *if* we compare things, nothing will appear sublime whose greatness is surpassed or even equalled by that of something else ; and, if this process of comparison is pursued, in the end nothing will be found sublime except the absolute totality (however it may be imagined). And this kind of sublimity, which arises from attempts to measure or compare, is often exceedingly striking. But it is only one kind. For it is an entire delusion—though a very common one in theories of the sublime—to suppose that we *must* attempt to measure or compare. On the contrary, in the majority of cases our impression of overwhelming greatness is accompanied neither by any idea that this greatness has a measure, nor by the idea that it is immeasurable or infinite.[1]

It will not do, then, to lay it down that the sublime is the beautiful which has immeasurable, incomparable, or infinite greatness. But I suggest that, after the explanations given, we may conveniently use the adjective 'unmeasured,' so long as we remember that this means one thing where we do not measure at all, and another thing where we try to measure and fail. And, this being so, it seems that we may say that *all* sublimity, and not only that in which the idea of infinite greatness or of the Infinite emerges, is an image of infinity; for in all, through a certain check or limitation and the overcoming of it, we reach the perception or the imaginative idea of something which, on the one hand, has a positive nature, and, on the other, is either *not* determined as finite or *is* determined as infinite. But we must not add that this makes the sublime superior to the 'beautiful.' For the 'beautiful' too, though in a different way, is an image of infinity. In 'beauty,' as we said, that which appears in a sensuous form seems to rest in that form, to be wholly embodied in it; it shows no tendency to pass beyond it, and intimates no reserve

---

[1] To avoid complication I have passed by the case where we compare the sublime thing with another thing and find it much greater without finding it immeasurably great. Here the greatness, it appears to me, is still un-measured. That is to say, we do not attempt to determine its amount, and if we did we should lose the impression of sublimity. We may *say*, perhaps, that it is ten, fifty, or a million times, as great; but these words no more represent mathematical calculations than Hamlet's 'forty thousand brothers.'

of force that might strain or break it. So that the 'beautiful' thing is a whole complete in itself, and in moments when beauty fills our souls we know what Wordsworth meant when he said 'the least of things seemed infinite,' though each thing, being but one of many, must from another point of view, here suppressed, be finite. 'Beauty,' then, we may perhaps say, is the image of the total presence of the Infinite within any limits it may choose to assume; sublimity the image of its boundlessness, and of its rejection of any pretension to independence or absoluteness on the part of its finite forms; the one the image of its immanence, the other of its transcendence.

Within an hour I could attempt no more than an outline of our subject. That is inevitable; and so is another defect, which I regret more. In analysing any kind of aesthetic experience we have to begin by disentangling the threads that meet in it; and when we can only make a beginning, no time is left for the further task of showing how they are interwoven. We distinguish, for example, one kind of sublimity from another, and we must do so; but in the actual experience, the single instance, these kinds often melt together. I take one case of this. Trying to overlook the field in which sublimity appears, we say that there is a sublimity of inorganic things, and of things vital, and of things spiritual, and that these kinds differ. And this is true; and perhaps it is also true that sometimes we experience one of these kinds, so to say, quite pure and unmixed with others. But it is not always, perhaps not usually so. More frequently kind mingles with kind, and we mutilate the experience when we name it after one of them. In life the imagination, touched at one point, tingles all over and responds at all points. It is offered an impression of physical or vital greatness, but at once it brings from the other end of its world reminiscences of quite another order, and fuses the impression with them. Or an appeal is made to the sense of spiritual greatness, but there rises before the imagination a vision with the outlines and hues of material Nature. Offer it a sunset— a mere collection of coloured lines and spots—and they become to it regrets and hopes and longings too deep for tears. Tell it of souls made perfect in bliss, and it sees an immeasurable rose, or city-walls that flash with the light of all the gems on earth. The truth that a sparrow and a mountain are different, and that Socrates is not Satan, interests it but little. What it cares for is the truth that, when they are sublime, they are all the same; for each becomes infinite, and it feels in each its own infinity.

1903.

NOTES[1]

I add here a few remarks on some points which it was not convenient to discuss in the lecture.

1. We have seen that in the apprehension of sublimity we do not always employ comparison or attempt to measure. To feel a thing overwhelmingly great it is not necessary to have before the mind either the idea of something less great, or any standard of greatness. To argue that this must be necessary because 'great' means nothing except as opposed to 'small,' is like arguing that I cannot have a perception of pride without thinking of humility.

This point seems to me quite clear. But a question remains. If we go below consciousness, what is it that happens in us? The apprehension of sublimity implies that we have received an exceedingly strong impression. This as a matter of fact must mean an impression very much stronger than something else; and this something else must be, so to say, a standard with which the impression is unconsciously compared. What then is it?

Stated in the most general terms, it must apparently be the usual or average strength of impressions.

But this unconscious standard takes particular concrete forms in various classes of cases. Not seldom it seems to be our sense of our own power or of average human power. This is especially so where the thing felt to be sublime is, in the relevant respect, *in eodem genere* with ourselves. A sublime lion, for example, is immensely superior to us, or to the average man, in muscular force and so in dangerousness, Tourgénieff's sparrow in courage and love, a god in all sorts of ways. And

[1] I am far from being satisfied with the ideas imperfectly expressed in the first and third of these Notes, but they require more consideration than I can give to them during the printing of the Second Edition. The reader is requested to take them as mere suggestions.

the use of this unconscious standard is probably the reason of the fact, noted in the lecture, that it is difficult to feel sublimity, as regards vital force, in a creature smaller than ourselves.

But this is not the only standard. A sublime lion is not only immensely stronger than we are, but is generally also exceptional among lions; and so with a sublime tree or bridge or thunderstorm. So that we seem also to use as unconscious standard the idea of the average of the kind to which the thing belongs. An average thunderstorm hardly seems sublime, and yet it is overwhelmingly superior to us in power.[1]

What, again, is the psychical machinery employed when we attempt to measure the shoreless sea, or time, and find them immeasurable? Is there any standard of the 'usual' here? I will leave this question to more skilled psychologists than myself.

2. Since the impression produced by sublimity is one of very exceptional strength, we are not able to feel it continuously for long, though we can repeat it after a pause. In this the sublime differs from the 'beautiful,' on which we like to *dwell* after our first surprise is over. A tragedy or symphony that was sublime from beginning to end could not be so experienced. Living among mountains, we feel their beauty more or less constantly, their sublimity only by flashes.

3. If our account of the impression produced by sublimity is true, why should not any sensation whatever produce this impression merely by gaining extraordinary strength? It seems to me it would, supposing at its normal strength it conformed to the general requirements of aesthetic experience, and supposing the requisite accession of strength did not remove this conformity. But this, in one respect at least, it would do. It would make the light, sound, smell, physiologically painful, and we should feel it as painful or even dangerous. We find this in the case of lightning. If it is to be felt as aesthetic it must not pass a certain degree of brightness; or, as we sometimes say, it must not be too 'near.'

[1] Hence a creature much less powerful than ourselves *may*, I suppose, be sublime, even from the mere point of view of vital energy. But I doubt if this is so in my own case. I have seen 'magnificent' or 'glorious' cocks and cats, but if I called them 'sublime' I should say rather more than I feel. I mention cocks, because Ruskin somewhere mentions a sublime cock; but I cannot find the passage, and this cock may have been sublime (if it really was so to Ruskin) from some other than 'vital' greatness.

HEGEL'S THEORY OF TRAGEDY

HEGEL'S THEORY OF TRAGEDY[1]

SINCE Aristotle dealt with tragedy, and, as usual, drew the main features of his subject with those sure and simple strokes which no later hand has rivalled, the only philosopher who has treated it in a manner both original and searching is Hegel. I propose here to give a sketch of Hegel's theory, and to add some remarks upon it. But I cannot possibly do justice in a sketch to a theory which fills many pages of the *Aesthetik*; which I must tear from its connections with the author's general view of poetry, and with the rest of his philosophy[2]; and which I must try to exhibit as far as possible in the language of ordinary literature. To estimate this theory, therefore, from my sketch would be neither safe nor just—all the more because, in the interest of immediate clearness, I have not scrupled to insert

[1] See, primarily, *Aesthetik*, iii. 479-581, and especially 525-581. There is much in *Aesthetik*, i. 219-306, and a good deal in ii. 1-243, that bears on the subject. See also the section on Greek religion in *Religionsphilosophie*, ii. 96-156, especially 131-6, 152-6; and the references to the death of Socrates in *Geschichte der Philosophie*, ii. 81 ff., especially 102-5. The works so far cited all consist of posthumous redactions of lecture-notes. Among works published by Hegel himself, the early essay on 'Naturrecht' (*Werke*, i. 386 ff.), and *Phaenomenologie d. Geistes*, 320-348, 527-542, deal with or bear on *Greek* tragedy. See also *Rechtsphilosophie*, 196, note. There is a note on *Wallenstein* in *Werke*, xvii. 411-4. These references are to the second edition of the works cited, where there are two editions.

[2] His theory of tragedy is connected with his view of the function of negation in the universe. No statement therefore which ignores his metaphysics and his philosophy of religion can be more than a fragmentary account of that theory.

without warning various remarks and illustrations
for which Hegel is not responsible.

On certain characteristics of tragedy the briefest
reminder will suffice. A large part of the nature of
this form of drama is common to the drama in all its
forms; and of this nothing need be said. It will be
agreed, further, that in all tragedy there is some sort
of collision or conflict—conflict of feelings, modes of
thought, desires, wills, purposes; conflict of persons
with one another, or with circumstances, or with
themselves; one, several, or all of these kinds of
conflict, as the case may be. Again,. it may be
taken for granted that a tragedy is a story of
unhappiness or suffering, and excites such feelings
as pity and fear. To this, if we followed the present
usage of the term, we should add that the story of
unhappiness must have an unhappy end; by which
we mean in effect that the conflict must close with
the death of one or more of the principal characters.
But this usage of the word 'tragedy' is comparatively recent; it leaves us without a name for many
plays, in many languages, which deal with unhappiness without ending unhappily; and Hegel takes
the word in its older and wider sense.

Passing on from these admitted characteristics of
tragedy, we may best approach Hegel's peculiar
view by observing that he lays particular stress on
one of them. That a tragedy is a story of suffering
is probably to many people the most obvious fact
about it. Hegel says very little of this; partly,
perhaps, because it is obvious, but more because
the essential point to him is not the suffering but its
cause, namely, the action or conflict. Mere suffering, he would say, is not tragic, but only the suffering that comes of a special kind of action. Pity for
mere misfortune, like fear of it, is not tragic pity or
fear. These are due to the spectacle of the conflict
and its attendant suffering, which do not appeal
simply to our sensibilities or our instinct of self-

preservation, but also to our deeper mind or spirit (*Geist*, a word which, with its adjective, I shall translate 'spirit,' 'spiritual,' because our words 'mind' and 'mental' suggest something merely intellectual).

The reason why the tragic conflict thus appeals to the spirit is that it is itself a conflict of the spirit. It is a conflict, that is to say, between powers that rule the world of man's will and action—his 'ethical substance.' The family and the state, the bond of parent and child, of brother and sister, of husband and wife, of citizen and ruler, or citizen and citizen, with the obligations and feelings appropriate to these bonds; and again the powers of personal love and honour, or of devotion to a great cause or an ideal interest like religion or science or some kind of social welfare—such are the forces exhibited in tragic action; not indeed alone, not without others less affirmative and perhaps even evil, but still in preponderating mass. And as they form the substance of man, are common to all civilised men, and are acknowledged as powers rightfully claiming human allegiance, their exhibition in tragedy has that interest, at once deep and universal, which is essential to a great work of art.

In many a work of art, in many a statue, picture, tale, or song, such powers are shown in solitary peace or harmonious co-operation. Tragedy shows them in collision. Their nature is divine, and in religion they appear as gods; but, as seen in the world of tragic action, they have left the repose of Olympus, have entered into human wills, and now meet as foes. And this spectacle, if sublime, is also terrible. The essentially tragic fact is the self-division and intestinal warfare of the ethical substance, not so much the war of good with evil as the war of good with good. Two of these isolated powers face each other, making incompatible demands. The family claims what the state refuses, love requires what honour forbids. The competing forces are both in themselves rightful, and so far the claim of each is equally justified; but the right of each is pushed into a wrong, because it ignores the right of the other, and demands that absolute sway which belongs to neither alone, but to the whole of which each is but a part.

And one reason why this happens lies in the nature of the characters through whom these claims are made. It is the nature of the tragic hero, at once his greatness and his doom, that he knows no shrinking or half-heartedness, but identifies himself wholly with the power that moves him, and will admit the justification of no other power. However varied and rich his inner life and character may be, in the conflict it is all concentrated in one point. Antigone *is* the determination to do her duty to her dead brother; Romeo is not a son or a citizen as well as a lover, he is lover pure and simple, and his love is the whole of him.

The end of the tragic conflict is the denial of both the exclusive claims. It is not the work of chance or blank fate; it is the act of the ethical substance itself, asserting its absoluteness against the excessive pretensions of its particular powers. In that sense, as proceeding from an absolute right which cancels claims based on right but pushed into wrong, it may be called the act of 'eternal justice.' Sometimes it can end the conflict peacefully, and the tragedy closes with a solution. Appearing as a divine being, the spiritual unity reconciles by some adjustment the claims of the contending powers (*Eumenides*); or at its bidding one of them softens its demand (*Philoctetes*); or again, as in the more beautiful solution of the *Oedipus Coloneus*, the hero by his own self-condemnation and inward purification reconciles himself with the supreme justice, and is accepted by it. But sometimes the quarrel is pressed to extremes; the denial of the one-sided claims involves the death of one or more of the persons concerned; and we have a catastrophe. The ultimate power thus appears as a destructive force. Yet even here, as Hegel insists, the end is not without an aspect of reconciliation. For that which is denied is not the rightful powers with which the combatants have identified themselves. On the contrary, those powers, and with them the only thing for which the combatants cared, are affirmed. What is denied is the exclusive and therefore wrongful assertion of their right.

Such in outline is Hegel's main view. It may be illustrated more fully by two examples, favourites of his, taken from Aeschylus and Sophocles. Clytemnestra has murdered Agamemnon, her husband and king. Orestes, their son, is impelled by filial piety to avenge his father, and is ordered by Apollo to do so. But to kill a mother is to sin against filial piety. The spiritual substance is divided against itself. The sacred bond of father and son demands what the equally sacred bond of son and mother forbids. When, therefore, Orestes has done the deed, the Furies of his murdered mother claim him for their prey. He appeals to Apollo, who resists their claim. A solution is arrived at without a catastrophe. The cause is referred to Athene, who institutes at Athens a court of sworn judges. The votes of this court being equally divided, Athene gives her casting-vote for Orestes; while the Furies are at last appeased by a promise of everlasting honour at Athens.

In the *Antigone*, on the other hand, to Hegel the 'perfect exemplar of tragedy,' the solution is negative. The brother of Antigone has brought against his native city an army of foreigners bent on destroying it. He has been killed in the battle, and Creon, the ruler of the city, has issued an edict forbidding anyone on pain of death to bury the corpse. In so doing he not only dishonours the dead man, but violates the rights of the gods of the dead. Antigone without hesitation disobeys the edict, and Creon, despite the remonstrance of his son, who is affianced to her, persists in exacting the penalty. Warned by the prophet Teiresias, he gives way, but too late. Antigone, immured in a rocky chamber to starve, has anticipated her death. Her lover follows her example, and his mother refuses to survive him. Thus Antigone has lost her life through her absolute assertion of the family against the state; Creon has violated the sanctity of the family, and in return sees his own home laid in ruins. But in this catastrophe neither the right of the family nor that of the state is denied; what is denied is the absoluteness of the claim of each.

The danger of illustrations like these is that they divert attention from the principle illustrated to questions about the interpretation of particular works. So it will be here. I cannot stay to discuss these questions, which do not affect Hegel's principle; but it will be well, before going further, to remove a misunderstanding of it which is generally to be found in criticisms of his treatment of the *Eumenides* and the *Antigone*. The main objection may be put thus : 'Hegel talks of equally justified powers or claims. But Aeschylus never meant that Orestes and the Furies were equally justified; for Orestes was acquitted. Nor did Sophocles mean that Antigone and Creon were equally right. And how can it have been equally the duty of Orestes to kill his mother and not to kill her?' But, in the first place, it is most important to observe that Hegel is not discussing at all what we should generally call the moral quality of the acts and persons concerned, or, in the ordinary sense, what it was their duty to do. And, in the second place, when he speaks of 'equally justified' powers, what he means, and, indeed, sometimes says, is that these powers are *in themselves* equally justified. The

family and the state, the bond of father and son,
the bond of mother and son, the bond of citizenship,
these are each and all, one as much as another,
powers rightfully claiming human allegiance.   It is
tragic that observance of one should involve the
violation of another.   These are Hegel's proposi-
tions, and surely they are true.   Their truth is quite
unaffected by the fact (assuming it is one) that in
the circumstances the act combining this observance
of one and violation of another was morally right,
or by the fact (if so it is) that one such act (say
Antigone's) was morally right, and another (say
Creon's) was morally wrong.   It is sufficient for
Hegel's principle that the violation should take
place, and that we should feel its weight.   We do
feel it.   We may approve the act of Antigone or
Orestes, but in approving it we still feel that it is
no light matter to disobey the law or to murder a
mother, that (as we might say) there is much justice
in the pleas of the Furies and of Creon, and that the
tragic effect depends upon these facts.   If, again,
it is objected that the underlying conflict in the
Antigone is not between the family and the state,
but between divine and human law, that objection,
if sound, might touch Hegel's interpretation,[1] but
it would not affect his principle, except for those
who recognise no obligation in human law ; and it
will scarcely be contended that Sophocles is to be
numbered among them.   On the other hand, it is,
I think, a matter for regret that Hegel employed
such words as 'right,' 'justified,' and 'justice.'
They do not mislead readers familiar with his
writings, but to others they suggest associations
with criminal law, or our everyday moral judgments,
or perhaps the theory of 'poetic justice' ; and these
are all out of place in a discussion on tragedy.

[1] I say 'might,' because Hegel himself in the *Phaenomenologie* uses
those very terms 'divine' and 'human law' in reference to the
Antigone.

Having determined in outline the idea or principle
of tragedy, Hegel proceeds to give an account of
some differences between ancient and modern works.
In the limited time at our disposal we shall do best
to confine ourselves to a selection from his remarks
on the latter. For in speaking of ancient tragedy
Hegel, who finds something modern in Euripides,
makes accordingly but little use of him for purposes of contrast, while his main point of view as
to Aeschylus and Sophocles has already appeared
in the illustrations we have given of the general
principle. I will only add, by way of preface, that
the pages about to be summarised leave on one,
rightly or wrongly, the impression that to his mind
the principle is more adequately realised in the best
classical tragedies than in modern works. But the
question whether this really was his deliberate
opinion would detain us too long from weightier
matters.[1]

Hegel considers first the cases where modern
tragedy resembles ancient in dealing with conflicts
arising from the pursuit of ends which may be called
substantial or objective and not merely personal.
And he points out that modern tragedy here shows
a much greater variety. Subjects are taken, for
example, from the quarrels of dynasties, of rivals
for the throne, of kings and nobles, of state and
church. Calderon shows the conflict of love and
honour regarded as powers imposing obligations.
Schiller in his early works makes his characters
defend the rights of nature against convention, or
of freedom of thought against prescription—rights
in their essence universal. Wallenstein aims at the
unity and peace of Germany; Karl Moor attacks
the whole arrangement of society; Faust seeks to
attain in thought and action union with the Absolute.
In such cases the end is more than personal; it
represents a power claiming the allegiance of the

[1] See Note at end of lecture.

individual; but, on the other hand, it does not
always or generally represent a great *ethical* institution or bond like the family or the state. We have
passed into a wider world.

But, secondly, he observes, in regard to modern
tragedy, that in a larger number of instances such
public or universal interests either do not appear
at all, or, if they appear, are scarcely more than
a background for the real subject. The real subject,
the impelling end or passion, and the ensuing conflict, is personal,—these particular characters with
their struggle and their fate. The importance
given to subjectivity—this is the distinctive mark
of modern sentiment, and so of modern art; and
such tragedies bear its impress. A part at least
of Hegel's meaning may be illustrated thus. We
are interested in the personality of Orestes or
Antigone, but chiefly as it shows itself in one
aspect, as identifying itself with a certain ethical
relation; and our interest in the personality is
inseparable and indistinguishable from our interest
in the power it represents. This is not so with
Hamlet, whose position so closely resembles that
of Orestes. What engrosses our attention is the
whole personality of Hamlet in his conflict, not with
an opposing spiritual power, but with circumstances
and, still more, with difficulties in his own nature.
No one could think of describing Othello as the
representative of an ethical family relation. His
passion, however much nobility he may show in
it, is personal. So is Romeo's love. It is not
pursued, like Posa's freedom of thought, as something universal, a right of man. Its right, if it
could occur to us to use the term at all, is Romeo's
right.

On this main characteristic of modern tragedy
others depend. For instance, that variety of subject
to which reference has just been made depends
on it. For when so much weight is attached to

personality, almost any fatal collision in which a
sufficiently striking character is involved may yield
material for tragedy.   Naturally, again, characteris-
ation has become fuller and more subtle, except in
dramas which are more or less an imitation of the
antique.   The characters in Greek tragedy are far
from being types or personified abstractions, as
those of classical French tragedy tend to be : they
are genuine individuals.   But still they are comparatively simple and easy to understand, and have
not the intricacy of the characters in Shakespeare.
These, for the most part, represent simply themselves ; and the loss of that interest which attached
to the Greek characters from their identification
with an ethical power, is compensated by an extraordinary subtlety in their portrayal, and also by
their possession of some peculiar charm or some
commanding superiority.   Finally, the interest in
personality explains the freedom with which characters more or less definitely evil are introduced in
modern tragedy.   Mephistopheles is as essentially
modern as Faust.   The passion of Richard or
Macbeth is not only personal, like that of Othello ;
it is egoistic and anarchic, and leads to crimes done
with a full knowledge of their wickedness ; but to
the modern mind the greatness of the personality
justifies its appearance in the position of hero.
Such beings as Iago and Goneril, almost portents
of evil, are not indeed made the heroes of tragedies;
but, according to Hegel, they would not have been
admitted in Greek tragedy at all.   If Clytemnestra
had been cited in objection as a parallel to Lady
Macbeth, he would have replied that Lady Macbeth
had not the faintest ground of complaint against
Duncan, while in reading the *Agamemnon* we are
frequently reminded that Clytemnestra's husband
was the sacrificer of their child.   He might have
added that Clytemnestra is herself an example of
the necessity, where one of the principal characters

inspires hatred or horror, of increasing the subtlety of the drawing or adding grandeur to the evil will.

It remains to compare ancient and modern tragedy in regard to the issue of the conflict. We have seen that Hegel attributes this issue in the former to the ethical substance or eternal justice, and so accounts for such reconciliation as we feel to be present even where the end is a catastrophe. Now, in the catastrophe of modern tragedy, he says, a certain justice is sometimes felt to be present; but even then it differs from the antique justice. It is in some cases more 'abstract': the end pursued by the hero, though it is not egoistic, is still presented rather as his particular end than as something rightful though partial; and hence the catastrophe appears as the reaction, not of an undivided ethical totality, but merely of the universal turning against a too assertive particular.[1] In cases, again, where the hero (Richard or Macbeth) openly attacks an ethical power and plunges into evil, we feel that he meets with justice, and only gets what he deserves; but then this justice is colder and more 'criminalistic' than that of ancient tragedy. Thus even when the modern work seems to resemble the ancient in its issue, the sense of reconciliation is imperfect. And partly for this reason, partly from the concentration of our interest on individuality as such, we desire to see in the individual himself some sort of reconciliation with his fate. What shape this will take depends, of course, on the story and the character of the hero. It may appear in a religious form, as his feeling that he is exchanging his earthly being for an indestructible happiness; or again, in his recognition of the justice of his fall; or at least he may show us that, in face of the forces that crush him to death, he maintains untouched the freedom and strength of his own will.

[1] This interpretation of Hegel's 'abstract' is more or less conjectural and doubtful.

But there remain, says Hegel, many modern tragedies where we have to attribute the catastrophe not to any kind of justice, but to unhappy circumstances and outward accidents. And then we can only feel that the individual whose merely personal ends are thwarted by mere particular circumstances and chances, pays the penalty that awaits existence in a scene of contingency and finitude. Such a feeling cannot rise above sadness, and, if the hero is a noble soul, it may become the impression of a dreadful external necessity. This impression can be avoided only when circumstance and accident are so depicted that they are felt to coincide with something in the hero himself, so that he is not simply destroyed by an outward force. So it is with Hamlet. ' This bank and shoal of time ' is too narrow for his soul, and the death that seems to fall on him by chance is also within him. And so in *Romeo and Juliet* we feel that the rose of a love so beautiful is too tender to bloom in the storm-swept valley of its birth. But such a feeling of reconciliation is still one of pain, an unhappy blessedness.[1] And if the situation displayed in a drama is of such a kind that we feel the issue to depend *simply* on the turn the dramatist may choose to give to the course of events, we are fully justified in our preference for a happy ending.

In this last remark (or rather in the pages misrepresented by it) Hegel, of course, is not criticising Shakespeare. He is objecting to the destiny-dramas of his own time, and to the fashionable indulgence in sentimental melancholy. Strongly as he asserted the essential function of negation throughout the universe, the affirmative power of the spirit, even in its profoundest divisions, was for him the deepest truth and the most inspiring theme. And

---

[1] Hegel's meaning does not fully appear in the sentences here condensed. The ' blessedness ' comes from the sense of greatness or beauty in the characters.

one may see this even in his references to Shakespeare. He appreciated Shakespeare's representation of extreme forms of evil, but, even if he was
fully satisfied of its justification, his personal preference lay in another direction, and while I do not
doubt that he thought *Hamlet* a greater work
than *Iphigenie*, I suspect he loved Goethe's play
the best.

Most of those who have thought about this
subject will agree that the ideas I have tried to
sketch are interesting and valuable ; but they suggest scores of questions. Alike in the account of
tragedy in general, and in that of the differences
between ancient and modern tragedy, everyone will
find statements to doubt and omissions to regret ;
and scarcely one of Hegel's interpretations of particular plays will escape objection. It is impossible
for me to touch on more than a few points ; and
to the main ideas I owe so much that I am more
inclined to dwell on their truth than to criticise
what seem to be defects. But perhaps after all
an attempt to supplement and amend may be the
best way of throwing some part of Hegel's meaning
more into relief. And I will begin with the attempt
to supplement.

He seems to be right in laying emphasis on the
action and conflict in tragedy rather than on the
suffering and misfortune. No mere suffering or
misfortune, no suffering that does not spring in
great part from human agency, and in some degree
from the agency of the sufferer, is tragic, however
pitiful or dreadful it may be. But, sufficient connection with these agencies being present, misfortune, the fall from prosperity to adversity, with the
suffering attending it, at once becomes tragic ; and
in many tragedies it forms a large ingredient, as
does the pity for it in the tragic feeling. Hegel, I
think, certainly takes too little notice of it ; and by

this omission he also withdraws attention from something the importance of which he would have admitted at once ; I mean the way in which suffering is borne. Physical pain, to take an extreme instance, is one thing : Philoctetes, bearing it, is another. And the noble endurance of pain that rends the heart is the source of much that is best worth having in tragedy.

Again, there is one particular kind of misfortune *not* obviously due to human agency, which undoubtedly may affect us in a tragic way. I mean that kind which suggests the idea of fate. Tragedies which represent man as the mere plaything of chance or a blank fate or a malicious fate, are never really deep : it is satisfactory to see that Maeterlinck, a man of true genius, has now risen above these ideas. But, where those factors of tragedy are present which Hegel emphasises, the impression of something fateful in what we call accident, the impression that the hero not only invites misfortune by his exceptional stature and exceptional daring, but is also, if I may so put it, strangely and terribly unlucky, is in many plays a genuine ingredient in tragic effect. It is so, for example, in the *Oedipus Tyrannus*. It is so even in dramas like Shakespeare's, which exemplify the saying that character is destiny. Hegel's own reference to the prominence of accident in the plot of *Hamlet* proves it. Othello would not have become Iago's victim if his own character had been different; but still, as we say, it is an extraordinary fatality which makes him the companion of the one man in the world who is at once able enough, brave enough, and vile enough to ensnare him. In the *Antigone* itself, and in the very catastrophe of it, accident plays its part : we can hardly say that it depends solely on the characters of Creon and Antigone that the one yields just too late to save the life of the other. Now, it may be said with truth that Hegel's whole account of the ultimate power in tragedy is a rationalisation of the idea of fate, but his remarks on this particular aspect of fate are neither sufficient nor satisfactory.

His insistence on the need for some element of reconciliation in a tragic catastrophe, and his remarks on the various forms it assumes, have the greatest value ; but one result of the omissions just noticed is that he sometimes exaggerates it, and at other times rates it too low. When he is speaking of the kind of tragedy he most approves, his language almost suggests that our feeling at the close of the conflict is, or should be, one of complete reconciliation. This it surely neither is nor can be. Not to mention the suffering and death we have witnessed, the very existence of the conflict, even if a supreme ethical power is felt to be asserted in its close, remains a painful fact, and, in large measure, a fact not understood. For, though we may be said to see, in one sense, how the opposition of spiritual powers arises, something in us, and that the best, still cries out against it. And even the perception or belief that it must needs be that offences come would not abolish our feeling that the necessity is terrible, or our pain in the woe of the guilty and the innocent. Nay, one may conjecture, the feeling and the pain would not vanish if we fully understood that the conflict and catastrophe were by a rational necessity involved in the divine and eternally accomplished purpose of the world. But this exaggeration in Hegel's language, if partly due to his enthusiasm for the affirmative, may be mainly, like some other defects, an accident of lecturing. In the *Philosophy of Religion*, I may add, he plainly states that in the solution even of tragedies like the *Antigone* something remains unresolved (ii. 135).

On the other hand, his treatment of the aspect of reconciliation in modern tragedy is in several respects insufficient. I will mention only one. He does not notice that in the conclusion of not a few

tragedies pain is mingled not merely with acquiescence, but with something like exultation. Is there
not such a feeling at the close of *Hamlet*, *Othello*,
and *King Lear*; and that although the end in the
last two cases touches the limit of legitimate pathos?
This exultation appears to be connected with our
sense that the hero has never shown himself so
great or noble as in the death which seals his failure.
A rush of passionate admiration, and a glory in the
greatness of the soul, mingle with our grief; and the
coming of death, so far from destroying these feelings, appears to leave them untouched, or even to
be entirely in harmony with them. If in such dramas
we may be said to feel that the ultimate power is no
mere fate, but a spiritual power, then we also feel
that the hero was never so near to this power as in
the moment when it required his life.

The last omission I would notice in Hegel's
theory is that he underrates the action in tragedy of
what may be called by a rough distinction moral
evil rather than defect. Certainly the part played
by evil differs greatly in different cases, but it is
never absent, not even from tragedies of Hegel's
favourite type. If it does not appear in the main
conflict, it appears in its occasion. You may say
that, while Iago and Macbeth have evil purposes,
neither the act of Orestes nor the vengeance of the
Furies, neither Antigone's breach of the edict nor
even Creon's insistence on her punishment, springs
from evil in them; but the situation with which
Orestes or Antigone has to deal, and so in a sense
the whole tragedy, arises from evil, the murder of
Agamemnon, and the attempt of Polyneices to bring
ruin on his native city. In fact, if we confine the
title 'tragedy' to plays ending with a catastrophe,
it will be found difficult to name great tragedies,
ancient or modern, in which evil has not directly or
indirectly a prominent part. And its presence has
an important bearing on the effect produced by the

catastrophe. On the one hand, it deepens the sense
of painful awe. The question why affirmative
spiritual forces should collide is hard enough ; but
the question why, together with them, there should
be generated violent evil and extreme depravity is
harder and more painful still. But, on the other
hand, the element of reconciliation in the catastrophe
is strengthened by recognition of the part played by
evil in bringing it about ; because our sense that
the ultimate power cannot endure the presence of
such evil is implicitly the sense that this power is
at least more closely allied with good. If it rejects
the exaggerated claims of its own isolated powers,
that which provokes from it a much more vehement
reaction must be still more alien to its nature.
This feeling is forcibly evoked by Shakespeare's
tragedies, and in many Greek dramas it is directly
appealed to by repeated reminders that what is
at work in the disasters is the unsleeping Ate which
follows an ancestral sin. If Aristotle did not in
some lost part of the *Poetics* discuss ideas like
this, he failed to give a complete rationale of Greek
tragedy.

I come lastly to the matter I have most at heart.
What I take to be the central idea in Hegel's
theory seems to me to touch the essence of tragedy.
And I will not assert that his own statement of it
fails to cover the whole field of instances. For he
does not teach, as he is often said to do, that tragedy
portrays only the conflict of such ethical powers as
the family and the state. He adds to these, as we
have seen, others, such as love and honour, together
with various universal ends ; and it may even be
maintained that he has provided in his general
statement for those numerous cases where, according
to himself, no substantial or universal ends collide,
but the interest is centred on 'personalities.' Nevertheless, when these cases come to be considered

more fully—and, in Hegel's view, they are the most
characteristically modern cases—we are not satisfied.
They naturally tend to appear as declensions from
the more ideal ancient form ; for how can a personality which represents only itself claim the interest
of one which represents something universal? And
further, they are sometimes described in a manner
which strikes the reader, let us say, of Shakespeare,
as both insufficient and misleading. Without raising,
then, unprofitable questions about the comparative
merits of ancient and modern tragedy, I should like
to propose a restatement of Hegel's general principle which would make it more obviously apply to
both.

If we omit all reference to ethical or substantial
powers and interests, what have we left? We have
the more general idea—to use again a formula not
Hegel's own—that tragedy portrays a self-division
and self-waste of spirit, or a division of spirit
involving conflict and waste. It is implied in this
that on *both* sides in the conflict there is a spiritual
value. The same idea may be expressed (again, I
think, not in Hegel's own words) by saying that the
tragic conflict is one not merely of good with evil,
but also, and more essentially, of good with good.
Only, in saying this, we must be careful to observe
that 'good' here means anything that has spiritual
value, not moral goodness alone,[1] and that 'evil'
has a similarly wide sense.

Now this idea of a division of spirit involving
conflict and waste covers the tragedies of ethical
and other universal powers, and it covers much
besides. According to it the collision of such
powers would be one kind of tragic collision, but
only one. *Why* are we tragically moved by the
conflict of family and state? Because we set a high
value on family and state. Why then should not
the conflict of anything else that has sufficient value

[1] Hegel himself expressly guards against this misconception.

affect us tragically? It does. The value must be
sufficient—a moderate value will not serve; and
other characteristics must be present which need
not be considered here. But, granted these conditions, *any* spiritual conflict involving spiritual
waste is tragic. And it is just one greatness of
modern art that it has shown the tragic fact in
situations of so many and such diverse kinds.
These situations have not the peculiar effectiveness of the conflicts preferred by Hegel, but they
may have an equal effectiveness peculiar to themselves.

Let me attempt to test these ideas by choosing a
most unfavourable instance—unfavourable because
the play seems at first to represent a conflict simply
of good and evil, and so, according both to Hegel's
statement and the proposed restatement, to be no
tragedy at all: I mean *Macbeth*. What is the
conflict here? It will be agreed that it does not
lie between two ethical powers or universal ends,
and that, as Hegel says, the main interest is in
personalities. Let us take it first, then, to lie
between Macbeth and the persons opposing him,
and let us ask whether there is not spiritual value
or good on both sides—not an equal amount of
good (that is not necessary), but enough good on
each to give the impression of spiritual waste. Is
there not such good in Macbeth? It is not a
question merely of moral goodness, but of good.
It is not a question of the use made of good, but
of its presence. And such bravery and skill in war
as win the enthusiasm of everyone about him; such
an imagination as few but poets possess; a conscience so vivid that his deed is to him beforehand
a thing of terror, and, once done, condemns him to
that torture of the mind on which he lies in restless
ecstasy; a determination so tremendous and a
courage so appalling that, for all this torment, he
never dreams of turning back, but, even when he

has found that life is a tale full of sound and fury, signifying nothing, will tell it out to the end though earth and heaven and hell are leagued against him ; are not these things, in themselves, good, and gloriously good? Do they not make you, for all your horror, admire Macbeth, sympathise with his agony, pity him, and see in him the waste of forces on which you place a spiritual value? It is simply on this account that he is for you, not the abstraction called a criminal who merely 'gets what he deserves' (art, like religion, knows no such thing), but a tragic hero, and that his war with other forces of indubitable spiritual worth is a tragic war.[1]

It is required by the restatement of Hegel's principle to show that in the external conflict of persons there is good on both sides. It is not required that this should be true, secondly, of both sides in the conflict within the hero's soul ; for the hero is only a part of the tragedy. Nevertheless in almost all cases, if not in all, it is true. It is obviously so where, as in the hero and also the heroine of the *Cid*, the contending powers in this internal struggle are love and honour. Even when love is of a quality less pure and has a destructive force, as in Shakespeare's Antony, it is clearly true. And it remains true even where, as in Hamlet and Macbeth, the contest seems to lie, and for most purposes might conveniently be said to lie, between forces simply good and simply the reverse. This is not really so, and the tragic effect depends upon the fact. It depends on our feeling that the elements in the man's nature are so inextricably blended that

---

[1] The same point may be put thus, in view of that dangerous word 'personality.' Our interest in Macbeth may be called interest in a personality ; but it is not an interest in some bare form of self-consciousness, nor yet in a person in the legal sense, but in a personality full of matter. This matter is not an ethical or universal end, but it must in a sense be universal—human nature in a particular form— or it would not excite the horror, sympathy, and admiration it does excite. Nor, again, could it excite these feelings if it were not composed largely of qualities on which we set a high value.

the good in him, that which we admire, instead of
simply opposing the evil, reinforces it. Macbeth's
imagination deters him from murder, but it also
makes the vision of a crown irresistibly bright. If
he had been less determined, nay, if his conscience
had been less maddening in its insistence that he
had thrown the precious jewel of his soul irretriev-
ably away, he might have paused after his first deed,
might even have repented. Yet his imagination,
his determination, and his conscience were things
good. Hamlet's desire to do his duty is a good
thing, but what opposes this desire is by no means
simply evil. It is something to which a substantial
contribution is made by the qualities we most admire
in him. Thus the nature of tragedy, as seen in the
external conflict, repeats itself on each side of this
conflict, and everywhere there is a spiritual value in
both the contending forces.

In showing that *Macbeth*, a tragedy as far removed as possible from the *Antigone* as understood
by Hegel, is still of one nature with it, and equally
answers to the account of tragedy proposed, it has
been necessary to ignore the great difference between
the two plays. But when once the common essence
of all tragedies has been determined, their differences become the interesting subject. They could
be distinguished according to the character of the
collisions on which they are built, or of the main
forces which move the principal agents. And it
may well be that, other things being equal (as they
never are), the tragedy in which the hero is, as we
say, a good man, is more tragic than that in which
he is, as we say, a bad one. The more spiritual
value, the more tragedy in conflict and waste. The
death of Hamlet or Othello is, so far, more tragic
than that of Macbeth, that of Macbeth than that of
Richard. Below Richard stands Iago, a figure still
tragic, but unfit for the hero's part; below him
persons like Regan or, in the very depth, Oswald,

characters no longer (at least in the dramatic sense) tragic at all. Moral evil, that is to say, so greatly diminishes the spiritual value we ascribe to the personality that a very large amount of good of some kind is required to bring this personality up to the tragic level, the destruction of evil as such being in no degree tragic. And again, it may well be that, other things being equal, the more nearly the contending forces approach each other in good- ness, the more tragic is the conflict; that the collision is, so far, more tragic in the *Antigone* than in *Macbeth*, and Hamlet's internal conflict than his struggle with outward enemies and obstacles. But it is dangerous to describe tragedy in terms that even appear to exclude *Macbeth*, or to describe *Macbeth*, even casually or by implication, in terms which imply that it portrays a conflict of mere evil with mere good.

The restatement of Hegel's main principle as to the conflict would involve a similar restatement as to the catastrophe (for we need not consider here those 'tragedies' which end with a solution). As before, we must avoid any reference to ethical or universal ends, or to the work of 'justice' in the catastrophe. We might then simply say that, as the tragic action portrays a self-division or intestinal conflict of spirit, so the catastrophe displays the violent annulling of this division or conflict. But this statement, which might be pretty generally accepted, would represent only half of Hegel's idea, and perhaps nothing of what is most characteristic and valuable in it. For the catastrophe (if I may put his idea in my own way) has two aspects, a negative and an affirmative, and we have ignored the latter. On the one hand it is the act of a power immeasurably superior to that of the con- flicting agents, a power which is irresistible and unescapable, and which overbears and negates whatever is incompatible with it. So far, it may

be called, in relation to the conflicting agents,[1]
necessity or fate ; and unless a catastrophe affects
us in ways corresponding with this aspect it is not
truly tragic. But then if this were all and this
necessity were merely infinite, characterless, external
force, the catastrophe would not only terrify (as it
should), it would also horrify, depress, or at best
provoke indignation or rebellion ; and these are not
tragic feelings. The catastrophe, then, must have
a second and affirmative aspect, which is the source
of our feelings of reconciliation, whatever form they
may assume. And this will be taken into account if
we describe the catastrophe as the violent self-
restitution of the divided spiritual unity. The
necessity which acts and negates in it, that is to
say, is yet of one substance with both the agents.
It is divided against itself in them ; they are *its*
conflicting forces ; and in restoring its unity through
negation it affirms them, so far as they are compatible with that unity. The qualification is essential,
since the hero, for all his affinity with that power, is,
as the living man we see before us, not so compatible. He must die, and his union with ' eternal
justice ' (which is more than ' justice ') must itself
be ' eternal ' or ideal. But the qualification does
not abolish what it qualifies. This is no occasion
to ask how in particular, and in what various ways
in various works, we feel the effect of this affirmative aspect in the catastrophe. But it corresponds
at least with that strange double impression which
is produced by the hero's death. He dies, and
our hearts die with him ; and yet his death
matters nothing to us, or we even exult. He is
dead ; and he has no more to do with death than
the power which killed him and with which he
is one.

[1] In relation to *both* sides in the conflict (though it may not need to
negate life in both). For the ultimate agent in the catastrophe is
emphatically not the finite power of one side. It is beyond both, and,
at any rate in relation to them, boundless.

I leave it to students of Hegel to ask whether he would have accepted the criticisms and modifications I have suggested. Naturally I think he would, as I believe they rest on truth, and am sure he had a habit of arriving at truth. But in any case their importance is trifling, compared with that of the theory which they attempt to strengthen and to which they owe their existence.

1901.

NOTE

Why did Hegel, in his lectures on Aesthetics, so treat of tragedy as to suggest the idea that the kind of tragedy which he personally preferred (let us for the sake of brevity call it 'ancient') is also the most adequate embodiment of the idea of tragedy? This question can be answered, I think, only conjecturally, but some remarks on it may have an interest for readers of Hegel (they are too brief to be of use to others).

One answer might be this. Hegel did not really hold that idea. But he was lecturing, not writing a book. He thought the principle of tragedy was more clearly and readily visible in ancient works than in modern; and so, for purposes of exposition, he emphasised the ancient form. And this fact, with his personal enthusiasm for certain Greek plays, leads the reader of the *Aesthetik* to misconstrue him.

Again, we must remember the facts of Hegel's life. He seems first to have reflected on tragedy at a time when his enthusiasm for the Greeks and their 'substantial' ethics was combined, not only with a contemptuous dislike for much modern 'subjectivity' (this he never ceased to feel), but with a certain hostility to the individualism and the un-political character of Christian morality. His first view of tragedy was thus, in effect, a theory of Aeschylean and Sophoclean tragedy; and it appears in the early essay on *Naturrecht* and more fully in the *Phaenomenologie*. Perhaps, then, when he came to deal with the subject more generally, he insensibly regarded the ancient form as the typical form, and tended to treat the modern rather as a modification of this type than as an alternative embodiment of the general idea of tragedy. The note in the *Rechtsphilosophie* (p. 196) perhaps favours this idea

But, whether it is correct or no, I believe that the impression produced by the *Aesthetik* is a true one, and that Hegel did deliberately consider the ancient form the more satisfactory. It would not follow, of course, from that opinion that he thought the advantage was all on one side, or considered this or that ancient poet greater than this or that modern, or wished that modern poets had tried to write tragedies of the Greek type. Tragedy would, in his view, be in somewhat the same position as Sculpture. Renaissance sculpture, he might say, has qualities in which it is superior to Greek, and Michael Angelo may have been as great an artist as Pheidias; but all the same for certain reasons Greek sculpture is, and probably will remain, sculpture *par excellence*. So, though not to the same extent, with tragedy.

And such a view would cohere with his general view of Art. For he taught that, in a sense, Classical Art is Art *par excellence*, and that in Greece beauty held a position such as it never held before and will not hold again. To explain in a brief note how this position bears upon his treatment of modern tragedy would be impossible: but if the student of Hegel will remember in what sense and on what grounds he held it; that he describes Beauty as the '*sinnliches* Scheinen der Idee'; that for him the new idea that distinguished Christianity and Romantic Art from Greek religion and Classical Art is that '*unendliche* Subjektivität' which implies a negative, though not merely negative, relation to sense; and that in Romantic Art this idea is not only exhibited in the religious sphere, but appears in the position given to personal honour, love, and loyalty, and indirectly in what Hegel calls 'die formelle Selbst-ständigkeit der individuellen Besonderheiten,' and in the fuller admission of common and un-beautiful reality into the realm of Beauty,—he will see how all this is connected with those characteristics of modern tragedy which Hegel regards as necessary and yet as, in part, drawbacks. This connection, which Hegel has no occasion to work out, will be apparent even from consideration of the introductory chapter on 'die romantische Kunstform,' *Aesthetik*, ii. 120-135.

There is one marked difference, I may add, between ancient and modern tragedy, which should be considered with reference to this subject, and which Hegel, I think, does not explicitly

point out. Speaking roughly, we may say that the former
includes, while the latter tends to ignore, the accepted religious
ideas of the time. The ultimate reason of this difference, on
Hegel's view, would be that the Olympian gods are themselves
the '*sinnliches* Scheinen der Idee,' and so are in the same
element as Art, while this is, on the whole, not so with modern
religious ideas. One result would be that Greek tragedy
represents the total Greek mind more fully than modern
tragedy can the total modern mind.

WORDSWORTH

WORDSWORTH [1]

'NEVER forget what, I believe, was observed to you by Coleridge, that every great and original writer, in proportion as he is great or original, must himself create the taste by which he is to be relished; he must teach the art by which he is to be seen. . . . My ears are stone-dead to this idle buzz, and my flesh as insensible as iron to these petty stings.' These sentences, from a letter written by Wordsworth to Lady Beaumont in 1807, may remind us of the common attitude of his reviewers in the dozen years when most of his best poetry was produced. A century has gone by, and there is now no English poet, either of that period or of any other, who has been the subject of criticism more just, more appreciative, we may even say more reverential. Some of this later criticism might have satisfied even that sense of wonder, awe, and solemn responsibility with which the poet himself regarded the operation of the spirit of poetry within him; and if we desire an interpretation of that spirit, we shall find a really astonishing number of excellent

[1] The following pages reproduce the two concluding lectures of a short course on the Age of Wordsworth, given at Oxford in April, 1903, and intended specially for undergraduates in the School of English Language and Literature. A few passages from the other lectures appear elsewhere in this volume. On the subject of the course may I advise any reader who may need the advice to consult Professor Herford's *The Age of Wordsworth*, a little book which is familiar to students of the history of English Literature, and the more admired the more they use it?

guides. Coleridge, Hazlitt, Arnold, Swinburne,
Brooke, Myers, Pater, Lowell, Legouis,—how easy
to add to this list of them! Only the other day
there came another, Mr. Walter Raleigh. And
that the best book on an English poet that has
appeared for some years should be a study of
Wordsworth is just what might have been expected. The whirligig of time has brought him a
full revenge.

I have no idea of attempting in these two lectures
another study, or even an estimate, of Wordsworth.
My purpose is much more limited. I think that
in a good deal of current criticism, and also in the
notions of his poetry prevalent among general
readers, a disproportionate emphasis is often laid
on certain aspects of his mind and writings. And
I should like to offer some words of warning as
to this tendency, and also some advice as to the
spirit in which he should be approached. I will
begin with the advice, though I am tempted at the
last moment to omit it, and simply to refer you to
Mr. Raleigh, who throughout his book has practised
what I am about to preach.

I.

There have been greater poets than Wordsworth, but none more original. He saw new
things, or he saw things in a new way. Naturally,
this would have availed us little if his new things
had been private fancies, or if his new perception had been superficial. But that was not so.
If it had been, Wordsworth might have won
acceptance more quickly, but he would not have
gained his lasting hold on poetic minds. As it
is, those in whom he creates the taste by which
he is relished, those who learn to love him (and
in each generation they are not a few), never let
him go. Their love for him is of the kind that
he himself celebrated, a settled passion, perhaps

'slow to begin,' but 'never ending,' and twined around the roots of their being. And the reason is that they find his way of seeing the world, his poetic experience, what Arnold meant by his 'criticism of life,' to be something deep, and therefore something that will hold. It continues to bring them joy, peace, strength, exaltation. It does not thin out or break beneath them as they grow older and wiser; nor does it fail them, much less repel them, in sadness or even in their sorest need. And yet—to return to our starting-point—it continues to strike them as original, and something more. It is not like Shakespeare's myriad-mindedness; it is, for good or evil or both, peculiar. They can remember, perhaps, the day when first they saw a cloud somewhat as Wordsworth saw it, or first really understood what made him write this poem or that; his unique way of seeing and feeling, though now familiar and beloved, still brings them not only peace, strength, exaltation, but a 'shock of mild surprise'; and his paradoxes, long known by heart and found full of truth, still remain paradoxes.

If this is so, the road into Wordsworth's mind must be through his strangeness and his paradoxes, and not round them. I do not mean that they are everywhere in his poetry. Much of it, not to speak of occasional platitudes, is beautiful without being peculiar or difficult; and some of this may be as valuable as that which is audacious or strange. But unless we get hold of that, we remain outside Wordsworth's centre; and, if we have not a most unusual affinity to him, we cannot get hold of that unless we realise its strangeness, and refuse to blunt the sharpness of its edge. Consider, for example, two or three of his statements; the statements of a poet, no doubt, and not of a philosopher, but still evidently statements expressing, intimating, or symbolising, what for him was the most vital truth. He said that the meanest

flower that blows could give him thoughts that
often lie too deep for tears. He said, in a poem
not less solemn, that Nature was the soul of all his
moral being ; and also that she can so influence us
that nothing will be able to disturb our faith that
all that we behold is full of blessings. After making
his Wanderer tell the heart-rending tale of Margaret, he makes him say that the beauty and
tranquillity of her ruined cottage had once so affected
him

> That what we feel of sorrow and despair
> From ruin and from change, and all the grief
> The passing shows of Being leave behind,
> Appeared an idle dream, that could not live
> Where meditation was.

He said that this same Wanderer could read in the
silent faces of the clouds unutterable love, and that
among the mountains all things for him breathed
immortality. He said to 'Almighty God,'

> But thy most dreaded instrument
> For working out a pure intent
> Is Man arrayed for mutual slaughter ;
> Yea, Carnage is thy daughter.

This last, it will be agreed, is a startling statement ;
but is it a whit more extraordinary than the others?
It is so only if we assume that we are familiar
with thoughts that lie too deep for tears, or if we
translate 'the soul of all my moral being' into
'somehow concordant with my moral feelings,' or
convert 'all that we behold' into 'a good deal that
we behold,' or transform the Wanderer's reading
of the silent faces of the clouds into an argument
from 'design.' But this is the road round Wordsworth's mind, not into it.[1]

---

[1] These statements, with the exception of the last, were chosen
partly because they all say, with the most manifest seriousness, much
the same thing that is said, with a touch of playful exaggeration, in
The Tables Turned, where occurs that outrageous stanza about 'one
impulse from a vernal wood' which Mr. Raleigh has well defended.
When all fitting allowance has been made for the fact that these

Again, with all Wordsworth's best poems, it is essential not to miss the unique tone of his experience. This doubtless holds good of any true poet, but not in the same way. With many poems there is little risk of our failing either to feel what is distinctive of the writer, or to appropriate what he says. What is characteristic, for example, in Byron's lines, *On this day I complete my thirty-sixth year*, or in Shelley's *Stanzas written in dejection near Naples*, cannot escape discovery, nor is there any difficulty in understanding the mood expressed. But with Wordsworth, for most readers, this risk is constantly present in some degree. Take, for instance, one of the most popular of his lyrics, the poem about the daffodils by the lake. It is popular partly because it remains a pretty thing even to those who convert it into something quite undistinctive of Wordsworth. And it is comparatively easy, too, to perceive and to reproduce in imagination a good deal that *is* distinctive; for instance, the feeling of the sympathy of the waves and the flowers and the breeze in their glee, and the Wordsworthian 'emotion recollected in tranquillity' expressed in the lines (written by his wife),

> They flash upon that inward eye
> Which is the bliss of solitude.

But there remains something still more intimately Wordsworthian :

> I wandered lonely as a Cloud
> That floats on high o'er vales and hills.

It is thrust into the reader's face, for these are the opening lines. But with many readers it passes unheeded, because it is strange and outside their

---

statements, and many like them, are 'poetic,' they ought to remain startling. Two of them—that from the story of Margaret (*Excursion*, I.), and that from the *Ode*, 1815—were made less so, to the injury of the passages, by the Wordsworth of later days, who had forgotten what he felt, or yielded to the objections of others.

own experience. And yet it is absolutely essential to the effect of the poem.

This poem, however, even when thoroughly conventionalised, would remain, as I said, a pretty thing; and it could scarcely excite derision. Our point is best illustrated from the pieces by which Wordsworth most earned ridicule, the ballad poems. They arose almost always from some incident which, for him, had a novel and arresting character and came on his mind with a certain shock; and if we do not get back to this through the poem, we remain outside it. We may, of course, get back to this and yet consider the poem to be more or less a failure. There is here therefore room for legitimate differences of opinion. Mr. Swinburne sees, no doubt, as clearly as Coleridge did, the intention of *The Idiot Boy* and *The Thorn*, yet he calls them 'doleful examples of eccentricity in dullness,' while Coleridge's judgment, though he criticised both poems, was very different. I believe (if I may venture into the company of such critics) that I see why Wordsworth wrote *Goody Blake and Harry Gill* and the *Anecdote for Fathers*, and yet I doubt if he has succeeded in either; but a great man, Charles James Fox, selected the former for special praise, and Matthew Arnold included the latter in a selection from which he excluded *The Sailor's Mother*.[1] Indeed, of all the poems at first most ridiculed there is probably not one that has not

---

[1] *Goody Blake*, to my mind, tries vainly to make the kind of impression overwhelmingly made by Coleridge's *Three Graves*. The question as to the *Anecdote for Fathers* is not precisely whether it makes you laugh, but whether it makes you laugh at the poet, and in such a way that the end fails to restore your sobriety. The danger is in the lines,

> And five times to the child I said,
> Why, Edward, tell me why?

The reiteration, with the struggle between the poet and his victim, is thoroughly Wordsworthian, and there are cases where it is managed with perfect success, as we shall see; but to me it has here the effect so delightfully reproduced in *Through the Looking-glass* ('I'll tell thee everything I can').

been praised by some excellent judge. But they were ridiculed by men who judged them without attempting first to get inside them. And this is fatal.

I may bring out the point by referring more fully to one of them. *Alice Fell* was beloved by the best critic of the nineteenth century, Charles Lamb; but the general distaste for it was such that it was excluded 'in policy' from edition after edition of Wordsworth's Poems; many still who admire *Lucy Gray* see nothing to admire in *Alice Fell*; and you may still hear the question asked, What could be made of a child crying for the loss of her cloak? And what, I answer, could be made of a man poking his stick into a pond to find leeches? What sense is there in asking questions about the subject of a poem, if you first deprive this subject of all the individuality it possesses in the poem? Let me illustrate this individuality methodically. A child crying for the loss of her cloak is one thing quite another is a child who has an imagination, and who sees the tattered remnants of her cloak whirling in the wheel-spokes of a post-chaise fiercely driven by strangers on lonesome roads through a night of storm in which the moon is drowned. She was alone, and, having to reach the town she belonged to, she got up behind the chaise, and her cloak was caught in the wheel. And she is fatherless and motherless, and her poverty (the poem is called *Alice Fell, or Poverty*) is so extreme that for the loss of her weather-beaten rag she does not 'cry'; she weeps loud and bitterly; weeps as if her innocent heart would break; sits by the stranger who has placed her by his side and is trying to console her, insensible to all relief; sends forth sob after sob as if her grief could never, never have an end; checks herself for a moment to answer a question, and then weeps on as if she had lost her only friend, and the thought would choke her very heart.

It was *this* poverty and *this* grief that Wordsworth described with his reiterated hammering blows. Is it not pathetic? And to Wordsworth it was more. To him grief like this is sublime. It is the agony of a soul from which something is torn away that was made one with its very being. What does it matter whether the thing is a woman, or a kingdom, or a tattered cloak? It is the passion that counts. Othello must not agonise for a cloak, but 'the little orphan Alice Fell' has nothing else to agonise for. Is all this insignificant? And then—for this poem about a child is right to the last line—next day the storm and the tragedy have vanished, and the new cloak is bought, of duffil grey, as warm a cloak as man can sell; and the child is as pleased as Punch.[1]

2.

I pass on from this subject to another, allied to it, but wider. In spite of all the excellent criticism of Wordsworth, there has gradually been formed, I think, in the mind of the general reader a partial and misleading idea of the poet and his work. This partiality is due to several causes: for instance, to the fact that personal recollections of Wordsworth have inevitably been, for the most part, recollections of his later years; to forgetfulness of his position in the history of literature, and of the restricted purpose of his first important poems; and to the insistence of some of his most influential critics, notably Arnold, on one particular source of his power—an insistence perfectly just, but accompanied now and then by a lack of sympathy with other aspects of his poetry. The result is an idea of him which is mainly true and really characteristic, but yet incomplete, and so, in a sense, untrue; a picture, I might say, somewhat like Millais' first portrait of Gladstone, which renders the inspiration,

[1] Some remarks on *We are seven* are added in a note at the end of the lecture.

the beauty, the light, but not the sternness or imperiousness, and not all of the power and fire. Let me try to express this idea, which, it is needless to say, I do not attribute, in the shape here given to it, to anyone in particular.

It was not Wordsworth's function to sing, like most great poets, of war, or love, or tragic passions, or the actions of supernatural beings. His peculiar function was 'to open out the soul of little and familiar things,' alike in nature and in human life. His 'poetry is great because of the extraordinary power with which he feels the joy offered to us in nature, the joy offered to us in the simple primary affections and duties.' His field was therefore narrow; and, besides, he was deficient in romance, his moral sympathies were somewhat limited, and he tended also to ignore the darker aspects of the world. But in this very optimism lay his strength. The gulf which for Byron and Shelley yawned between the real and the ideal, had no existence for him. For him the ideal was realised, and Utopia a country which he saw every day, and which, he thought, every man might see who did not strive, nor cry, nor rebel, but opened his heart in love and thankfulness to sweet influences as universal and perpetual as the air. The spirit of his poetry was also that of his life—a life full of strong but peaceful affections; of a communion with nature in keen but calm and meditative joy; of perfect devotion to the mission with which he held himself charged; and of a natural piety gradually assuming a more distinctively religious tone. Some verses of his own best describe him, and some verses of Matthew Arnold his influence on his readers. These are his own words (from *A Poet's Epitaph*) :

> But who is he, with modest looks,
> And clad in homely russet brown?
> He murmurs near the running brooks
> A music sweeter than their own.

He is retired as noontide dew,
Or fountain in a noon-day grove ;
And you must love him, ere to you
He will seem worthy of your love.

The outward shows of sky and earth,
Of hill and valley, he has viewed ;
And impulses of deeper birth
Have come to him in solitude.

In common things that round us lie
Some random truths he can impart,
—The harvest of a quiet eye
That broods and sleeps on his own heart.

But he is weak ; both man and boy,
Hath been an idler in the land :
Contented if he might enjoy
The things which others understand.

And these are the words from Arnold's *Memorial Verses* :

He too upon a wintry clime
Had fallen—on this iron time
Of doubts, disputes, distractions, fears
He found us when the age had bound
Our souls in its benumbing round—
He spoke, and loosed our heart in tears.
He laid us as we lay at birth
On the cool flowery lap of earth ;
Smiles broke from us and we had ease.
The hills were round us, and the breeze
Went o'er the sunlit fields again ;
Our foreheads felt the wind and rain.
Our youth returned : for there was shed
On spirits that had long been dead,
Spirits dried up and closely furled,
The freshness of the early world.

Ah, since dark days still bring to light
Man's prudence and man's fiery might,
Time may restore us in his course
Goethe's sage mind and Byron's force ;
But where will Europe's latter hour
Again find Wordsworth's healing power ?
Others will teach us how to dare,
And against fear our breast to steel ;
Others will strengthen us to bear—
But who, ah who, will make us feel ?

> The cloud of mortal destiny,
> Others will front it fearlessly—
> But who, like him, will put it by?
>
> Keep fresh the grass upon his grave,
> O Rotha! with thy living wave.
> Sing him thy best! for few or none
> Hears thy voice right, now he is gone.

Those last words are enough to disarm dissent. No, that voice will never again be heard quite right now Wordsworth is gone. Nor is it, for the most part, dissent that I wish to express. The picture we have been looking at, though we may question the accuracy of this line or that, seems to me, I repeat, substantially true. But is there nothing missing? Consider this picture, and refuse to go beyond it, and then ask if it accounts for all that is most characteristic in Wordsworth. How did the man in the picture ever come to write the Immortality *Ode*, or *Yew-trees*, or why should he say,

> For I must tread on shadowy ground, must sink
> Deep—and, aloft ascending, breathe in worlds
> To which the heaven of heavens is but a veil?

How, again, could he say that Carnage is God's daughter, or write the *Sonnets dedicated to National Liberty and Independence*, or the tract on the Convention of Cintra? Can it be true of him that many of his best-known poems of human life— perhaps the majority—deal with painful subjects, and not a few with extreme suffering? Should we expect him to make an 'idol' of Milton, or to show a 'strong predilection for such geniuses as Dante and Michael Angelo'? He might easily be 're-served,' but is it not surprising to find him described as haughty, prouder than Lucifer, inhumanly arrogant? Why should his forehead have been marked by the 'severe worn pressure of thought,' or his eyes have looked so 'supernatural . . . like fires, half burning, half smouldering, with a sort of acrid fixture of regard, and seated at the further end of two caverns'?   In all this there need be nothing inconsistent with the picture we have been looking at; but that picture fails to suggest it.   In that way the likeness it presents is only partial, and I propose to emphasise some of the traits which it omits or marks too faintly.[1]

And first as to the restriction of Wordsworth's field.   Certainly his field, as compared with that of some poets, is narrow; but to describe it as confined to external nature and peasant life, or to little and familiar things, would be absurdly untrue, as a mere glance at his Table of Contents suffices to show.   And its actual restriction was not due to any false theory, nor mainly to any narrowness of outlook.   It was due, apart from limitation of endowment, on the one hand to that diminution of poetic energy which in Wordsworth began comparatively soon, and on the other, especially in his best days, to deliberate choice; and we must not assume without question that he was inherently incapable of doing either what he would not do, or what, in his last five and thirty years, he could no longer do.

There is no reason to suppose that Wordsworth undervalued or objected to the subjects of such poets as Homer and Virgil, Chaucer and Spenser, Shakespeare and Milton.   And when, after writing his part of the *Lyrical Ballads,* he returned from Germany and settled in the Lake Country, the subjects he himself revolved for a great poem were not concerned with rural life or humble persons. Some old 'romantic' British theme, left unsung by Milton; some tale of Chivalry, dire enchantments, war-like feats; vanquished Mithridates passing north and becoming Odin; the fortunes of the followers of Sertorius; de Gourgues' journey of

[1] The phrases quoted in this paragraph are taken chiefly from Hazlitt and De Quincey.

vengeance to Florida; Gustavus; Wallace and his
exploits in the war for his country's independence,—
these are the subjects he names first. And, though
his 'last and favourite aspiration' was towards

> Some philosophic song
> Of Truth that cherishes our daily life,

—that song which was never completed—yet, some
ten years later, he still hoped, when it should be
finished, to write an epic. Whether at any time
he was fitted for the task or no, he wished to
undertake it; and his addiction, by no means
entire even in his earlier days, to little and
familiar things was due, not at all to an opinion
that they are the only right subjects or the best,
nor merely to a natural predilection for them, but
to the belief that a particular kind of poetry was
wanted at that time to counteract its special
evils. There prevailed, he thought, a 'degrading
thirst after outrageous stimulation.' The violent
excitement of public events, and 'the increasing
accumulation of men in cities, where the uniformity
of their occupations produces a craving for extraordinary incident, which the rapid communication
of intelligence hourly gratifies,' had induced a
torpor of mind which only yielded to gross and
sensational effects—such effects as were produced
by 'frantic novels,' of the Radcliffe or Monk Lewis
type, full of mysterious criminals, gloomy castles
and terrifying spectres. He wanted to oppose to
this tendency one as far removed from it as
possible; to write a poetry even *more* alien to it
than Shakespeare's tragedies or Spenser's stories of
knights and dragons; to show men that wonder
and beauty can be felt, and the heart be moved,
even when the rate of the pulse is perfectly normal.
In the same way, he grieved Coleridge by refusing
to interest himself in the Somersetshire fairies, and
declared that he desired for his scene no planet

but the earth, and no region of the earth stranger
than England and the lowliest ways in England.
And, being by no means merely a gentle shepherd,
but a born fighter who was easily provoked and
could swing his crook with uncommon force, he
asserted his convictions defiantly and carried them
out to extremes. And so in later days, after he
had somewhat narrowed, when in the Seventh
Book of the *Excursion* he made the Pastor protest
that poetry was not wanted to multiply and aggra-
vate the din of war, or to propagate the pangs and
turbulence of passionate love, he did this perhaps
because the world which would not listen to him [1]
was enraptured by *Marmion* and the earlier poems
of Byron.

How great Wordsworth's success might have
been in fields which he deliberately avoided, it is
perhaps idle to conjecture. I do not suppose it
would have been very great, but I see no reason
to believe that he would have failed. With regard,
for instance, to love, one cannot read without a
smile his reported statement that, had he been a
writer of love-poetry, it would have been natural
to him to write it with a degree of warmth which
could hardly have been approved by his principles,
and which might have been undesirable for the
reader. But one may smile at his naïveté without
disbelieving his statement. And, in fact, Wordsworth neither wholly avoided the subject nor failed
when he touched it. The poems about Lucy are
not poems of passion, in the usual sense, but they
surely are love-poems. The verses *'Tis said thaῐ
some have died for love*, excluded from Arnold's
selection but praised by Ruskin, are poignant
enough. And the following lines from *Vaudracour
and Julia* make one wonder how this could be to

[1] The publication of the *Excursion* seems to have been postponed
for financial reasons. One edition of a thousand copies sufficed the
world for thirteen years.

Arnold the only poem of Wordsworth's that he could not read with pleasure :

> Arabian fiction never filled the world
> With half the wonders that were wrought for him.
> Earth breathed in one great presence of the spring ;
> Life turned the meanest of her implements,
> Before his eyes, to price above all gold ;
> The house she dwelt in was a sainted shrine ;
> Her chamber-window did surpass in glory
> The portals of the dawn ; all paradise
> Could, by the simple opening of a door,
> Let itself in upon him :—pathways, walks,
> Swarmed with enchantment, till his spirit sank,
> Surcharged, within him, overblest to move
> Beneath a sun that wakes a weary world
> To its dull round of ordinary cares ;
> A man too happy for mortality !

As a whole, *Vaudracour and Julia* is a failure, but these lines haunt my memory, and I cannot think them a poor description of that which they profess to describe. This is not precisely 'passion,' and, I admit, they do not prove Wordsworth's capacity to deal with passion. The main reason for doubting whether, if he had made the attempt, he would have reached his highest level, is that, so far as we can see, he did not strongly feel— perhaps hardly felt at all—that the *passion* of love is a way into the Infinite ; and a thing must be no less than this to Wordsworth if it is to rouse all his power. Byron, it seemed to him, had

> dared to take
> Life's rule from passion craved for passion's sake ;[1]

and he utterly repudiated that. 'The immortal mind craves objects that endure.'

Then there is that 'romance' which Wordsworth abjured. In using the word I am employing the familiar distinction between two tendencies of the Romantic Revival, one called naturalistic and one called, in a more special sense, romantic, and

---

[1] *Evening Voluntaries*, iv. We know that he refers to Byron.

signalised, among other ways, by a love of the
marvellous, the supernatural, the exotic, the worlds
of mythology. It is a just and necessary distinction : the *Ancient Mariner* and *Michael* are
very dissimilar. But, like most distinctions of the
kind, it becomes misleading when it is roughly
handled or pushed into an antithesis; and it would
be easy to show that these two tendencies exclude
one another only in their inferior examples, and
that the better the example of either, the more it
shows its community with the other. There is
not a great deal of truth to nature in *Lalla Rookh*,
but there is plenty in the *Ancient Mariner*: in
certain poems of Crabbe there is little romance, but
there is no want of it in *Sir Eustace Grey* or in
Peter Grimes. Taking the distinction, however,
as we find it, and assuming, as I do, that it lay
beyond Wordsworth's power to write an *Ancient
Mariner*, or to tell us of

> magic casements opening on the foam
> Of perilous seas in faery lands forlorn,

we are not therefore to conclude that he was by
nature deficient in romance and incapable of writing
well what he refused to write. The indications are
quite contrary. Not to speak here of his own
peculiar dealings with the supernatural, his vehement
defence (in the *Prelude*) of fairy-tales as food for
the young is only one of many passages which show
that in his youth he lived in a world not haunted
only by the supernatural powers of nature. He
delighted in 'Arabian fiction.' The 'Arabian sands'
(*Solitary Reaper*) had the same glamour for him as
for others. His dream of the Arab and the two
books (*Prelude*, v.) has a very curious romantic
effect, though it is not romance *in excelsis*, like
Kubla Khan. His love of Spenser; his very
description of him,

> Sweet Spenser, moving through his clouded heaven
> With the moon's beauty and the moon's soft pace ;

the very lines, so characteristic of his habitual attitude, in which he praises the Osmunda fern as

> lovelier, in its own retired abode
> On Grasmere's beach, than Naiad by the side
> Of Grecian brook, or Lady of the Mere
> Sole-sitting by the shores of old romance,[1]

—these, and a score of other passages, all point the same way. He would not carry his readers to the East, like Southey and Moore and Byron, nor, like Coleridge, towards the South Pole; but when it suited his purpose, as in *Ruth*, he could write well enough of un-English scenery:

> He told of the magnolia, spread
> High as a cloud, high overhead,
> The cypress and her spire;
> Of flowers that with one scarlet gleam
> Cover a hundred leagues, and seem
> To set the hills on fire.

He would not choose Endymion or Hyperion for a subject, for he was determined to speak of what Englishmen may see every day; but what he wrote of Greek religion in the *Excursion* is full of imagination and brought inspiration to Keats, and the most famous expression in English of that longing for the perished glory of Greek myth which appears in much Romantic poetry came from Wordsworth's pen:

> Great God! I'd rather be
> A Pagan suckled in a creed outworn;
> So might I, standing on this pleasant lea,
> Have glimpses that would make me less forlorn;
> Have sight of Proteus rising from the sea;
> Or hear old Triton blow his wreathed horn.

As for war, Wordsworth neither strongly felt, nor at all approved, that elementary love of fighting which, together with much nobler things, is gratified by some great poetry. And assuredly he could not, even if he would, have rivalled the last canto of

---

[1] *Poems on the Naming of Places*, iv. Keats need not have been ashamed to write the last line.

Marmion, nor even the best passages in the *Siege of Corinth.* But he is not to be judged by his intentional failures. The martial parts of the *White Doe of Rylstone* are, with few exceptions, uninteresting, if not painfully tame. The former at least they were meant to be. The *Lay of the Last Minstrel* was on every tongue. The modest poet was as stiff-necked a person as ever walked the earth; and he was determined that no reader of his poem who missed its spiritual interest should be interested in anything else. Probably he overshot his mark. For readers who could understand him the effect he aimed at would not have been weakened by contrast with an outward action narrated with more spirit and sympathy. But, however that may be, he did what he meant to do. In the *Song at the Feast of Brougham Castle,* again, the warlike close of the Song was not written for its own sake. It was designed with a view to the transition to the longer metre, the thought of peace in communion with nature, and the wonderful stanza ' Love had he found in huts where poor men lie.' But, for the effect of this transition, it was necessary for Wordsworth to put his heart into the martial close of the Song; and surely it has plenty of animation and glory. Its author need not have shrunk from the subject of war if he had wished to handle it *con amore.*

The poet whose portrait we drew when we began might have been the author of the *White Doe,* and perhaps of *Brougham Castle,* and possibly of the *Happy Warrior.* He could no more have composed the *Poems dedicated to National Independence and Liberty* than the political sonnets of Milton. And yet Wordsworth wrote nothing more characteristic than these *Poems,* which I am not going to praise, since Mr. Swinburne's praise of them is, to my mind, not less just than eloquent. They are characteristic in many ways. The later are, on the whole, decidedly inferior to the earlier. Even in this little series,

which occupies the first fifteen years of the century,
the decline of Wordsworth's poetic power and the
increasing use of theological ideas are clearly visible.
The Odes, again, are much inferior to the majority
of the Sonnets. And this too is characteristic.
The entire success of the *Ode to Duty* is exceptional,
and it is connected with the fact that the poem is
written in regular stanzas of a simple metrical
scheme. The irregular Odes are never thus successful. Wordsworth could not command the tone of
sustained rapture, and where his metrical form is
irregular his ear is uncertain. The Immortality Ode,
like *King Lear*, is its author's greatest product, but
not his best piece of work. The Odes among the
Poems which we are now considering are declama-
tory, even violent, and yet they stir comparatively
little emotion, and they do not sing. The sense of
massive passion, concentrated, and repressing the
utterance it permits itself, is that which most moves
us in his political verse. And the Sonnet suited this.

The patriotism of these *Poems* is equally characteristic. It illustrates Wordsworth's total rejection
of the Godwinian ideas in which he had once in
vain sought refuge, and his belief in the necessity
and sanctity of forms of association arising from
natural kinship. It is composed, we may say, of
two elements. The first is the simple love of
country raised to a high pitch, the love of 'a lover
or a child'; the love that makes it for some men
a miserable doom to be forced to live in a foreign
land, and that makes them feel their country's
virtues and faults, and joys and sorrows, like
those of the persons dearest to them. We talk as
if this love were common. It is very far from
common; but Wordsworth felt it.[1] The other
element in his patriotism I must call by the dreaded
name of 'moral,' a name which Wordsworth did not

---

[1] ''Tis past, that melancholy dream,'—so he describes his sojourn in
Germany.

dread, because it meant for him nothing stereotyped or narrow. His country is to him the representative of freedom, left, as he writes in 1803,

> the only light
> Of Liberty that yet remains on earth.

This Liberty is, first, national independence; and that requires military power, the maintenance of which is a primary moral duty.[1] But neither military power nor even national independence is of value in itself; and neither could be long maintained without that which gives value to both. This is the freedom of the soul, plain living and high thinking, indifference to the externals of mere rank or wealth or power, domestic affections not crippled (as they may be) by poverty. Wordsworth fears for his country only when he doubts whether this inward freedom is not failing;[2] but he seldom fears for long. England, in the war against Napoleon, is to him almost what the England of the Long Parliament and the Commonwealth was to Milton,—an elect people, the chosen agent of God's purpose on the earth. His ideal of life, unlike Milton's in the stress he lays on the domestic affections and the influence of nature, is otherwise of the same Stoical cast. His country is to him, as to Milton,

> An old and haughty nation, proud in arms.[3]

And his own pride in it is, like Milton's, in the highest degree haughty. It would be calumnious to say that it recalls the description of the English given by the Irishman Goldsmith,

> Pride in their port, defiance in their eye,
> I see the lords of human kind pass by;

[1] Wordsworth's Letter to Major-General Pasley (*Prose Works*, i.) contains an excellent statement both of his views on this duty and of his hostility to mere militarism.

[2] I am writing of the years of the Napoleonic War. Later, he lost courage, as he himself said. But it is not true that he ever ceased to sympathise with the cause of national independence in Europe.

[3] [This great line, as I am reminded, refers to the Welsh (*Comus*, 33); but it does not seem necessary to change the quotation.]

for Wordsworth had not the faintest wish to see his countrymen the lords of human kind, nor is there anything vulgar in his patriotism ; but there *is* pride in his port and defiance in his eye. And, lastly, the character of his ideal and of this national pride, with him as with Milton, is connected with personal traits,—impatience of constraint, severity, a certain austere passion, an inclination of imagination to the sublime.

3.

These personal traits, though quite compatible with the portrait on which I am commenting, are not visible in it. Nor are others, which belong especially, but not exclusively, to the younger Wordsworth. He had a spirit so vehement and affections so violent (it is his sister's word) as to inspire alarm for him. If he had been acquainted with that excuse for impotent idleness and selfishness, 'the artistic temperament,' he might have made out a good claim to it. He was from the beginning self-willed, and for a long time he appeared aimless. He would not work at the studies of his university : he preferred to imagine a university in which he *would* work. He had a passion for wandering which was restrained only by want of means, and which opened his heart to every pedlar or tramp whom he met. After leaving Cambridge he would not fix on a profession. He remained, to the displeasure of his relatives, an idler in the land or out of it ; and as soon as he had £900 of capital left to him he determined *not* to have a profession. Sometimes he worked hard at his poetry, even heroically hard ; but he did not work methodically, and often he wrote nothing foɪ weeks, but loafed and walked and enjoyed himself He was not blind like Milton, but the act of writing was physically disagreeable to him, and he made his woman-kind write to his dictation.

He would not conform to rules, or attend to the dinner-bell, or go to church (he made up for this neglect later). 'He wrote his *Ode to Duty*,' said one of his friends, 'and then he had done with that matter.' He never 'tired' of his 'unchartered freedom.' In age, if he wanted to go out, whatever the hour and whatever the weather, he must have his way. 'In vain one reminded him that a letter needed an answer or that the storm would soon be over. It was very necessary for him to do what he liked.' If the poetic fit was on him he could attend to nothing else. He was passionately fond of his children, but, when the serious illness of one of them coincided with an onset of inspiration, it was impossible to rouse him to a sense of danger. At such times he was as completely possessed as any wild poet who ruins the happiness of everyone dependent on him. But he has himself described the tyranny of inspiration, and the reaction after it, in his *Stanzas written in Thomson's Castle of Indolence*. It is almost beyond doubt, I think, that the first portrait there is that of himself; and though it is idealised it is probably quite as accurate as the portrait in *A Poet's Epitaph*. In the *Prelude* he tells us that, though he rarely at Cambridge betrayed by gestures or looks his feelings about nature, yet, when he did so, some of his companions said he was mad. Hazlitt, describing his manner of reading his own poetry in much later years, says, 'It is clear that he is either mad or inspired.'

Wordsworth's lawlessness was of the innocuous kind, but it is a superstition to suppose that he was a disgustingly well-regulated person. It is scarcely less unjust to describe his poetic sympathies as narrow and his poetic morality as puritanical. The former, of course, had nothing like the range of minds like Chaucer, or Shakespeare, or Browning, or the great novelists. Wordsworth's want of humour would by itself have made that impossible;

and, in addition, though by no means wanting in psychological curiosity, he was not much interested in complex natures. Simple souls, and especially simple souls that are also deep, were the natures that attracted him: and in the same way the passions he loved to depict are not those that storm themselves out or rush to a catastrophe, but those that hold the soul in a vice for long years. But, these limitations admitted, it will not be found by anyone who reviews the characters in the smaller poems and the *Excursion* (especially Book vii.), that Wordsworth's poetic sympathies are narrow. They are wider than those of any imaginative writer of his time and country except Scott and perhaps Crabbe.

Nor is his morality narrow. It is serious, but it is human and kindly and not in the least ascetic. 'It is the privilege of poetic genius,' he says in his defence of Burns, 'to catch a spirit of pleasure wherever it can be found—in the walks of nature and in the business of men. The poet, trusting to primary instincts, luxuriates among the felicities of love and wine, and is enraptured while he describes the fairer aspects of war: nor does he shrink from the company of the passion of love though immoderate—from convivial pleasure though intemperate—nor from the presence of war though savage and recognised as the handmaid of desolation. Who but some impenetrable dunce or narrow-minded puritan in works of art ever read without delight the picture which Burns has drawn of the convivial exaltation of the rustic adventurer Tam o' Shanter?' There is no want of sympathy in Wordsworth's own picture of the 'convivial exaltation' of his Waggoner. It is true that he himself never describes a scene in which, to quote his astonishing phrase, 'conjugal fidelity archly bends to the service of general benevolence,' and that his treatment of sexual passion is always grave and, in a true sense, moral; but it is plain and manly and perfectly free from timidity or monkishness. It would really be easier to make out against Wordsworth a charge of excessive tolerance than a charge of excessive rigidity. A beggar is the sort of person he likes. It is all very well for him to say that he likes the Old Cumberland Beggar because, by making people give, he keeps love alive in their hearts. It may be so—he says so, and I always believe him. But that was not his only reason; and it is clear to me that, when he met the tall gipsy-beggar, he gave her money because she was beautiful and queenly, and that he delighted in her two lying boys because of their gaiety and joy in life. Neither has he the least objection to a thief. The grandfather and grandson who go pilfering together, two infants separated by ninety years, meet with nothing but smiles from him. The Farmer of Tilsbury Vale, after thirty years of careless hospitality, found himself ruined. He borrowed money, spent some of it in paying a few of his other debts, and absconded to London.

> But this he did all in the *ease* of his heart.

And for this reason, and because in London he keeps the ease of his heart and continues to love the country, Wordsworth dismisses him with a blessing. What he cannot bear is torpor. He passes a knot of gipsies in the morning; and, passing them again after his twelve hours of joyful rambling, he finds them just as they were, sunk in sloth; and he breaks out,

> Oh, better wrong and strife,
> Better vain deeds and evil than such life.

He changed this shocking exclamation later, but it represents his original feeling, and he might have trusted that only an 'impenetrable dunce or narrow-minded puritan' would misunderstand him.[1]

---

[1] In saying that what Wordsworth could not bear was torpor, of course I do not mean that he could bear faithlessness, ingratitude, cruelty, and the like. He had no tolerance for such things, either in

Wordsworth's morality is of one piece with his optimism and with his determination to seize and exhibit in everything the element of good. But this is a subject far too large for treatment here, and I can refer to it only in the most summary way. What Arnold precisely meant when he said that Wordsworth 'put by' the cloud of human destiny I am not sure. That Wordsworth saw this cloud and looked at it steadily is beyond all question. I am not building on such famous lines as

> The still sad music of humanity,

or

> the fierce confederate storm
> Of Sorrow, barricadoed evermore
> Within the walls of cities;

or

> Amid the groves, under the shadowy hills,
> The generations are prepared; the pangs,
> The internal pangs, are ready; the dread strife
> Of poor humanity's afflicted will
> Struggling in vain with ruthless destiny;

for, although such quotations could be multiplied, isolated expressions, even when not dramatic,[1] would prove little. But I repeat the remark already made, that if we review the subjects of many of Wordsworth's famous poems on human life,—the subjects, for example, of *The Thorn, The Sailor's Mother, Ruth, The Brothers, Michael, The Affliction of Margaret, The White Doe of Rylstone,* the story of Margaret in *Excursion,* i., half the stories told in *Excursion,* vi. and vii.—we find ourselves in the presence of poverty, crime, insanity, ruined innocence, torturing hopes doomed to extinction, solitary

his poetry or in his life. 'I could kick such a man across England with my naked foot,' the old poet burst forth when he heard of a base action. This reminds one of Browning, whose antinomian morality was not so very unlike Wordsworth's. And neither poet would have found it difficult to include the worst vices under the head of torpor or 'the unlit lamp and the ungirt loin.'

[1] The third quotation is from a speech by the Solitary (*Excursion,* vi.).

anguish, even despair. Ignore the manner in which
Wordsworth treated his subjects, and you will have
to say that his world, so far as humanity is concerned, is a dark world,—at least as dark as that
of Byron. Unquestionably then he saw the cloud
of human destiny, and he did not avert his eyes
from it. Nor did he pretend to understand its darkness. The world was to him in the end 'this
unintelligible world,' and the only 'adequate support
for the calamities of mortal life' was faith.[1] But he
was profoundly impressed, through the experience
of his own years of crisis, alike by the dangers of
despondency, and by the superficiality of the views
which it engenders. It was for him (and here, as
in other points, he shows his natural affinity to
Spinoza) a condition in which the soul, concentrated
on its own suffering, for that very reason loses hold
both of its own being and of the reality of which it
forms a part. His experience also made it impossible
for him to doubt that what he grasped

> At times when most existence with herself
> Is satisfied,

—and these are the times when existence is most
united in love with other existence—was, in a special
sense or degree, the truth, and therefore that the
evils which we suffer, deplore, or condemn, cannot
really be what they seem to us when we merely
suffer, deplore, or condemn them. He set himself
to *see* this, as far as he could, and to show it. He
sang of pleasure, joy, glee, blitheness, love, wherever
in nature or humanity they assert their indisputable
power ; and turning to pain and wrong, and gazing
at them steadfastly, and setting himself to present
the facts with a quiet but unsparing truthfulness, he
yet endeavoured to show what he had seen, that
sometimes pain and wrong are the conditions of a

---

[1] The second half of this sentence, true of the Wordsworth of the
Excursion, is perhaps not quite true of his earlier mind.

happiness and good which without them could not
have been, that no limit can be set to the power
of the soul to transmute them into its own substance,
and that, in suffering and even in misery, there may
still be such a strength as fills us with awe or with
glory. He did not pretend, I repeat, that what he
saw sufficed to solve the riddle of the painful earth.
'Our being rests' on 'dark foundations,' and 'our
haughty life is crowned with darkness.' But still
what he showed was what he *saw*, and he saw it
in the cloud of human destiny. We are not here
concerned with his faith in the sun behind that
cloud ; my purpose is only to insist that he 'fronted'
it 'fearlessly.'

4.

After quoting the lines from *A Poet's Epitaph*,
and Arnold's lines on Wordsworth, I asked how
the man described in them ever came to write
the *Ode* on Immortality, or *Yew-trees*, or why he
should say,

> For I must tread on shadowy ground, must sink
> Deep—and, aloft ascending, breathe in worlds
> To which the heaven of heavens is but a veil.

The aspect of Wordsworth's poetry which answers
this question forms my last subject.

We may recall this aspect in more than one way.
First, not a little of Wordsworth's poetry either
approaches or actually enters the province of the
sublime. His strongest natural inclination tended
there. He himself speaks of his temperament as
'stern,' and tells us that

> to the very going out of youth
> [He] too exclusively esteemed *that* love,
> And sought *that* beauty, which, as Milton says,
> Hath terror in it.

This disposition is easily traced in the imaginative

impressions of his childhood as he describes them in the *Prelude*. His fixed habit of looking

> with feelings of fraternal love
> Upon the unassuming things that hold
> A silent station in this beauteous world,

was only formed, it would seem, under his sister's influence, after his recovery from the crisis that followed the ruin of his towering hopes in the French Revolution. It was a part of his endeavour to find something of the distant ideal in life's familiar face. And though this attitude of sympathy and humility did become habitual, the first bent towards grandeur, austerity, sublimity, retained its force. It is evident in the political poems, and in all those pictures of life which depict the unconquerable power of affection, passion, resolution, patience, or faith. It inspires much of his greatest poetry of Nature. It emerges occasionally with a strange and thrilling effect in the serene, gracious, but sometimes stagnant atmosphere of the later poems,—for the last time, perhaps, in that magnificent stanza of the *Extempore Effusion upon the Death of James Hogg* (1835),

> Like clouds that rake the mountain-summits,
> Or waves that own no curbing hand,
> How fast has brother followed brother
> From sunshine to the sunless land !

Wordsworth is indisputably the most sublime of our poets since Milton.

We may put the matter, secondly, thus. However much Wordsworth was the poet of small and humble things, and the poet who saw his ideal realised, not in Utopia, but here and now before his eyes, he was, quite as much, what some would call a mystic. He saw everything in the light of 'the visionary power.' He was, for himself,

> The transitory being that beheld
> This Vision.

He apprehended all things, natural or human, as the expression of something which, while manifested in them, immeasurably transcends them. And nothing can be more intensely Wordsworthian than the poems and passages most marked by this visionary power and most directly issuing from this apprehension. The bearing of these statements on Wordsworth's inclination to sublimity will be obvious at a glance.

Now we may prefer the Wordsworth of the daffodils to the Wordsworth of the yew-trees, and we may even believe the poet's mysticism to be moonshine ; but it is certain that to neglect or throw into the shade this aspect of his poetry is neither to take Wordsworth as he really was nor to judge his poetry truly, since this aspect appears in much of it that we cannot deny to be first-rate. Yet there is, I think, and has been for some time, a tendency to this mistake. It is exemplified in Arnold's Introduction and has been increased by it, and it is visible in some degree even in Pater's essay. Arnold wished to make Wordsworth more popular ; and so he was tempted to represent Wordsworth's poetry as much more simple and unambitious than it really was, and as much more easily apprehended than it ever can be. He was also annoyed by attempts to formulate a systematic Wordsworthian philosophy ; partly, doubtless, because he knew that, however great the philosophical value of a poet's ideas may be, it cannot by itself determine the value of his poetry ; but partly also because, having himself but little turn for philosophy, he was disposed to regard it as illusory ; and further because, even in the poetic sphere, he was somewhat deficient in that kind of imagination which is allied to metaphysical thought. This is one reason of his curious failure to appreciate Shelley, and of the evident irritation which Shelley produced in him. And

it is also one reason why, both in his *Memorial
Verses* and in the introduction to his selection
from Wordsworth, he either ignores or depreciates
that aspect of the poetry with which we are just
now concerned. It is not true, we must bluntly
say, that the cause of the greatness of this poetry
'is simple and may be told quite simply.' It is
true, and it is admirably said, that this poetry ' is
great because of the extraordinary power with
which Wordsworth feels the joy offered to us in
nature, the joy offered to us in the simple primary
affection and duties.' But this is only half the truth.

Pater's essay is not thus one-sided. It is, to my
mind, an extremely fine piece of criticism. Yet the
tendency to which I am objecting does appear in
it. Pater says, for example, that Wordsworth is
the poet of nature, 'and of nature, after all, in her
modesty. The English Lake country has, of course,
its grandeurs. But the peculiar function of Wordsworth's genius, as carrying in it a power to open
out the soul of apparently little and familiar things,
would have found its true test had he become the
poet of Surrey, say! and the prophet of its life.'
This last sentence is, in one sense, doubtless true.
The ' function ' referred to could have been exercised in Surrey, and was exercised in Dorset and
Somerset, as well as in the Lake country. And
this function was a ' peculiar function of Wordsworth's genius.' But that it was *the* peculiar
function of his genius, or more peculiar than that
other function which forms our present subject, I
venture to deny ; and for the full exercise of this
latter function, it is hardly hazardous to assert,
Wordsworth's childhood in a mountain district, and
his subsequent residence there, were indispensable.
This will be doubted for a moment, I believe, only
by those readers (and they are not a few) who
ignore the *Prelude* and the *Excursion*. But the
Prelude and the *Excursion*, though there are dull

pages in both, contain much of Wordsworth's best
and most characteristic poetry.   And even in a
selection like Arnold's, which, perhaps wisely, makes
hardly any use of them, many famous poems will be
found which deal with nature but not with nature
'in her modesty.'

My main object was to insist that the 'mystic,'
'visionary,' 'sublime,' aspect of Wordsworth's poetry
must not be slighted.   I wish to add a few remarks
on it, but to consider it fully would carry us far
beyond our bounds ; and, even if I attempted the
task, I should not formulate its results in a body of
doctrines.   Such a formulation is useful, and I see
no objection to it in principle, as one method of
exploring Wordsworth's mind with a view to the
better apprehension of his poetry.   But the method
has its dangers, and it is another matter to put
forward the results as philosophically adequate, or to
take the position that ' Wordsworth was first and fore-
most a philosophical thinker, a man whose intention
and purpose it was to think out for himself, faithfully
and seriously, the questions concerning man and
nature and human life ' (Dean Church).   If this were
true, he should have given himself to philosophy and
not to poetry ; and there is no reason to think that
he would have been eminently successful.   Nobody
ever was so who was not forced by a special natural
power and an imperious impulse into the business
of 'thinking out,' and who did not develope this
power by years of arduous discipline.   Wordsworth
does not show it in any marked degree; and,
though he reflected deeply and acutely, he was
without philosophical training.   His poetry is immensely interesting as an imaginative expression
of the same mind which, in his day, produced in
Germany great philosophies.   His poetic experience,
his intuitions, his single thoughts, even his large
views, correspond in a striking way, sometimes in
a startling way, with ideas methodically developed

by Kant, Schelling, Hegel, Schopenhauer. They remain admirable material for philosophy ; and a philosophy which found itself driven to treat them as moonshine would probably be a very poor affair. But they are like the experience and the utterances of men of religious genius : great truths are enshrined in them, but generally the shrine would have to be broken to liberate these truths in a form which would satisfy the desire to understand. To claim for them the power to satisfy that desire is an error, and it tempts those in whom that desire is predominant to treat them as mere beautiful illusions.

Setting aside, then, any questions as to the ultimate import of the 'mystic' strain in Wordsworth's poetry, I intend only to call attention to certain traits in the kind of poetic experience which exhibits it most plainly. And we may observe at once that in this there is always traceable a certain hostility to 'sense.' I do not mean that hostility which is present in *all* poetic experience, and of which Wordsworth was very distinctly aware. The regular action of the senses on their customary material produces, in his view, a 'tyranny' over the soul. It helps to construct that every-day picture of the world, of sensible objects and events 'in disconnection dead and spiritless,' which we take for reality. In relation to this reality we become passive slaves ;[1] it lies on us with a weight 'heavy as frost and deep almost as life.' It is the origin alike of our torpor and our superficiality. *All* poetic experience frees us from it to some extent, or breaks into it, and so may be called hostile to sense. But this experience is, broadly speaking, of two different kinds. The perception of the daffodils as dancing in glee, and in sympathy with other gleeful beings, shows us a living, joyous, loving world, and so a 'spiritual' world, not a merely 'sensible' one. But

---

[1] This is just the opposite of the 'wise passiveness' of imaginative but unreflective feeling.

the hostility to sense is here no more than a hostility
to *mere* sense : this 'spiritual' world is itself the
sensible world more fully apprehended : the daffodils
do not change or lose their colour in disclosing their
glee.   On the other hand, in the kind of experience
which forms our present subject, there is always
some feeling of definite contrast with the limited
sensible world.   The arresting feature or object is
felt in some way *against* this background, or even as
in some way a denial of it.   Sometimes it is a
visionary unearthly light resting on a scene or on
some strange figure.   Sometimes it is the feeling
that the scene or figure belongs to the world of
dream.   Sometimes it is an intimation of boundlessness, contradicting or abolishing the fixed limits of
our habitual view.   Sometimes it is the obscure
sense of 'unknown modes of being,' unlike the
familiar modes.   This kind of experience, further,
comes often with a distinct shock, which may
bewilder, confuse or trouble the mind.   And, lastly,
it is especially, though not invariably, associated
with mountains, and again with solitude.   Some of
these bald statements I will go on to illustrate, only
remarking that the boundary between these modes
of imagination is, naturally, less marked and more
wavering in Wordsworth's poetry than in my brief
analysis.

We may begin with a poem standing near this
boundary, the famous verses *To the Cuckoo*, 'O
blithe new-comer.' It stands near the boundary
because, like the poem on the Daffodils, it is
entirely happy.   But it stands unmistakably on the
further side of the boundary, and is, in truth, more
nearly allied to the *Ode* on Immortality than to the
poem on the Daffodils.   The sense of sight is
baffled, and its tyranny broken.   Only a cry is heard,
which makes the listener look a thousand ways, so
shifting is the direction from which it reaches him.
It seems to come from a mere 'voice,' 'an invisible

thing,' 'a mystery.' It brings him 'a tale of visionary hours,'—hours of childhood, when he sought this invisible thing in vain, and the earth appeared to his bewildered but liberated fancy 'an unsubstantial fairy place.' And still, when he hears it, the great globe itself, we may say, fades like an unsubstantial pageant ; or, to quote from the Immortality *Ode*, the 'shades of the prison house' melt into air. These words are much more solemn than the Cuckoo poem ; but the experience is of the same type, and 'the visionary gleam' of the ode, like the 'wandering voice' of the poem, is the expression through sense of something beyond sense.

Take another passage referring to childhood. It is from the *Prelude*, ii. Here there is something more than perplexity. There is apprehension, and we are approaching the sublime :

> One summer evening (led by her [1]) I found
> A little boat tied to a willow tree
> Within a rocky cave, its usual home.
> Straight I unloosed her chain, and stepping in
> Pushed from the shore. It was an act of stealth
> And troubled pleasure, nor without the voice
> Of mountain-echoes did my boat move on ;
> Leaving behind her still, on either side,
> Small circles glittering idly in the moon,
> Until they melted all into one track
> Of sparkling light. But now, like one who rows,
> Proud of his skill, to reach a chosen point
> With an unswerving line, I fixed my view
> Upon the summit of a craggy ridge,
> The horizon's utmost boundary ; far above
> Was nothing but the stars and the grey sky.
> She was an elfin pinnace ; lustily
> I dipped my oars into the silent lake,
> And, as I rose upon the stroke, my boat
> Went heaving through the water like a swan ;
> When, from behind that craggy steep till then
> The horizon's bound, a huge peak, black and huge,
> As if with voluntary power instinct,
> Upreared its head. I struck and struck again,

[1] Nature.

And growing still in stature the grim shape
Towered up between me and the stars, and still,
For so it seemed, with purpose of its own
And measured motion like a living thing,
Strode after me. With trembling oars I turned,
And through the silent water stole my way
Back to the covert of the willow tree ;
There in her mooring-place I left my bark,—
And through the meadows homeward went, in grave
And serious mood ; but after I had seen
That spectacle, for many days, my brain
Worked with a dim and undetermined sense
Of unknown modes of being ; o'er my thoughts
There hung a darkness, call it solitude
Or blank desertion. No familiar shapes
Remained, no pleasant images of trees,
Of sea or sky, no colours of green fields ;
But huge and mighty forms, that do not live
Like living men, moved slowly through the mind
By day, and were a trouble to my dreams.

The best commentary on a poem is generally to be found in the poet's other works. And those last dozen lines furnish the best commentary on that famous passage in the *Ode*, where the poet, looking back to his childhood, gives thanks for it,—not however for its careless delight and liberty,

> But for those obstinate questionings
> Of sense and outward things,
> Fallings from us, vanishings ;
> Blank misgivings of a Creature
> Moving about in worlds not realised,
> High instincts before which our mortal Nature
> Did tremble like a guilty thing surprised.

Whether, or how, these experiences afford 'intimations of immortality' is not in question here ; but it will never do to dismiss them so airily as Arnold did. Without them Wordsworth is not Wordsworth.

The most striking recollections of his childhood have not in all cases this manifest affinity to the *Ode*, but wherever the visionary feeling appears in them (and it appears in many), this affinity is still traceable. There is, for instance, in *Prelude*, xii., the description of the crag, from which, on a wild dark day, the boy watched eagerly the two highways below for the ponies that were coming to take him home for the holidays. It is too long to quote, but every reader of it will remember

> the wind and sleety rain,
> And all the business of the elements,
> The single sheep, and the one blasted tree,
> And the bleak music from that old stone wall,
> The noise of wood and water, and the mist
> That on the line of each of those two roads
> Advanced in such indisputable shapes.

Everything here is natural, but everything is apocalyptic. And we happen to know why. Wordsworth is describing the scene in the light of memory. In that eagerly expected holiday his father died ; and the scene, as he recalled it, was charged with the sense of contrast between the narrow world of common pleasures and blind and easy hopes, and the vast unseen world which encloses it in beneficent yet dark and inexorable arms. The visionary feeling has here a peculiar tone ; but always, openly or covertly, it is the intimation of something illimitable, over-arching or breaking into the customary 'reality.' Its character varies ; and so sometimes at its touch the soul, suddenly conscious of its own infinity, melts in rapture into that infinite being ; while at other times the ' mortal nature' stands dumb, incapable of thought, or shrinking from some presence

> Not un-informed with Phantasy, and looks
> That threaten the profane.

This feeling is so essential to many of Wordsworth's most characteristic poems that it may almost be called their soul ; and failure to understand them frequently arises from obtuseness to it. It appears in a mild and tender form, but quite openly, in the lines *To a Highland Girl*, where the child, and the rocks and trees and lake and road by her home, seem to the poet

> Like something fashioned in a dream.

It gives to *The Solitary Reaper* its note of remote-
ness and wonder ; and even the slight shock of
bewilderment due to it is felt in the opening line of
the most famous stanza :

> Will no one tell me what she sings ?

Its etherial music accompanies every vision of the
White Doe, and sounds faintly to us from far away
through all the tale of failure and anguish.   Without
it such shorter narratives as *Hartleap Well* and
Resolution and Independence would lose the imaginative atmosphere which adds mystery and grandeur
to the apparently simple ' moral.'

In *Hartleap Well* it is conveyed at first by slight
touches of contrast.   Sir Walter, in his long pursuit
of the Hart, has mounted his third horse.

> Joy sparkled in the prancing courser's eyes ;
> The horse and horseman are a happy pair ;
> But, though Sir Walter like a falcon flies,
> There is a doleful silence in the air.
>
> A rout this morning left Sir Walter's hall,
> That as they galloped made the echoes roar ;
> But horse and man are vanished, one and all ;
> Such race, I think, was never seen before.

At last even the dogs are left behind, stretched one
by one among the mountain fern.

> Where is the throng, the tumult of the race ?
> The bugles that so joyfully were blown ?
> —This chase it looks not like an earthly chase ;
> Sir Walter and the Hart are left alone.

Thus the poem begins.   At the end we have the
old shepherd's description of the utter desolation of
the spot where the waters of the little spring had
trembled with the last deep groan of the dying
stag, and where the Knight, to commemorate his
exploit, had built a basin for the spring, three pillars
to mark the last three leaps of his victim, and a
pleasure-house, surrounded by trees and trailing
plants, for the summer joy of himself and his

paramour. But now 'the pleasure-house is dust,'
and the trees are grey, 'with neither arms nor
head':

> Now, here is neither grass nor pleasant shade;
> The sun on drearier hollow never shone;
> So will it be, as I have often said,
> Till trees, and stones, and fountain all are gone.

It is only this feeling of the presence of mysterious
inviolable Powers, behind the momentary powers of
hard pleasure and empty pride, that justifies the
solemnity of the stanza :

> The Being, that is in the clouds and air,
> That is in the green leaves among the groves,
> Maintains a deep and reverential care
> For the unoffending creatures whom he loves.

Hartleap Well is a beautiful poem, but whether
it is entirely successful is, perhaps, doubtful. There
can be no sort of doubt as to *Resolution and
Independence*, probably, if we must choose, the
most Wordsworthian of Wordsworth's poems, and
the best test of ability to understand him. The
story, if given in a brief argument, would sound
far from promising. We should expect for it, too,
a ballad form somewhat like that of *Simon Lee*.
When we read it, we find instead lines of extraordinary grandeur, but, mingled with them, lines
more pedestrian than could be found in an impressive
poem from any other hand,—for instance,

> And, drawing to his side, to him did say,
> 'This morning gives us promise of a glorious day.'

or,

> 'How is it that you live, and what is it you do?'

We meet also with that perplexed persistence, and
that helpless reiteration of a question (in this case
one already clearly answered), which in other poems
threatens to become ludicrous, and on which a
writer with a keener sense of the ludicrous would
hardly have ventured. Yet with all this, and by

dint of all this, we read with bated breath, almost
as if we were in the presence of that 'majestical'
Spirit in *Hamlet*, come to 'admonish' from another
world, though not this time by terror. And one
source of this effect is the confusion, the almost
hypnotic obliteration of the habitual reasoning mind,
that falls on the poet as he gazes at the leech-
gatherer, and hears, without understanding, his
plain reply to the enquiry about himself and the
prosaic 'occupation' he 'pursues':

> The old man still stood talking by my side;
> But now his voice to me was like a stream
> Scarce heard; nor word from word could I divide;
> And the whole body of the man did seem
> Like one whom I had met with in a dream;
> Or like a man from some far region sent,
> To give me human strength, by apt admonishment.

The same question was asked again, and the answer
was repeated.   But

> While he was talking thus, the lonely place,
> The old man's shape, and speech, all troubled me.

'Trouble' is a word not seldom employed by the
poet to denote the confusion caused by some visionary experience.   Here are, again, the fallings from
us, vanishings, blank misgivings, dim fore-feelings of
the soul's infinity.

Out of many illustrations I will choose three more.
There is in the *Prelude*, iv., the passage (so strongly
resembling *Resolution and Independence* that I
merely refer to it) where Wordsworth describes an
old soldier suddenly seen, leaning against a mile-
stone on the moon-lit road, all alone:

> No living thing appeared in earth or air;
> And, save the flowing water's peaceful voice,
> Sound there was none . . .
>   . . . still his form
> Kept the same awful steadiness—at his feet
> His shadow lay, and moved not.

His shadow proves he was no ghost; but a ghost

was never ghostlier than he.   And by him we may
place the London beggar of *Prelude*, vii.:

> How oft, amid those overflowing streets,
> Have I gone forward with the crowd, and said
> Unto myself, 'The face of every one
> That passes by me is a mystery!'
> Thus have I looked, nor ceased to look, oppressed
> By thoughts of what and whither, when and how,
> Until the shapes before my eyes became
> A second-sight procession, such as glides
> Over still mountains, or appears in dreams;
> And once, far-travelled in such mood, beyond
> The reach of common indication, lost
> Amid the moving pageant, I was smitten
> Abruptly, with the view (a sight not rare)
> Of a blind Beggar, who, with upright face,
> Stood, propped against a wall, upon his chest
> Wearing a written paper, to explain
> His story, whence he came, and who he was.
> Caught by the spectacle my mind turned round
> As with the might of waters; an apt type
> This label seemed of the utmost we can know.
> Both of ourselves and of the universe;
> And, on the shape of that unmoving man,
> His steadfast face and sightless eyes, I gazed,
> As if admonished from another world.

Still more curious psychologically is the passage,
in the preceding book of the *Prelude*, which tells
us of a similar shock and leads to the description of
its effects.   The more prosaically I introduce the
passage, the better.   Wordsworth and Jones ('Jones,
as from Calais southward you and I') set out to
walk over the Simplon, then traversed only by a
rough mule-track.   They wandered out of the way,
and, meeting a peasant, discovered from his answers
to their questions that, without knowing it, they '*had
crossed the Alps*.'   This may not sound important,
and the italics are Wordsworth's, not mine.   But
the next words are these:

> Imagination—here the Power so called
> Through sad incompetence of human speech,
> That awful Power rose from the mind's abyss
> Like an unfathered vapour that enwraps,

At once, some lonely traveller.   I was lost;
Halted without an effort to break through;
But to my conscious soul I now can say—
'I recognise thy glory': in such strength
Of usurpation, when the light of sense
Goes out, but with a flash that has revealed
The invisible world, doth greatness make abode,
There harbours; whether we be young or old,
Our destiny, our being's heart and home,
Is with infinitude, and only there;
With hope it is, hope that can never die,
Effort, and expectation, and desire,
And something evermore about to be.

And what was the result of this shock?   The poet
may answer for himself in some of the greatest lines
in English poetry.   The travellers proceeded on
their way down the Defile of Gondo.

Downwards we hurried fast,
And, with the half-shaped road which we had missed,
Entered a narrow chasm.   The brook and road
Were fellow-travellers in this gloomy strait,
And with them did we journey several hours
At a slow pace.   The immeasurable height
Of woods decaying, never to be decayed,
The stationary blasts of waterfalls,
And in the narrow rent at every turn
Winds thwarting winds, bewildered and forlorn,
The torrents shooting from the clear blue sky,
The rocks that muttered close upon our ears,
Black drizzling crags that spake by the way-side
As if a voice were in them, the sick sight
And giddy prospect of the raving stream,
The unfettered clouds and region of the Heavens,
Tumult and peace, the darkness and the light—
Were all like workings of one mind, the features
Of the same face, blossoms upon one tree;
Characters of the great Apocalypse,
The types and symbols of Eternity,
Of first, and last, and midst, and without end.[1]

[1] I add here some notes which would have disturbed the lecture,
but may be of use to the student of Wordsworth's mind who cares
to return to them.
     The collocation of the last two quotations shows how, for Words-
worth, 'the visionary power' arises from, and testifies to, the mind's
infinity, and how the feeling of this is, or involves, or is united
with, a feeling or idea of *the* infinite or 'one mind,' and of union with

I hardly think that 'the poet of Surrey, say, and the prophet of its life' could have written thus. And of all the poems to which I have lately referred, and all the passages I have quoted, there are but two or three which do not cry aloud that their

it. This connection of ideas (as to which I purposely use vague alternative terms, because I do not want to theorise the poet's experience), is frequent or constant in Wordsworth, and it ought always to be borne in mind in regard to his language about 'immortality' or 'eternity.' His sense or consciousness of 'immortality,' that is to say, is at once a consciousness that he (in some sense of that word) is potentially infinite, and a consciousness that 'he' belongs to, is part of, is the home of, or is, an 'active principle' which is eternal, indivisible, and the 'soul of all the worlds' (cf. opening of *Excursion*, ix.). Whatever we may make of this connection of ideas, unless we realise it we shall remain entirely outside Wordsworth's mind in passages like that just referred to, and in passages where he talks of 'acts of immortality in Nature's course,' or says that to the Wanderer 'all things among the mountains breathed immortality,' or says that he has been unfolding 'far-stretching views of immortality,' though he may not appear to us to have touched in any way on the subject. Nature and Man (in one sense) are for Wordsworth 'transitory,' but Nature always and everywhere *reveals* 'immortality,' and Man (in another sense) *is* 'immortal.' Unquestionably for Wordsworth he is so. In what precise sense he is so for Wordsworth may not be discoverable, but the only chance of discovering it is to forget what we or anybody else, except Wordsworth, may mean by 'man' and 'immortal,' and to try to get into *his* mind.

There is an illuminating passage on 'the visionary power' and the mind's infinity or immortality, in *Prelude*, ii. :

and hence, from the same source,
Sublimer joy; for I would walk alone,
Under the quiet stars, and at that time
Have felt whate'er there is of power in sound
To breathe an elevated mood, by form
Or image unprofaned; and I would stand,
If the night blackened with a coming storm,
Beneath some rock, listening to notes that are
The ghostly language of the ancient earth,
Or make their dim abode in distant winds.
Thence did I drink the visionary power;
And deem not profitless those fleeting moods
Of shadowy exultation: not for this,
That they are kindred to our purer mind
And intellectual life; but that the soul,
Remembering how she felt, but what she felt
Remembering not, retains an obscure sense
Of possible sublimity, whereto
With growing faculties she doth aspire,
With faculties still growing, feeling still
That whatsoever point they gain, they yet
Have something to pursue.

An interesting point, worth fuller treatment, is the connection of this feeling of infinity and the endless passing of limits with Wordsworth's love of wandering, wanderers, and high roads. See, for

birth-place was the moor or the mountain, and that severed from their birth-place they would perish. The more sublime they are, or the nearer they approach sublimity, the more is this true. The cry of the cuckoo in *O blithe new-comer*, though visionary, is not sublime ; but, echoed by the mountain, it is

> Like—but oh, how different ![1]

It was among the mountains that Wordsworth, as he says of his Wanderer, *felt* his faith. It was there that all things

> Breathed immortality, revolving life,
> And greatness still revolving ; infinite.
> There littleness was not ; the least of things
> Seemed infinite ; and there his spirit shaped
> Her prospects, nor did he believe,—he *saw*.

And even if we count his vision a mere dream, still he put into words, as no other poet has, the spirit of the mountains.

> Two voices are there ; one is of the sea,
> One of the mountains ; each a mighty voice.

And of the second of these we may say that 'few or none hears it right' now he is gone.

Partly because he is the poet of mountains he is, even more pre-eminently, the poet of solitude. For there are tones in the mountain voice scarcely audible except in solitude, and the reader whom Wordsworth's greatest poetry baffles could have no better advice offered him than to do what he has probably never done in his life—to be on a mountain alone. But for Wordsworth not this solitude only,

---

instance, *Prelude*, xiii., 'Who doth not love to follow with his eye The windings of a public way?' And compare the enchantment of the question, *What, are you stepping westward?*

> 'twas a sound
> Of something without place or bound.

[1] *Yes, it was the mountain echo*, placed in Arnold's selection, with his usual taste, next to the earlier poem *To the Cuckoo*.

but all solitude and all things solitary had an extraordinary fascination.

> The outward shows of sky and earth,
> Of hill and valley, he has viewed ;
> And impulses *of deeper birth*
> Have come to him in solitude.

The sense of solitude, it will readily be found, is
essential to nearly all the poems and passages we
have been considering, and to some of quite a
different character, such as the Daffodil stanzas.
And it is not merely that the poet is alone ; what he
sees is so too. If the leech-gatherer and the
soldier on the moon-lit road had not been solitary
figures, they would not have awaked 'the visionary
power' ; and it is scarcely fanciful to add that if the
boy who was watching for his father's ponies had
had beside him any more than

> The *single* sheep and the *one* blasted tree,

the mist would not have advanced along the roads
'in such indisputable shapes.' With Wordsworth
that power seems to have sprung into life at once
on the perception of loneliness. What is lonely is a
spirit. To call a thing lonely or solitary is, with
him, to say that it opens a bright or solemn vista
into infinity. He himself 'wanders lonely as a
cloud' : he seeks the 'souls of lonely places' : he
listens in awe to

> One voice, the solitary raven . . .
> An iron knell, with echoes from afar :

against the distant sky he descries the shepherd,

> A solitary object and sublime,
> Above all height ! like an aerial cross
> Stationed alone upon a spiry rock
> Of the Chartreuse, for worship.

But this theme might be pursued for hours, and I
will refer only to two poems more. The editor of
the *Golden Treasury*, a book never to be thought
of without gratitude, changed the title *The Solitary*

Reaper into *The Highland Reaper*. He may have
had his reasons. Perhaps he had met some one who
thought that the Reaper belonged to Surrey. Still
the change was a mistake : the 'solitary' in Wordsworth's title gave the keynote. The other poem is
Lucy Gray. 'When I was little,' a lover of Wordsworth once said, 'I could hardly bear to read *Lucy
Gray*, it made me feel so lonely.' Wordsworth
called it *Lucy Gray, or Solitude*, and this young
reader understood him. But there is too much
reason to fear that for half his readers his 'solitary
child' is generalised into a mere 'little girl,' and
that they never receive the main impression he
wished to produce. Yet his intention is announced
in the opening lines, and as clearly shown in the
lovely final stanzas, which give even to this ballad
the visionary touch which distinguishes it from *Alice
Fell* :

> Yet some maintain that to this day
> She is a living child ;
> That you may see sweet Lucy Gray
> Upon the lonesome wild.
>
> O'er rough and smooth she trips along,
> And never looks behind ;
> And sings a solitary song
> That whistles in the wind.

The solitariness which exerted so potent a spell
on Wordsworth had in it nothing 'Byronic.' He
preached in the *Excursion* against the solitude of
'self-indulging spleen.' He was even aware that he
himself, though free from that weakness, had felt

> perhaps too much
> The self-sufficing power of Solitude.[1]

No poet is more emphatically the poet of community. A great part of his verse—a part as
characteristic and as precious as the part on which
I have been dwelling—is dedicated to the affections
of home and neighbourhood and country, and to
that soul of joy and love which links together all

[1] This was Coleridge's opinion.

Nature's children, and 'steals from earth to man, from man to earth.' And this soul is for him as truly the presence of 'the Being that is in the clouds and air' and in the mind of man as are the power, the darkness, the silence, the strange gleams and mysterious visitations which startle and confuse with intimations of infinity. But solitude and solitariness were to him, in the main, one of these intimations. They had not for him merely the 'eeriness' which they have at times for everyone, though that was essential to some of the poems we have reviewed. They were the symbol of power to stand alone, to be 'self-sufficing,' to dispense with custom and surroundings and aid and sympathy—a self-dependence at once the image and the communication of 'the soul of all the worlds.' Even when they were full of 'sounds and sweet airs that give delight and hurt not,' the solitude of the Reaper or of Lucy, they so appealed to him. But they appealed also to that austerer strain which led him to love 'bare trees and mountains bare,' and lonely places, and the bleak music of the old stone wall, and to dwell with awe, and yet with exultation, on the majesty of that 'unconquerable mind' which through long years holds its solitary purpose, sustains its solitary passion, feeds upon its solitary anguish. For this mind, as for the blind beggar or the leech-gatherer, the 'light of sense' and the sweetness of life have faded or 'gone out'; but in it 'greatness makes abode,' and it 'retains its station proud,' 'by form or image unprofaned.' Thus, in whatever guise it might present itself, solitariness 'carried far into his heart' the haunting sense of an 'invisible world'; of some Life beyond this 'transitory being' and 'unapproachable by death';

> Of Life continuous, Being unimpaired;
> That hath been, is, and where it was and is
> There shall endure,—existence unexposed
> To the blind walk of mortal accident;

From diminution safe and weakening age;
While man grows old, and dwindles, and decays;
And countless generations of mankind
Depart; and leave no vestige where they trod.

For me, I confess, all this is far from being 'mere poetry'—partly because I do not believe that any such thing as 'mere poetry' exists. But whatever kind or degree of truth we may find in all this, everything in Wordsworth that is sublime or approaches sublimity has, directly or more remotely, to do with it. And without this part of his poetry Wordsworth would be 'shorn of his strength,' and would no longer stand, as he does stand, nearer than any other poet of the Nineteenth Century to Milton.

NOTE.

I take this opportunity of airing a heresy about *We are Seven.*
Wordsworth's friend, James Tobin, who saw the *Lyrical Ballads*
while they were going through the press, told him that this poem
would make him everlastingly ridiculous, and entreated him in
vain to cancel it. I have forgotten how it was received in 1798,
but it has long been one of the most popular of the ballad poems,
and I do not think I have ever heard it ridiculed. I wonder,
however, what its readers take to be the 'moral' of it, for I have
never been able to convince myself that the 'moral' given in
the poem itself truly represents the imaginative impression from
which the poem arose.

The 'moral' is in this instance put at the beginning, in the
mutilated opening stanza :-

> —————— A simple child,
> That lightly draws its breath,
> And feels its life in every limb,
> What should it know of death?

Wordsworth, in composing, began his poem with the end; and
when it was all but finished he recited it to Dorothy and
Coleridge, and observed that a prefatory stanza was wanted,
and that he should enjoy his tea better if he could add it first.
Coleridge at once threw off the stanza as we have it, except that
the first line ran, 'A simple child, dear brother Jim,'—this Jim, who
rhymes with 'limb,' being the James Tobin who protested
afterwards against the poem. The stanza was printed in the
Lyrical Ballads as Coleridge made it, Wordsworth objecting
to the words 'dear brother Jim' as ludicrous, but (apparently)
giving way for the sake of the joke of introducing Tobin.

Now the poem gains in one way by this stanza, which has a

felicity of style such as Wordsworth perhaps would not have achieved in expressing the idea. And the idea was not only accepted by Wordsworth, but, according to his own account, he had mentioned in substance what he wished to be expressed. It must seem, therefore, outrageous to hint a doubt whether the stanza truly represents the imaginative experience from which the poem arose; and I can only say, in excuse, that this doubt does not spring from reflection, or from knowledge of Coleridge's authorship of the stanza, for I do not remember ever having read *We are Seven* without feeling it or without saying to myself at the end, 'This means more than the first stanza says.' And, however improbable, it cannot be called impossible that even so introspective a poet as Wordsworth might misconstrue the impression that stirred him to write. I will take courage, therefore, to confess the belief that what stirred him was the coincidence of the child's feelings with some of those feelings of his own childhood which he described in the Immortality *Ode*, and once or twice in conversation, and which, in a less individual and peculiar form, he attributes, in the Essay on Epitaphs, to children in general. But, rather than argue the point, I will refer to one or two passages. ' At that time I could not believe that I should lie down quietly in the grave, and that my body would moulder into dust' (remark recorded by Bishop Wordsworth, *Prose Works*, ed. Grosart, iii. 464). Is not this the condition of the child in *We are Seven*? 'Nothing,' he says to Miss Fenwick, 'was more difficult for me in childhood than to admit the notion of death as a state applicable to my own being' (*ib*. iii. 194). He then quotes the first stanza of *We are Seven*. It is true that thereupon he expressly distinguishes his own case from the child's, attributing the difficulty in her case to 'animal vivacity.' But I have already fully admitted that Wordsworth's direct testimony goes against me; and I have now only to call attention to a passage in the Essay on Epitaphs. In that essay Wordsworth begins by saying that the custom of raising monuments to the dead 'proceeded obviously from a two-fold desire; first, to guard the remains of the deceased from irreverent approach or from savage violation, and, secondly, to preserve their memory.' But these desires, in his opinion, resolve themselves into one, and both proceed from the consciousness or fore-feeling of immortality, also described as 'an intimation or assurance within us, that some part of our nature is imperishable.' And he goes on thus : 'If we look back upon the days of childhood, we shall find that the time is not in remembrance when, with respect to our own individual Being, the mind was without this assurance. . . . Forlorn, and cut off from communication with the best part of his nature, must that man be, who should derive the sense of immortality, as it exists in the mind of a child, from the same unthinking gaiety or liveliness of animal spirits with which the lamb in the meadow or any other irrational creature is endowed; to an inability arising from the imperfect state of his faculties to come, in any point of his being, into contact with a notion of death; or to an unreflecting acquiescence in what had been instilled into him!' Now Coleridge's stanza, and Wordsworth's own distinction between the child and himself, do come at least very near to attributing the child's inability to realise the fact of death to that very liveliness of animal spirits which, as a sufficient cause of it, is here indignantly repudiated. According to the present passage, this inability ought to have been traced to that 'sense' or 'consciousness' of immortality which is inherent in human nature. And (whether or no Wordsworth rightly describes this sense) it was *this*, I suggest, that, unknown to himself, arrested him in the child's persistent ignoring of the fact of death. The poem is thus allied to the Immortality *Ode*. The child is in possession of one of those 'truths that wake to perish never,' though the tyranny of the senses and the deadening influence of custom obscure them as childhood passes away. When the conversation took place (in 1793), and even when the poem was written (1798), Wordsworth had not yet come to regard the experiences of his own childhood as he saw them later (*Tintern Abbey*, 1798, shows this), and so he gave to the poem a moral which is not adequate to it. Or perhaps he accepted from Coleridge a formulation of his moral which was not quite true even to his own thoughts at that time. It is just worth observing as possibly significant that the child in *We are Seven* is not described as showing any particular 'animal vivacity': she strikes one as rather a quiet, though determined, little person.

These remarks, of course, can have no interest for those readers who feel no misgivings, such as I have always felt, in reading the poem. But many, I think, must feel them.

SHELLEY'S VIEW OF POETRY

SHELLEY'S VIEW OF POETRY

THE ideas of Wordsworth and of Coleridge about poetry have often been discussed and are familiar. Those of Shelley are much less so, and in his eloquent exposition of them there is a radiance which almost conceals them from many readers. I wish, at the cost of all the radiance, to try to see them and show them rather more distinctly. Even if they had little value for the theory of poetry, they would still have much as material for it, since they allow us to look into a poet's experience in conceiving and composing. And, in addition, they throw light on some of the chief characteristics of Shelley's own poetry.

His poems in their turn form one of the sources from which his ideas on the subject may be gathered. We have also some remarks in his letters and in prose pieces dealing with other topics. We have the prefaces to those of his works which he himself published. And, lastly, there is the *Defence of Poetry*. This essay was written in reply to an attack made on contemporary verse by Shelley's friend Peacock,—not a favourable specimen of Peacock's writing. The *Defence*, we can see, was hurriedly composed, and it remains a fragment, being only the first of three projected parts. It contains a good deal of historical matter, highly interesting, but too extensive to be made use of here. Being polemical, it no doubt exaggerates such of

Shelley's views as collided with those of his anta-
gonist. But, besides being the only full expression
of these views, it is the most mature, for it was
written within eighteen months of his death. It
appears to owe very little either to Wordsworth's
Prefaces or to Coleridge's *Biographia Literaria*;
but there are a few reminiscences of Sidney's
Apology, which Shelley had read just before he
wrote his own *Defence*; and it shows, like much
of his mature poetry, how deeply he was influenced
by the more imaginative dialogues of Plato.

I.

Any one familiar with the manner in which Shelley
in his verse habitually represents the world could
guess at his general view of poetry. The world to
him is a melancholy place, a 'dim vast vale of tears,'
illuminated in flashes by the light of a hidden but
glorious power. Nor is this power, as that favourite
metaphor would imply, wholly outside the world.
It works within it as a soul contending with obstruc-
tion and striving to penetrate and transform the
whole mass. And though the fulness of its glory
is concealed, its nature is known in outline. It
is the realised perfection of everything good and
beautiful on earth; or, in other words, all such
goodness and beauty is its partial manifestation.
'All,' I say : for the splendour of nature, the love of
lovers, every affection and virtue, any good action
or just law, the wisdom of philosophy, the creations
of art, the truths deformed by superstitious religion,
—all are equally operations or appearances of the
hidden power. It is of the first importance for the
understanding of Shelley to realise how strong in
him is the sense and conviction of this unity in life :
it is one of his Platonic traits. The intellectual
Beauty of his *Hymn* is absolutely the same thing
as the Liberty of his *Ode*, the 'Great Spirit' of Love
that he invokes to bring freedom to Naples, the

One which in *Adonaïs* he contrasts with the Many,
the Spirit of Nature of *Queen Mab*, and the Vision
of *Alastor* and *Epipsychidion*. The skylark of the
famous stanzas is free from our sorrows, not because
it is below them, but because, as an embodiment of
that perfection, it knows the rapture of love without
its satiety, and understands death as we cannot.
The voice of the mountain, if a whole nation could
hear it with the poet's ear, would 'repeal large
codes of fraud and woe'; it is the same voice as
the reformer's and the martyr's. And in the far-off
day when the 'plastic stress' of this power has
mastered the last resistance and is all in all, outward
nature, which now suffers with man, will be redeemed
with him, and man, in becoming politically free, will
become also the perfect lover. Evidently, then,
poetry, as the world now is, must be one of the
voices of this power, or one tone of its voice. To
use the language so dear to Shelley, it is the revelation of those eternal ideas which lie behind the
many-coloured, ever-shifting veil that we call reality
or life. Or rather, it is one such revelation among
many.

When we turn to the *Defence of Poetry* we meet
substantially the same view. There is indeed a
certain change; for Shelley is now philosophising
and writing prose, and he wishes not to sing from
the mid-sky, but, for a while at least, to argue with
his friend on the earth. Hence at first we hear
nothing of that perfect power at the heart of things,
and poetry is considered as a creation rather than
a revelation. But for Shelley, we soon discover,
this would be a false antithesis. The poet creates,
but this creation is no mere fancy of his; it represents 'those forms which are common to universal
nature and existence,' and 'a poem is the very
image of life expressed in its eternal truth.' We
notice, further, that the more voluntary and conscious work of invention and execution is regarded

as quite subordinate in the creative process. In
that process the mind, obedient to an influence
which it does not understand and cannot control,
is driven to produce images of perfection which
rather form themselves in it than are formed by it.
The greatest stress is laid on this influence or
inspiration; and in the end we learn that the origin
of the whole process lies in certain exceptional
moments when visitations of thought and feeling,
elevating and delightful beyond all expression, but
always arising unforeseen and departing unbidden,
reach the soul; that these are, as it were, the inter-
penetration of a diviner nature through our own;
and that the province of the poet is to arrest these
apparitions, to veil them in language, to colour
every other form he touches with their evanescent
hues, and so to 'redeem from decay the visitations
of the divinity in man.'

Even more decided is the emphasis laid on the
unity of all the forms in which the 'divinity' or
ideal power thus attests its presence. Indeed,
throughout a large part of the essay, that 'Poetry'
which Shelley is defending is something very much
wider than poetry in the usual sense. The enemy
he has to meet is the contention that poetry and its
influence steadily decline as civilisation advances,
and that they are giving place, and ought to give
place, to reasoning and the pursuit of utility. His
answer is that, on the contrary, imagination has been,
is, and always will be, the prime source of everything that has intrinsic value in life. Reasoning, he
declares, cannot create, it can only operate upon the
products of imagination. Further, he holds that the
predominance of mere reasoning and mere utility
has become in great part an evil; for while it has
accumulated masses of material goods and moral
truths, we distribute the goods iniquitously and fail
to apply the truths, because, for want of imagination,
we have not sympathy in our hearts and do not feel

what we know. The 'Poetry' which he defends,
therefore, is the whole creative imagination with all
its products. And these include not merely literature
in verse, but, first, whatever prose writing is allied
to that literature; and, next, all the other fine arts;
and, finally, all actions, inventions, institutions, and
even ideas and moral dispositions, which imagination
brings into being in its effort to satisfy the longing
for perfection. Painters and musicians are poets.
Plato and Bacon, even Herodotus and Livy, were
poets, though there is much in their works which
is not poetry. So were the men who invented the
arts of life, constructed laws for tribes or cities, disclosed, as sages or founders of religion, the excellence
of justice and love. And every one, Shelley would
say, who, perceiving the beauty of an imagined
virtue or deed, translates the image into a fact, is
so far a poet. For all these things come from
imagination.

Shelley's exposition of this, which is probably the
most original part of his theory, is not very clear;
but, if I understand his meaning, that which he
takes to happen in all these cases might be thus
described. The imagination—that is to say, the
soul imagining—has before it, or feels within it,
something which, answering perfectly to its nature,
fills it with delight and with a desire to realise what
delights it. This something, for the sake of brevity,
we may call an idea, so long as we remember that
it need not be distinctly imagined and that it is
always accompanied by emotion. The reason why
such ideas delight the imagining soul is that they
are, in fact, images or forebodings of its own perfection—of itself become perfect—in one aspect or
another. These aspects are as various as the
elements and forms of its own inner life and outward existence; and so the idea may be that of the
perfect harmony of will and feeling (a virtue), or of
the perfect union of soul with soul (love), or of the

perfect order of certain social relations or forces (a
law or institution), or of the perfect adjustment of
intellectual elements (a truth); and so on. The
formation and expression of any such idea is thus
the work of Poetry in the widest sense ; while at the
same time (as we must add, to complete Shelley's
thought) any such idea is a gleam or apparition of
the perfect Intellectual Beauty.

I choose this particular title of the hidden power
or divinity in order to point out (what the reader is
left to observe for himself) that the imaginative idea
is always regarded by Shelley as beautiful. It is,
for example, desirable for itself and not merely as a
means to a further result ; and it has the formal
characters of beauty. For, as will have been noticed
in the instances given, it is always the image of an
order, or harmony, or unity in variety, of the elements
concerned. Shelley sometimes even speaks of their
'rhythm.' For example, he uses this word in
reference to an action ; and I quote the passage
because, though it occurs at some distance from the
exposition of his main view, it illustrates it well.
He is saying that the true poetry of Rome, unlike
that of Greece, did not fully express itself in poems.
' The true poetry of Rome lived in its institutions :
for whatever of beautiful, true and majestic they
contained, could have sprung only from the faculty
which creates the order in which they consist. The
life of Camillus ; the death of Regulus ; the expectation of the senators, in their god-like state, of the
victorious Gauls ; the refusal of the Republic to
make peace with Hannibal after the battle of
Cannæ '—these he describes as 'a rhythm and order
in the shows of life,' an order not arranged with
a view to utility or outward result, but due to the
imagination, which, 'beholding the beauty of this
order, created it out of itself according to its own
idea.'

2.

If this, then, is the nature of Poetry in the widest sense, how does the poet, in the special sense, differ from other unusually creative souls? Not essentially in the inspiration and general substance of his poetry, but in the kind of expression he gives to them. In so far as he is a poet, his medium of expression, of course, is not virtue, or action, or law; poetry is one of the arts. And, again, it differs from the rest, because its particular vehicle is language. We have now to see, therefore, what Shelley has to say of the form of poetry, and especially of poetic language.

First, he claims for language the highest place among the vehicles of artistic expression, on the ground that it is the most direct and also the most plastic. It is itself produced by imagination instead of being simply encountered by it, and it has no relation except to imagination; whereas any more material medium has a nature of its own, and relations to other things in the material world, and this nature and these relations intervene between the artist's conception and his expression of it in the medium. It is to the superiority of its vehicle that Shelley attributes the greater fame which poetry has always enjoyed as compared with other arts. He forgets (if I may interpose a word of criticism) that the media of the other arts have, on their side, certain advantages over language, and that these perhaps counterbalance the inferiority which he notices. He would also have found it difficult to show that language, on its physical side, is any more a product of imagination than stone or pigments. And his idea that the medium in the other arts is an obstacle intervening between conception and expression is, to say the least, one-sided. A sculptor, painter, or musician, would probably reply that it is only the qualities of his medium that

enable him to express at all ; that what he
expresses is inseparable from the vehicle of expression ; and that he has no conceptions which are
not from the beginning sculpturesque, pictorial, or
musical. It is true, no doubt, that his medium is
an obstacle as well as a medium ; but this is also
true of language.

But to resume. Language, Shelley goes on to
say, receives in poetry a peculiar form. As it represents in its meaning a perfection which is always an
order, harmony, or rhythm, so it itself, as so much
sound, *is* an order, harmony, or rhythm. It is
measured language, which is not the proper vehicle
for the mere recital of facts or for mere reasoning.
For Shelley, however, this measured language is
not of necessity metrical. The order or measure
may remain at the stage which it reaches in beautiful
prose, like that of Plato, the melody of whose
language, Shelley declares, is the most intense it is
possible to conceive. It may again advance to
metre ; and he admits that metrical form is convenient, popular, and preferable, especially in poetry
containing much action. But he will not have any
new great poet tied down to it. It is not essential,
while measure is absolutely so. For it is no mere
accident of poetry that its language is measured,
nor does a delight in this measure mean little. As
sensitiveness to the order of the relations of sounds
is always connected with sensitiveness to the order
of the relations of thoughts, so also the harmony of
the words is scarcely less indispensable than their
meaning to the communication of the influence of
poetry. ' Hence,' says Shelley, ' the vanity of translation : it were as wise to cast a violet into a crucible
that you might discover the formal principle of its
colour and odour, as seek to transfuse from one
language into another the creations of a poet.'
Strong words to come from the translator of the
Hymn to Mercury and of Agathon's speech in the

Symposium![1] And is not all that Shelley says of
the difference between measured and unrhythmical
language applicable, at least in some degree, to the
difference between metrical and merely measured
language? Could he really have supposed that
metre is no more than a 'convenience,' which con-
tributes nothing of any account to the influence of
poetry? But I will not criticise. Let me rather
point out how surprising, at first sight, and how
significant, is Shelley's insistence on the importance
of measure or rhythm. No one could assert more
absolutely than he the identity of the general substance of poetry with that of moral life and action, of
the other arts, and of the higher kinds of philosophy.
And yet it would be difficult to go beyond the
emphasis of his statement that the formal element
(as he understood it) is indispensable to the effect
of poetry.

Shelley, however, nowhere considers this element
more at length. He has no discussions, like those
of Wordsworth and Coleridge, on diction. He
never says, with Keats, that he looks on fine phrases
like a lover. We hear of his deep-drawn sigh of
satisfaction as he finished reading a passage of
Homer, but not of his shouting his delight, as he
ramped through the meadows of Spenser, at some
marvellous flower. When in his letters he refers
to any poem he is reading, he scarcely ever mentions
particular lines or expressions; and we have no
evidence that, like Coleridge and Keats, he was a
curious student of metrical effects or the relations of
vowel-sounds. I doubt if all this is wholly accidental.
Poetry was to him so essentially an effusion of
aspiration, love and worship, that we can imagine
his feeling it almost an impiety to break up its unity
even for purposes of study, and to give a separate

---

[1] Statements equally emphatic on this subject may be found in a
passage quoted by Mrs. Shelley, in a footnote to Shelley's letter to
John Gisborne, Nov. 16, 1819 (Letter XXX. in Mrs. Shelley's edition).
Cf. also Letter XXXIII. to Leigh Hunt, Nov. 1819.

attention to its means of utterance. And what he
does say on the subject confirms this impression.
In the first place, as we have seen, he lays great
stress on inspiration; and his statements, if exaggerated and misleading, must still reflect in some degree
his own experience. No poem, he asserts, however
inspired it may be, is more than a feeble shadow of
the original conception; for when composition begins,
inspiration is already on the decline. And so in a
letter he speaks of the detail of execution destroying
all wild and beautiful visions. Still, inspiration, if
diminished by composition, is not wholly dispelled;
and he appeals to the greatest poets of his day
whether it is not an error to assert that the finest
passages of poetry are produced by labour and study.
Such toil he would restrict to those parts which
connect the inspired passages, and he speaks with
contempt of the fifty-six various readings of the first
line of the *Orlando Furioso*. He seems to exaggerate on this matter because in the *Defence* his foe
is cold reason and calculation. Elsewhere he writes
more truly of the original conception as being obscure
as well as intense;[1] from which it would seem to
follow that the feeble shadow, if darker, is at least
more distinct than the original. He forgets, too,
what is certainly the fact, that the poet in reshaping
and correcting is able to revive in some degree the
fire of the first impulse. And we know from himself
that his greatest works cost him a severe labour not
confined to the execution, while his manuscripts show
plenty of various readings, if never so many as fifty-
six in one line.

Still, what he says is highly characteristic of his
own practice in composition. He allowed the rush
of his ideas to have its way, without pausing to

---

[1] I cannot find the passage or passages to which I referred in
making this statement, and therefore I do not vouch for its accuracy.
Cf. from the fragment *Fiordispina*,

    The ardours of a vision which obscure
    The very idol of its portraiture.

complete a troublesome line or to find a word that
did not come; and the next day (if ever) he filled
up the gaps and smoothed the ragged edges. And
the result answers to his theory. Keats was right
in telling him that he might be more of an artist.
His language, indeed, unlike Wordsworth's or
Byron's, is, in his mature work, always that of a
poet; we never hear his mere speaking voice; but
he is frequently diffuse and obscure, and even in
fine passages his constructions are sometimes trailing
and amorphous. The glowing metal rushes into
the mould so vehemently that it overleaps the
bounds and fails to find its way into all the
little crevices. But no poetry is more manifestly
inspired, and even when it is plainly imperfect it
is sometimes so inspired that it is impossible to
wish it changed. It has the rapture of the mystic,
and that is too rare to lose. Tennyson quaintly
said of the hymn *Life of Life*: 'He seems to go
up into the air and burst.' It is true: and, if we
are to speak of poems as fireworks, I would not
compare *Life of Life* with a great set piece of
Homer or Shakespeare that illumines the whole
sky; but, all the same, there is no more thrilling
sight than the heavenward rush of a rocket, and
it bursts at a height no other fire can reach.

In addition to his praise of inspiration Shelley
has some scattered remarks on another point which
show the same spirit. He could not bear in poetic
language any approach to artifice, or any sign that
the writer had a theory or system of style. He
thought Keats's earlier poems faulty in this respect,
and there is perhaps a reference to Wordsworth
in the following sentence from the Preface to the
Revolt of Islam: 'Nor have I permitted any system
relating to mere words to divert the attention of
the reader, from whatever interest I may have
succeeded in creating, to my own ingenuity in
contriving,—to disgust him according to the rules

of criticism. I have simply clothed my thoughts in what appeared to me the most obvious and appropriate language. A person familiar with nature, and with the most celebrated productions of the human mind, can scarcely err in following the instinct, with respect to selection of language, produced by that familiarity.'[1] His own poetic style certainly corresponds with his intention. It cannot give the kind of pleasure afforded by what may be called without disparagement a learned and artful style, such as Virgil's or Milton's; but, like the best writing of Shakespeare and Goethe, it is, with all its individuality, almost entirely free from mannerism and the other vices of self-consciousness, and appears to flow so directly from the thought that one is ashamed to admire it for itself. This is equally so whether the appropriate style is impassioned and highly figurative, or simple and even plain. It is indeed in the latter case that Shelley wins his greatest, because most difficult, triumph. In the dialogue part of *Julian and Maddalo* he has succeeded remarkably in keeping the style quite close to that of familiar though serious conversation, while making it nevertheless unmistakably poetic. And the *Cenci* is an example of a success less complete only because the problem was even harder. The ideal of the style of tragic drama in the nineteenth or twentieth century should surely be, not to reproduce with modifications the style of Shakespeare, but to do what Shakespeare did—to idealise, without deserting, the language of contemporary speech. Shelley in the *Cenci* seems to me to have come nearest to this ideal.

[1] Cf. from the Preface to the *Cenci*: ' I entirely agree with those modern critics who assert that, in order to move men to true sympathy, we must use the familiar language of men. . . . But it must be the real language of men in general, and not that of any particular class to whose society the writer happens to belong.'

3.

So much for general exposition. If now we consider more closely what Shelley says of the substance of poetry, a question at once arises. He may seem to think of poetry solely as the direct expression of perfection in some form, and accordingly to imagine its effect as simply joy or delighted aspiration. Much of his own poetry, too, is such an expression ; and we understand when we find him saying that Homer embodied the ideal perfection of his age in human character, and unveiled in Achilles, Hector, and Ulysses 'the truth and beauty of friendship, patriotism, and persevering devotion to an object.' But poetry, it is obvious, is not wholly, perhaps not even mainly, of this kind. What is to be said, on Shelley's theory, of his own melancholy lyrics, those 'sweetest songs' that 'tell of saddest thought'? What of satire, of the epic of conflict and war, or of tragic exhibitions of violent and destructive passion? Does not his theory reflect the weakness of his own practice, his tendency to portray a thin and abstract ideal instead of interpreting the concrete detail of nature and life ; and ought we not to oppose to it a theory which would consider poetry simply as a representation of fact?

To this last question I should answer No. Shelley's theory, rightly understood, will take in, I think, everything really poetic. And to a considerable extent he himself shows the way to meet these doubts. He did not mean that the *immediate* subject of poetry must be perfection in some form. The poet, he says, can colour with the hues of the ideal everything he touches. If so, he may write of absolutely anything so long as he *can* so colour it, and nothing would be excluded from his province except those things (if any such exist) in which no positive relation to the ideal, however indirect, can be shown or intimated. Thus to take the instance

of Shelley's melancholy lyrics, clearly the lament
which arises from loss of the ideal, and mourns the
evanescence of its visitations or the desolation of its
absence, is indirectly an expression *of* the ideal; and
so on his theory is the simplest song of unhappy
love or the simplest dirge. Further, he himself
observes that, though the joy of poetry is often
unalloyed, yet the pleasure of the 'highest portions
of our being is frequently connected with the pain
of the inferior,' that 'the pleasure that is in sorrow
is sweeter than the pleasure of pleasure itself,' and
that not sorrow only, but 'terror, anguish, despair
itself, are often the chosen expressions of an
approximation to the highest good.' That, then,
which appeals poetically to such painful emotions
will again be an indirect portrayal of the ideal; and
it is clear, I think, that this was how Shelley in the
Defence regarded heroic and tragic poetry, whether
narrative or dramatic, with its manifestly imperfect
characters and its exhibition of conflict and wild
passion. He had, it is true, another and an unsatis-
factory way of explaining the presence of these
things in poetry; and I will refer to this in a
moment. But he tells us that the Athenian tragedies
represent the highest idealisms (his name for ideals)
of passion and of power (not merely of virtue); and
that in them we behold ourselves, 'under a thin
disguise of circumstance, stripped of all but that
ideal perfection and energy which every one feels to
be the internal type of all that he loves, admires,
and would become.' He writes of Milton's Satan
in somewhat the same strain. The Shakespearean
tragedy from which he most often quotes is one
in which evil holds the stage, *Macbeth*; and he was
inclined to think *King Lear*, which certainly is no
direct portrait of perfection, the greatest drama
in the world. Lastly, in the Preface to his own
Cenci he truly says that, while the story is fearful
and monstrous, 'the poetry which exists in these

tempestuous sufferings and crimes,' if duly brought
out, 'mitigates the pain of the contemplation of moral
deformity' : so that he regards Count Cenci himself
as a *poetic* character, and therefore as in *some* sense
an expression of the ideal. He does not further
explain his meaning. Perhaps it was that the perfection which poetry is to exhibit includes, together
with those qualities which win our immediate and
entire approval or sympathy, others which are
capable of becoming the instruments of evil. For
these, the energy, power and passion of the soul
though they may be perverted, are in themselves
elements of perfection; and so, even in their per-
version or their combination with moral deformity,
they retain their value, they are not simply ugly or
horrible, but appeal through emotions predominantly
painful to the same love of the ideal which is directly
satisfied by pictures of goodness and beauty. Now
to these various considerations we shall wish to add
others ; but if we bear these in mind, I believe we
shall find Shelley's theory wide enough, and must
hold that the substance of poetry is never mere fact,
but is always ideal, though its method of representation is sometimes more direct, sometimes more
indirect.

Nevertheless, he does not seem to have made his
view quite clear to himself, or to hold to it consistently. We are left with the impression, not
merely that he personally preferred the direct
method (as he was, of course, entitled to do), but
that his use of it shows a certain weakness, and
also that even in theory he unconsciously tends to
regard it as the primary and proper method, and
to admit only by a reluctant after-thought the
representation of imperfection. Let me point out
some signs of this. He considered his own *Cenci*
as a poem inferior in kind to his other main works,
even as a sort of accommodation to the public.
With all his modesty he knew what to think of the

neglected *Prometheus* and *Adonaïs*, but there is
no sign that he, any more than the world, was
aware that the character of Cenci was a creation
without a parallel in our poetry since the seventeenth
century. His enthusiasm for some second-rate and
third-rate Italian paintings, and his failure to understand Michael Angelo, seem to show the same
tendency. He could not enjoy comedy : it seemed
to him simply cruel : he did not perceive that to
show the absurdity of the imperfect is to glorify the
perfect. And, as I mentioned just now, he wavers
in his view of the representation of heroic and tragic
imperfection. We find in the Preface to *Prometheus
Unbound* the strange notion that Prometheus is a
more poetic character than Milton's Satan because
he is free from Satan's imperfections, which are said
to interfere with the interest. And in the *Defence*
a similar error appears. Achilles, Hector, Ulysses,
though they exhibit ideal virtues, are, he admits,
imperfect. Why, then, did Homer make them so?
Because, he seems to reply, Homer's contemporaries
regarded their vices (*e.g.* revengefulness and deceit-
fulness) as virtues. Homer accordingly had to
conceal in the costume of these vices the unspotted
beauty that he himself imagined; and, like Homer,
'few poets of the highest class have chosen to
exhibit the beauty of their conceptions in its naked
truth and splendour.' Now, this idea, to say nothing
of its grotesque improbability in reference to Homer,
and its probable baselessness in reference to most
other poets, is quite inconsistent with that truer
view of heroic and tragic character which was
explained just now. It is an example of Shelley's
tendency to abstract idealism or spurious Platonism.
He is haunted by the fancy that if he could only
get at the One, the eternal Idea, in complete
aloofness from the Many, from life with all its
change, decay, struggle, sorrow and evil, he would
have reached the true object of poetry : as if the

whole finite world were a mere mistake or illusion,
the sheer opposite of the infinite One, and in no
way or degree its manifestation. Life, he says—

> Life, like a dome of many-coloured glass,
> Stains the white radiance of eternity;

but the other side, the fact that the many colours
are the white light broken, he tends to forget, by
no means always, but in one, and that not the least
inspired, of his moods. This is the source of that
thinness and shallowness of which his view of the
world and of history is justly accused, a view in
which all imperfect being is apt to figure as absolutely
gratuitous, and everything and everybody as pure
white or pitch black. Hence also his ideals of good,
whether as a character or as a mode of life, resting
as they do on abstraction from the mass of real
existence, tend to lack body and individuality; and
indeed, if the existence of the many is a mere
calamity, clearly the next best thing to their dis-
appearance is that they should all be exactly alike
and have as little character as possible. But we
must remember that Shelley's strength and weakness
are closely allied, and it may be that the very
abstractness of his ideal was a condition of that
quivering intensity of aspiration towards it in which
his poetry is unequalled. We must not go for this
to Homer and Shakespeare and Goethe; and if we
go for it to Dante, we shall find, indeed, a mind far
vaster than Shelley's, but also that dualism of
which we complain in him, and the description of
a heaven which, equally with Shelley's regenerated
earth, is no place for mere mortality. In any case,
as we have seen, the weakness in his poetical practice, though it occasionally appears also as a defect
in his poetical theory, forms no necessary part of it.

4.

I pass to his views on a last point. If the business
of poetry is somehow to express ideal perfection, it

may seem to follow that the poet should embody in his poems his beliefs about this perfection and the way to approach it, and should thus have a moral purpose and aim to be a teacher. And in regard to Shelley this conclusion seems the more natural because his own poetry allows us to see clearly some of his beliefs about morality and moral progress. Yet alike in his Prefaces and in the *Defence* he takes up most decidedly the position that the poet ought neither to affect a moral aim nor to express his own conceptions of right and wrong. ' Didactic poetry,' he declares, ' is my abhorrence : nothing can be equally well expressed in prose that is not tedious and supererogatory in verse.'[1] 'There was little danger,' he tells us in the *Defence*, 'that Homer or any of the eternal poets' should make a mistake in this matter ; but 'those in whom the poetical faculty, though great, is less intense, as Euripides, Lucan, Tasso, Spenser, have frequently affected a moral aim, and the effect of their poetry is diminished in exact proportion to the degree in which they compel us to advert to this purpose.' These statements may appeal to us, but are they consistent with Shelley's main views of poetry ? To answer this question we must observe what exactly it is that he means to condemn.

Shelley was one of the few persons who can literally be said to *love* their kind. He held most strongly, too, that poetry does benefit men, and benefits them morally. The moral purpose, then, to which he objects cannot well be a poet's general purpose of doing moral as well as other good through his poetry—such a purpose, I mean, as he may cherish when he contemplates his life and his life's work. And, indeed, it seems obvious that nobody with any humanity or any sense can object to that, except through some intellectual confusion. Nor, secondly, does Shelley mean, I think, to condemn

[1] Preface to *Prometheus Unbound.*

even the writing of a particular poem with a view
to a particular moral or practical effect; certainly,
at least, if this was his meaning he was condemning
some of his own poetry. Nor, thirdly, can he be
referring to the portrayal of moral ideals; for that
he regarded as one of the main functions of poetry,
and in the very place where he says that didactic
poetry is his abhorrence he also says, by way of
contrast, that he has tried to familiarise the minds
of his readers with beautiful idealisms of moral
excellence. It appears, therefore, that what he is
really attacking is the attempt to give, in the strict
sense, moral *instruction*, to communicate doctrines,
to offer argumentative statements of opinion on
right and wrong, and more especially, I think, on
controversial questions of the day. An example
would be Wordsworth's discourse on education at
the end of the *Excursion*, a discourse of which
Shelley, we know, had a very low opinion. In
short, his enemy is not the purpose of producing
a moral effect, it is the appeal made for this purpose
to the reasoning intellect. He says to the poet:
By all means aim at bettering men; you are a man,
and are bound to do so; but you are also a poet,
and therefore your proper way of doing so is not
by reasoning and preaching. His idea is of a
piece with his general championship of imagination, and it is quite consistent with his main view of
poetry.[1]

---

[1] I do not discuss the adequacy of Shelley's position, or assert that
he held it quite clearly or consistently. In support of my interpretation
of it I may refer to the Preface to the *Cenci*. There he repudiates the
idea of making the dramatic exhibition of the story 'subservient to
what is vulgarly called a moral purpose,' and, as the context shows,
he identifies such a treatment of the story with the 'enforcement' of
a 'dogma.'
This passage has a further interest. The dogma which Shelley
would not enforce in his tragedy was that 'no person can truly be
dishonoured by the act of another, and the fit return to make to the
most enormous injuries is kindness and forbearance, and a resolution
to convert the injurer from his dark passions by peace and love'; and
accordingly he held that 'if Beatrice had thought in this manner she

What, then, are the *grounds* of this position?
They are not clearly set out, but we can trace
several, and they are all solid. Reasoning on moral
subjects, moral philosophy, was by no means 'tedious'
to Shelley; it seldom is to real poets. He loved it,
and (outside his *Defence*) he rated its value very
high.[1] But he thought it tedious and out of place
in poetry, because it can be equally well expressed
in 'unmeasured' language—much better expressed,
one may venture to add. You invent an art in
order to effect by it a particular purpose which
nothing else can effect as well. How foolish, then,
to use this art for a purpose better served by something else! I know no answer to this argument,
and its application is far wider than that given to
it by Shelley. Secondly, Shelley remarks that a
poet's own conceptions on moral subjects are usually
those of his place and time, while the matter of his
poem ought to be eternal, or, as we say, of permanent
and universal interest. This, again, seems true, and
has a wide application; and it holds good even
when the poet, like Shelley himself, is in rebellion
against orthodox moral opinion; for his heterodox
opinions will equally show the marks of his place
and time, and constitute a perishable element in his
work. Doubtless no poetry can be without a perishable element; but that poetry has least of it which
interprets life least through the medium of systematic
and doctrinal ideas. The veil which time and place

would have been wiser and better.' How inexcusable then is the not
uncommon criticism on the *Cenci* that he represents Beatrice as a
perfect character and justifies her murder of 'the injurer.'

Shelley's position in the *Defence*, it may be added, is in total
disagreement with his youthful doctrine and practice. In 1811 he
wrote to Miss Hitchener, 'My opinion is that all poetical beauty ought
to be subordinate to the inculcated moral,' and a large part of *Queen
Mab* is frankly didactic. Even there, however, he reserved most of
the formal instruction for the Notes, perceiving that 'a poem very
didactic is . . . very stupid.'

[1] 'I consider poetry very subordinate to moral and political science,'
he says in a letter to Peacock, Jan. 1819.

have hung between Homer or Shakespeare and the
general reader of to-day is almost transparent, while
even a poetry so intense as that of Dante and Milton
is impeded in its passage to him by systems which
may be unfamiliar, and, if familiar, may be distasteful.

Lastly—and this is Shelley's central argument—
as poetry itself is directly due to imaginative inspiration and not to reasoning, so its true moral effect
is produced through imagination and not through
doctrine. Imagination is, for Shelley, 'the great
instrument of moral good.' The 'secret of morals
is love.' It is not 'for want of admirable doctrines
that men hate and despise and censure and deceive
and subjugate one another': it is for want of love.
And love is 'a going out of our own nature, and an
identification of ourselves with the beautiful which
exists in thought, action or person not our own.'
'A man,' therefore, 'to be greatly good must
imagine intensely and comprehensively.' And
poetry ministers to moral good, the effect, by acting
on its cause, imagination. It strengthens imagination
as exercise strengthens a limb, and so it indirectly
promotes morality. It also fills the imagination with
beautiful impersonations of all that we should wish
to be. But moral reasoning does not act upon the
cause, it only analyses the effect; and the poet has
no right to be content to analyse what he ought
indirectly to create. Here, again, in his eagerness,
Shelley cuts his antitheses too clean, but the defect
is easily made good, and the main argument is
sound.

Limits of time will compel me to be guilty of the
same fault in adding a consideration which is in the
spirit of Shelley's. The chief moral effect claimed
for poetry by Shelley is exerted, primarily, by
imagination on the emotions; but there is another
influence, exerted primarily through imagination on
the understanding. Poetry is largely an interpretation of life; and, considering what life is, that

must mean a moral interpretation. This, to have poetic value, must satisfy imagination; but we value it also because it gives us knowledge, a wider comprehension, a new insight into ourselves and the world.[1] Now, it may be held—and this view answers to a very general feeling among lovers of poetry now—that the most deep and original moral interpretation is not likely to be that which most shows a moral purpose or is most governed by reflective beliefs and opinions, and that as a rule we learn most from those who do not try to teach us, and whose opinions may even remain unknown to us: so that there is this weighty objection to the appearance of such purpose and opinions, that it tends to defeat its own intention. And the reason that I wish to suggest is this, that always we get most from the *genius* in a man of genius and not from the rest of him. Now, although poets often have unusual powers of reflective thought, the specific genius of a poet does not lie there, but in imagination. Therefore his deepest and most original interpretation is likely to come by the way of imagination. And the specific way of imagination is not to clothe in imagery consciously held ideas; it is to produce half-consciously a matter from which, when produced, the reader may, if he chooses, extract ideas. Poetry (I must exaggerate to be clear), psychologically considered, is not the *expression* of ideas or of a view of life; it is their discovery or creation, or rather both discovery and creation in one. The interpretation contained in *Hamlet* or *King Lear* was not brought ready-made to the old stories. What was brought to them was the huge substance of Shakespeare's imagination, in which all his experience and thought was latent; and this, dwelling and working on the stories with nothing but a

---

[1] And, I may add, the more it does this, so long as it does it imaginatively, the more does it satisfy imagination, and the greater is its *poetic* value.

dramatic purpose, and kindling into heat and motion,
gradually discovered or created in them a meaning
and a mass of truth about life, which was brought
to birth by the process of composition, but never
preceded it in the shape of ideas, and probably
never, even after it, took that shape to the poet's
mind. And *this* is the interpretation which we find
inexhaustibly instructive, because Shakespeare's
genius is in it. On the other hand, however much
from curiosity and personal feeling towards him we
may wish to know his opinions and beliefs about
morals or religion or his own poems or Queen
Elizabeth, we have not really any reason to suppose
that their value would prove extraordinary. And
so, to apply this generally, the opinions, reasonings
and beliefs of poets are seldom of the same quality
as their purely imaginative product. Occasionally,
as with Goethe, they are not far off it ; but sometimes they are intense without being profound, and
more eccentric than original; and often they are
very sane and sound, but not very different from
those of wise men without genius. And therefore
poetry is not the place for them. For we want in
poetry a moral interpretation, but not the interpretation we have already. As a rule the genuine
artist's quarrel with ' morality ' in art is not really
with morality, it is with a stereotyped or narrow
morality ; and when he refuses in his art to consider
things from what he calls the moral point of view,
his reasons are usually wrong, but his instinct is
right.

Poetry itself confirms on the whole this contention,
though doubtless in these last centuries a great poet's
work will usually reveal more of conscious reflection
than once it did. Homer and Shakespeare show no
moral aim and no system of opinion. Milton was
far from justifying the ways of God to men by the
argumentation he put into divine and angelic lips ;
his truer moral insight is in the creations of his

genius ; for instance, in the character of Satan or the picture of the glorious humanity of Adam and Eve. Goethe himself could never have told the world what he was going to express in the First Part of *Faust* : the poem told *him*, and it is one of the world's greatest. He knew too well what he was going to express in the Second Part, and with all its wisdom and beauty it is scarcely a great poem. Wordsworth's original message was delivered, not when he was a Godwinian semi-atheist, nor when he had subsided upon orthodoxy, but when his imagination, with a few hints from Coleridge, was creating a kind of natural religion ; and this religion itself is more profoundly expressed in his descriptions of his experience than in his attempts to formulate it. The moral virtue of Tennyson is in poems like *Ulysses* and parts of *In Memoriam*, where sorrow and the consciousness of a deathless affection or an unquenchable desire for experience forced an utterance ; but when in the *Idylls* he tried to found a great poem on explicit ideas about the soul and the ravages wrought in it by lawless passion, he succeeded but partially, because these ideas, however sound, were no product of his genius. And so the moral virtue of Shelley's poetry lay, not in his doctrines about the past and future of man, but in an intuition, which was the substance of his soul, of the unique value of love. In the end, for him, the truest name of that perfection called Intellectual Beauty, Liberty, Spirit of Nature, is Love. Whatever in the world has any worth is an expression of Love. Love sometimes talks. Love talking musically is Poetry.

1904.

THE LONG POEM
IN THE AGE OF WORDSWORTH

THE LONG POEM
IN THE AGE OF WORDSWORTH[1]

THE poetry of the age of Wordsworth, we are all agreed, is one of the glories of our literature. It is surpassed, many would add, by the poetry of no other period except the Elizabethan. But it has obvious flaws, of which perhaps we are becoming more and more distinctly conscious now ; and, apart from these definite defects, it also leaves with us, when we review it, a certain feeling of disappointment. It is great, we say to ourselves, but why is it not greater still ? It shows a wonderful abundance of genius : why does it not show an equal accomplishment ?

I.

Matthew Arnold, in his essay on *The Function of Criticism at the Present Time*, gave an answer to this question. ' It has long seemed to me,' he wrote, ' that the burst of creative activity in our literature, through the first quarter of this century, had about it, in fact, something premature . . . And

---

[1] The material of these pages belongs in part to the course mentioned on p. 99, and in part to a lecture given in November, 1905. They have in consequence defects which I have not found it possible to remove ; and they also open questions too large and difficult for a single lecture. This is one reason why I have not referred to the prevalence of the novel in the nineteenth century, a prevalence which doubtless influenced both the character and the popularity of the long poems. I hope the reader will not gain from the lecture the false impression that the writer's admiration for those poems is lukewarm, or that he has any tendency to reaction against the Romantic Revival of Wordsworth's time.

this prematureness comes from its having proceeded
without having its proper data, without sufficient
materials to work with.   In other words, the English poetry of the first quarter of this century, with
plenty of energy, plenty of creative force, did not
know enough.   This makes Byron so empty of
matter, Shelley so incoherent, Wordsworth even,
profound as he is, yet so wanting in completeness
and in variety.'   The statement that this poetry
' did not know enough' means, of course, for Arnold,
not that it lacked information, reading, ideas of a
kind, but that it lacked 'criticism.'   And this means
that it did not live and move freely in an atmosphere of the best available ideas, of ideas gained by
a free, sincere, and continued effort, in theology,
philosophy, history, science, to see things as they
are.   In such an atmosphere Goethe lived.   There
was not indeed in Goethe's Germany, nor was there
in the England of our poets, the 'national glow
of life and thought' that prevailed in the Athens of
Pericles or the England of Elizabeth.   That happiest
atmosphere for poetry was wanting in both countries.
But there was for Goethe 'a sort of equivalent for it
in the complete culture and unfettered thinking of a
large body of Germans,' a culture produced by a
many-sided learning and a long and widely-combined
critical effort.   It was this that our poets lacked.

Now, if this want existed, as Arnold affirms, it
may not have had all the importance he ascribes to
it, but considerable importance it must have had.
And as to its existence there can hardly be a doubt.
One of the most striking characteristics of Wordsworth's age is the very unusual superiority of the
imaginative literature to the scientific.   I mean by
the 'scientific' literature that of philosophy, theology,
history, politics, economics, not only that of the
sciences of Nature, which for our present purpose
are perhaps the least important.   In this kind of
literature Wordsworth's age has hardly an author

to show who could for a moment be placed
on a level with some five of the poets, with
the novelists Scott and Jane Austen, or with the
poetic critics Lamb, Hazlitt, and Coleridge. It
has no writers to compare with Bacon, Newton,
Hume, Gibbon, Johnson, or Burke. It is the
time of Paley, Godwin, Stewart, Bentham, Mitford,
Lingard, Coleridge the philosopher and theologian.
These are names worthy of all respect, but they
represent a literature quite definitely of the second
rank. And this great disproportion between the
two kinds of literature, we must observe, is a
peculiar phenomenon. If we go back as far as the
Elizabethan age we shall find no parallel to it.
The one kind was doubtless superior to the
other in Shakespeare's time, possibly even in
Milton's ; but Hooker and Bacon and Taylor and
Clarendon and Hobbes are not separated from the
best poets of their day by any startling difference of quality ;[1] while in the later periods, right
down to the age of Wordsworth, the scientific
literature quite holds its own, to say no more, with
the imaginative. Nor in the Germany of Wordsworth's own time is there that gap between the two
that we find in England. In respect of genius the
philosophers, for example, though none of them was
the equal of Goethe, were as a body not at all
inferior to the poets. The case of England in
Wordsworth's age is anomalous.

This peculiarity must be symptomatic, and it must
have been influential. It confirms Arnold's view
that the intellectual atmosphere of the time was not
of the best. If we think of the periodical literature
—of the *Quarterly* and *Edinburgh* and *Blackwood*—
we shall be still more inclined to assent to that
view. And when we turn to the poets themselves,
and especially to their prose writings, letters, and

---

[1] This, and not the permanent value of the scientific product,
is the point.

recorded conversation, and even to the critiques of
Hazlitt, of Lamb, and of Coleridge, we cannot
reject it. Assuredly we read with admiration, and
the signs of native genius we meet with in abundance
—in greater abundance, I think, than in the poetry
and criticism of Germany, if Goethe is excepted.
But the freedom of spirit, the knowledge, the superiority to prejudice and caprice and fanaticism, the
openness to ideas, the atmosphere that is all about us
when we read Lessing, Goethe, Schiller, Heine, we
do not find. Can we imagine any one of those four
either inspired or imprisoned as Shelley was by the
doctrines of Godwin? Could any of them have seen
in the French Revolution no more significance than
Scott appears to have detected? How cramped are
the attitudes, sympathetic or antipathetic, of nearly
all our poets towards the Christian religion! Could
anything be more *borné* than Coleridge's professed
reason for not translating *Faust*?[1] Is it possible
that a German poet with the genius of Byron or
Wordsworth could have inhabited a mental world
so small and so tainted with vulgarity as is opened
to us by the brilliant letters of the former, or could
have sunk, like the latter, to suggesting that the
cholera was a divine condemnation of Catholic
Emancipation and the Reform Bill?

But if we accept Arnold's statement as to the
intellectual atmosphere of the poetry of Wordsworth's time, a question will remain. Was he right
in regarding this atmosphere as the sole, or even
as the chief, cause of the fact (if it is one) that the
poetry does not fully correspond in greatness with
the genius of the poets? And before we come to
this question we must put another. Is the fact
really as it has just been stated? I do not think
so. The disappointment that we feel attends, it
seems to me, mainly our reading of the long poems.
Reviewing these in memory, and asking ourselves

[1] *Table-talk*, Feb. 16, 1833.

how many we can unreservedly call 'great,' we
hesitate. Beyond doubt there is great poetry in
some of them, fine poetry in many ; but that does
not make a great whole. Which of them is great
as a whole ? Not the *Prelude* or the *Excursion*,
still less *Endymion* or *The Revolt of Islam* or *Childe
Harold*, which hardly pretends to unity. *Christabel*,
the wonderful fragment, is a fragment; so is
Hyperion; *Don Juan*, also unfinished, becomes
more discursive the further it proceeds, and in
spirit is nowhere great. All the principal poets
wrote dramas, or at least dramatic pieces; and
some readers think that in *Manfred*, and still more
certainly in *Cain*, we have great poems, while others
think this of *Prometheus Unbound* and *The Cenci*.
But if as to one or more of these we assent, is our
judgment quite confident, and can we say that any
of them *satisfy* us, like some works of earlier times?
We are thus satisfied, it seems to me, only when we
come to poems of smaller dimensions, like *The
Ancient Mariner*, or *The Eve of Saint Agnes*, or
Adonais, or *The Vision of Judgment*, or when we
read the lyrics. To save time I will confine myself
to the latter.

Within this sphere we have no longer that
impression of genius which fails to reach full
accomplishment. I would go further. No poet, of
course, of Wordsworth's age is the equal of Shakespeare or of Milton ; and there are certain qualities,
too, of lyrical verse in which the times of Shakespeare and of Milton are superior to that of Wordsworth. But if we take the better part of the lyrical
poetry of these three periods in the mass, or again
in a representative selection, it will not be the latest
period, I think, that need fear the comparison. In
the original edition of the *Golden Treasury*, Book I.
(Wyatt to Shakespeare) occupies forty pages ; Book
II. (the rest of the seventeenth century) sixty-five ;
Book IV., which covers the very much shorter

period from Wordsworth to Hood, close on a
hundred and forty. 'Book I.,' perhaps most of us
would say, 'should be longer, and Book IV. a good
deal shorter : some third-rate pieces are included in
it, and Wordsworth is over-represented. And the
Elizabethan poems are mostly quite short, while the
Nineteenth Century poets shine equally in the
longer kinds of lyric. And Mr. Palgrave excluded
the old ballads, but admitted poems like Coleridge's
Love and Wordsworth's *Ruth* (seven whole pages).
And in any case we cannot judge by mere quantity.'
No; but still quantity must count for something,
and the *Golden Treasury* is a volume excellent in
selection, arrangement, and taste. It does, I think,
leave the impression that the age of Wordsworth
was our greatest period in lyrical poetry. And if
Book I. were swelled to the dimensions of Book IV.,
this impression would not be materially altered ; it
might even be deepened. For the change would
force into notice the comparative monotony of the
themes of the earlier poetry, and the immensely
wider range of the thought and emotion that attain
expression in the later. It might also convince us
that, on the whole, this more varied material is
treated with a greater intensity of feeling, though on
this point it is difficult to be sure, since we recognise
what may be called the conventions of an earlier
age, and are perhaps a little blind to those of a time
near our own.

Now the eminence of Wordsworth's age in lyrical
poetry, even if it is not also a pre-eminence, is a
significant fact. It may mean that the whole poetic
spirit of the time was lyrical in tendency ; and this
may indirectly be a cause of that sense of disappointment which mingles with our admiration of
the long poems. I will call attention, therefore, to
two or three allied facts. (1) The longer poems of
Campbell are already dead ; he survives only in
lyrics. This is also true of Moore. In spite of fine

passages (and the battle in *Marmion* is in certain qualities superior to anything else of the time) Scott's longer poems cannot be classed with the best contemporary poetry ; but in some of his ballads and songs he attains that rank. (2) Again, much of the most famous narrative poetry is semi-lyrical in form, as a moment's thought of Scott, Byron, and Coleridge will show. Some of it (for instance, several of Byron's tales, or Wordsworth's *White Doe of Rylstone*) is strongly tinged with the lyrical spirit. The centre of interest is inward. It is an interest in emotion, thought, will, rather than in scenes, events, actions, which express and re-act on emotions, thoughts, will. It would hardly be going too far to say that in the most characteristic narrative poetry the balance of outward and inward is rarely attained.[1] (3) The same tendencies are visible in much of the dramatic writing. Byron's regular dramas, for instance, if they ever lived, are almost forgotten ; but *Heaven and Earth*, which is still alive, is largely composed of lyrics, and the first two acts of *Manfred* are full of them. *Prometheus Unbound* is called 'a lyrical drama.' Though it has some very fine and some very beautiful blank verse passages (usually undramatic), its lyrics are its glory; and this is even more the case with *Hellas*. It would be untrue to say that the comparative failure of most of the dramas of the time is principally due to the lyrical spirit, but many of them show it. (4) The strength of this spirit may be illustrated lastly by a curious fact. The ode is one of the longest and most ambitious forms of lyric, and some of the most

---

[1] The narrative poems that satisfy most, because in their way they come nearest to perfection, will be found, I believe, to show this balance. Such, for instance, are *The Eve of St. Agnes, Lamia, Michael, The Vision of Judgment*, some of Crabbe's tales. It does not follow, of course, that such poems must contain the greatest poetry. Crabbe, for example, was probably the best artist of the day in narrative ; but he does not represent the full ideal spirit of the time.

famous poems of Wordsworth, Coleridge, and Keats are odes. But the greatest of the lyrists, who wrote the Odes to Liberty and Naples and the West Wind, found the limits even of the ode too narrow for his 'flight of fire.' If *Lycidas* and *L'Allegro* and Spenser's *Epithalamion* are lyrical poems, and if we are not arbitrarily to determine that nothing shall be called lyrical which exceeds a certain length, *Adonais* will be a lyrical elegy in fifty-five Spenserian stanzas, and the *Lines written among the Euganean Hills* and *Epipsychidion* will be lyrics consisting respectively of 370 and 600 lines.

It will however be agreed that in general a lyrical poem may be called short as compared with a narrative or drama. It is usual, further, to say that lyrical poetry is 'subjective,' since, instead of telling or representing a story of people, actions, and events, it expresses the thoughts and feelings of the poet himself. This statement is ambiguous and in other ways defective ; but it will be admitted to have a basis in fact. It may be suggested, then, that the excellence of the lyrical poetry of Wordsworth's time, and the imperfection of the long narratives and dramas, may have a common origin. Just as it was most natural to Homer or to Shakespeare to express the imaginative substance of his mind in the 'objective' shape of a world of persons and actions ostensibly severed from his own thoughts and feelings, so, perhaps, for some reason or reasons, it was most natural to the best poets of this later time to express that substance in the shape of impassioned reflections, aspirations, prophecies, laments, outcries of joy, murmurings of peace. The matter of these might, in another sense of the word, be 'objective' enough, a matter of general human interest, not personal in any exclusive way ; but it appeared in the form of the poet's thought and feeling. Just because he most easily expressed it thus, he succeeded less completely when he attempted the more objective form of utterance; and for the same reason it was especially important that he should be surrounded and penetrated by an atmosphere of wide, deep, and liberal 'criticism.' For he not only lived among ideas; he expressed ideas, and expressed them *as* ideas.

These suggestions seem to be supported by other phenomena of the poetry. The 'subjective' spirit extends, we saw, into many of the longer poems. This is obvious when it can plausibly be said, as in Byron's case, that the poet's one hero is himself. It appears in another way when the poem, through its story or stories, displays the poet's favourite ideas and beliefs. The *Excursion* does this; most of Shelley's longer poems do it. And the strength of this tendency may be seen in an apparent contradiction. One of the marks of the Romantic Revival is a disposition to substitute the more concrete and vivid forms of narrative and drama for the eighteenth century form of satiric or so-called didactic reflection. Yet most of the greater poets, especially in their characteristic beginnings, show a strong tendency to reflective verse; Coleridge, for example, in *Religious Musings*, Byron in the first two cantos of *Childe Harold*, Shelley in *Queen Mab*, and Keats in *Sleep and Poetry*. These are not, like the *Pleasures of Memory* and *Pleasures of Hope*, continuations of the traditional style; they are thoroughly Romantic; and yet they are reflective. Scott, indeed, goes straight to the objective forms; but then Scott, for good and evil, was little affected by the spiritual upheaval of his time. Those who were deeply affected by it, directly or indirectly, had their minds full of theoretic ideas. They were groping after, or were already inflamed by, some explicit view of life, and of life seen in relation to an ideal which it revealed or contradicted. And this view of life, at least at first, pressed for utterance in a more or less abstract shape, or became a sort of soul or second meaning within those appearances of nature, or actions of men, or figures and fantasies of youthful imagination, which formed the ostensible subject of the poetry.

Considered in this light, the following facts become very significant. Wordsworth, now about thirty, and the author of many characteristic lyrics, on returning from Germany and settling at Grasmere, begins to meditate a long poem. He tells us in the *Prelude* of the subjects he thought of. They are good subjects, legendary and historical, stories of action, not at all theoretical.[1] But it will not do : his mind 'turns recreant to her task.' He has another hope, a 'favourite aspiration' towards 'a philosophic song of Truth.' But even this will not do ; it is premature ; even Truth (I venture to suggest) is not inward enough. He must first tell the story of his own mind : the subject of his long poem must be Poetry itself. He tells this story, to our great gain, in the *Prelude* ; and it is the story of the steps by which he came to see reality, Nature and Man, as the partial expression of the ideal, of an all-embracing and perfect spiritual life or Being. Not till this is done can he proceed to the *Excursion*, which, together with much reflection and even argumentation, contains pictures of particular men.

'This for our greatest'; but it is not his history alone. The first longer poem of Shelley which can be called mature was *Alastor*. And what is its subject? The subject of the *Prelude*; the story of a Poet's soul, and of the effect on it of the revelation of its ideal. The first long poem of Keats was *Endymion*. The tendency to the concrete was strong in Keats; he has been called, I think, an Elizabethan born out of due time ; and *Endymion*, like *Venus and Adonis*, is a mythological story. But it is by no means that

[1] See p. 110.

alone. The infection of his time was in him. The
further subject of *Endymion* is again the subject of the
Prelude, the story of a poet's soul smitten by love of
its ideal, the Principle of Beauty, and striving for
union with it, for the ' wedding ' of the mind of man
' with this goodly universe in love and holy passion.'
What, again, is the subject of *Epipsychidion*? The
same.

> There was a Being whom my spirit oft
> Met on its visioned wanderings, far aloft
> In the clear golden prime of my youth's dawn.

The poem is all about the search of the poet's soul
for this ideal Being. And the *Sensitive Plant* is
this soul, and the Lady of the Garden this Being.
And *Prince Athanase* is the same soul, and if the
poem had been continued the Being would soon
have appeared. Is it not an astonishing proof of
Shelley's powers that the *Cenci* was ever written?
Shelley, when he died, had half escaped—Keats,
some time before he died, had quite escaped—from
that bewitching inward world of the poet's soul
and its shadowy adventures. Could that well be
the world of what we call emphatically a 'great
poem'?

2.

Let us review for a moment the course of our
discussion. I have been suggesting that, if our
pleasure and glory in the poetry of Wordsworth's
age is tinged with disappointment, this does not
extend to the lyrical poetry; that the lyrical spirit,
or, more generally, an inward or subjective tendency, shows itself in many of the longer works;
and that their imperfection is partly due to it.
Now, let me suggest that the atmosphere of adequate 'criticism' which Arnold misses in the age
and its poetry, while doubtless it would have influenced favourably even the lyrics, and much more
the larger works, could hardly have diminished the

force of that tendency, and that the main difficulty
lay *there*.   But, before developing this idea further,
I propose to leave for a time the English poetry of
Wordsworth's age, to look beyond it, and to ask
certain questions.

First, granted that in that age the atmosphere of
'criticism' was more favourable in Germany than in
England, how many long poems were produced in
Germany that we can call without hesitation or
qualification 'great'?   Were *any* produced except
by Goethe?   And, if we admit (as I gladly do) that
he produced several, was not the *main* reason simply
that he was born with more poetic genius than any
of his contemporaries, just as Dante and Shakespeare
and Milton were?   And again, with this native
genius and his long laborious life, did he produce
anything like as many great poems as might have
been expected?   And, if not, why not?   I do not
suggest that his general culture, so superior to that
of his English contemporaries, did not help him;
but are we sure that it did not also hinder him?
And is it not also significant that, in spite of his
love of new ideas, he felt an instinctive dread of the
influence of philosophy, in the strict sense, as of
something dangerous to the poetic modes of vision
and creation?

Secondly, if we look beyond the first quarter of
the century to the second and third, do we find in
Europe a large number of those emphatically great
poems, solid coherent structures of concrete imagination?   It seems more than doubtful.   To confine
ourselves to English examples, is it not the case
that Tennyson is primarily a lyrical poet, that the
best of his longer poems, *Maud* and *In Memoriam*,
are lyrical, and that the most ambitious, the narrative *Idylls of the King*, is, as a whole, not great?
Is the *Ring and the Book*, however fine in parts, a
great whole, or comparable as a whole with *Andrea
del Sarto* or *Rabbi ben Ezra*?   And is any one of

Browning's dramas a great play? What these questions suggest is that, while the difficulty about the long poem affects in an extreme degree the age of Wordsworth, it affects in some degree the time that follows. Its beginnings, too, are traceable before the nineteenth century. In fact it is connected with essential characteristics of modern poetry and art; and these characteristics are connected with the nature of modern life, and the position of the artist within that life. I wish to touch on this huge subject before returning to the age of Wordsworth.

Art, we may say, has become free, and, in a sense, universal. The poet is no longer the minstrel of king or nobles, nor even of a city or country. Literature, as Goethe foretold, becomes increasingly European, and more than European; and the poet, however national, is a citizen of the Republic of Letters. No class of subject, again, has any prerogative claim on him. Whatever, in any time or place, is human, whatever has been conceived as divine, whatever belongs even to external nature, he may choose, as it suits his bent or offers a promising material. The world is all before him; and it is a world which the increase of knowledge has made immensely wide and rich. His art, further, has asserted its independence. Its public exhibition must conform to the law; but otherwise it neither asks the approval nor submits to the control of any outward authority; and it is the handmaid of nothing. It claims a value for itself, as an expression of mind co-ordinate with other expressions, theoretic and practical; satisfying a need and serving a purpose that none of them can fulfil; subject only, as they too are subject, to the unity of human nature and human good. Finally, in respect of the methods of his art the poet claims and enjoys the same freedom. The practice of the past, the 'rules' of the past (if they existed or exist), are without authority for him. It is improbable beforehand that a violent breach with them will lead him to a real advance, just as it is improbable that such a breach with the morals or the science of his day will do so. But there is no certainty beforehand; and if he fails, he expects blame not because he innovates, but because he has failed by innovating.

The freedom of modern art, and the universality of its field, are great things, and the value of the second is easily seen in the extraordinary variety of subject-matter in the longer poems of the nineteenth century. But in candid minds most recitals of our modern advantages are followed by a melancholy sense of our feebleness in using them. And so in some degree it is here. The unrivalled opportunities fail to produce unrivalled works. And we can see that the deepest cause of this is not a want of native genius or of acquired skill or even of conscientious labour, but the fact that the opportunities themselves bring danger and difficulty. The poet who knows everything and may write about anything has, after all, a hard task. Things must have been easier, it seems to us, for an artist whose choice, if his aim was high, was restricted to a cycle of ideas and stories, mythological, legendary, or historical, or all together, concerning beings divine, daemonic, angelic, or heroic. His matter, as it existed in the general imagination, was already highly poetical. If not created by imagination, it was shaped or coloured by it; a world not of bodiless thoughts and emotions, but of scenes, figures, actions, and events. For the most part he lived in unity with it; it appealed to his own religious and moral feelings and beliefs, sometimes to his patriotic feelings; and he wrote, painted, or carved, for people who shared with him both his material and his attitude towards it. It belonged usually to the past, but he did not view it over a great gulf of time with the eye of a scientific historian. If he wished to robe it in the vesture of the life around him, he was checked by no scruples as to truth; and the life around him can seldom, we think, have appeared to him repulsively prosaic. Broad statements like these require much qualification; but, when it is supplied, they may still describe periods in which perhaps most of the greatest architecture, sculpture, painting, and poetry has come into being.

How different the position of the artist has now become we see at a glance, and I confine myself to some points which specially concern the difficulty of the long poem. If a poem is to be anything like great it must, in one sense, be concerned with the present. Whatever its 'subject' may be, it must express something living in the mind from which it comes and the minds to which it goes. Wherever its body is, its soul must be here and now. What subject, then, in the measureless field of choice, is the poet to select and fashion into a body? The outward life around him, as he and his critics so often lament, appears uniform, ugly, and rationally regulated, a world of trousers, machinery and policemen. Law— the rule, however imperfect, of the general reasonable will—is a vast achievement and priceless possession; but it is not favourable to striking events or individual actions on the grand scale. Beneath the surface, and breaking through it, there is doubtless an infinity of poetic matter; but this is inward, or it fails to appear in impressive forms; and therefore it may suit the lyric or idyll, the monologue or short story, the prose drama or novel, but hardly the long poem or high tragedy. Even war, for reasons not hard to find, is no longer the subject that it was.

But when the poet turns to a subject distant in place or time or both, new troubles await him. If he aims at complete truth to time and place the soul of the present will hardly come into his work. Yet he lives in an age of history and science, and these hamper as well as help him. The difficulty is not that he is bound to historical or scientific truth, for in principle, I venture to say, he is free. If he *can* satisfy imagination by violating them he is justified. It is no function of his to attain or propagate them ; and a critic who objected, say, to the First Part of *Faust* on the ground that it puts a modern spirit into the legend, would rightly be laughed at. It is its triumph to do so and yet to succeed. But then success is exceedingly difficult. For the poet lives in a time when the violation of truth is *prima facie* felt to be a fault, something that does require justification by the result. Further, he has himself to start from a clear consciousness of difference between the present and the past, the spirit and the story, and has to produce on this basis a harmony of spirit and story. And again, living in an age of analytical thought, he is likely—all the more likely, if he has much greatness of mind—to be keenly interested in ideas ; and so he is exposed to the temptation of using as the spirit of the old story some highly reflective idea—an idea not only historically alien to his material, but perhaps not very poetical, or again not very deep, because it belongs to him rather as philosopher than poet, while his genius is that of a poet.

The influence of some of these difficulties might readily be shown in the Second Part of *Faust* or in *Prometheus Unbound*, especially where we perceive in a figure or action some symbolical meaning, but find this meaning deficient in interest or poetic truth, or are vexed by the doubt how far it ought to be pursued.[1] But the matter is more easily illustrated by the partial failure of the *Idylls of the King*. We have no right to condemn beforehand an attempt to modernise the Arthurian legends. Tennyson's treatment of them, even his outrage on the story of Tristram, might conceivably have been justified by the result. And, indeed, in the *Holy Grail* and

[1] Demogorgon is an instance of such a figure.

the *Passing of Arthur* his treatment, to my mind, was more than justified. But, in spite of countless beauties, the total result of the *Idylls* was disappointing, not merely from the defects of this or that poem, but because the old unity of spirit and story was broken up, and the new was neither equal to the old nor complete in itself. For the main semi-allegorical idea, having already the disadvantage of not being poetic in its origin, was, as a reflective idea, by no means profound, and it led to such inconsistency in the very centre of the story as the imagination refuses to accept. Tennyson's Lancelot might have wronged the Arthur who is merely a blameless king and represents Conscience; but Tennyson's Lancelot would much rather have killed himself than be systematically treacherous to the friend and lover-husband who appears in *Guinevere*.[1]

These difficulties belong in some measure to the whole modern time—the whole time that begins with the Renaissance; but they become so much clearer and so much more serious with the advance of knowledge and criticism, that in speaking of them I have been referring specially to the last century. There are other difficulties not so closely connected

---

[1] This incongruity is not the only cause of the discomfort with which many lovers of Tennyson read parts of Arthur's speech in that Idyll; but it is the main cause, and, unlike other defects, it lies in the plan of the story. It may be brought out further thus. So far as Arthur is merely the blameless king and representative of Conscience, the attitude of a judge which he assumes in the speech is appropriate, and, again, Lancelot's treachery to him is intelligible and, however wrong, forgivable. But then this Arthur or Conscience could never be a satisfactory husband, and ought not to astound or shock us by uttering his recollections of past caresses. If, on the other hand, these utterances are appropriate, and if all along Lancelot and Guinevere have had no reason to regard Arthur as cold and wholly absorbed in his public duties, Lancelot has behaved not merely wrongly but abominably, and as the Lancelot of the *Idylls* could not have behaved. The truth is that Tennyson's design requires Arthur to be at once perfectly ideal and completely human. And this is not imaginable.

Having written this criticism, I cannot refrain from adding that I think the depreciation of Tennyson's genius now somewhat prevalent a mistake. I admire and love his poetry with all my heart, and regard him as considerably our greatest poet since the time of Wordsworth.

with that advance, and I will venture some very
tentative remarks on one of these, which also has
increased with time. It has to do with the kind of
life commonly lived by our poets. Is there not some
significance in the fact that the most famous of our
narrative poets were all three, in their various ways
and degrees, public men, or in contact with great
affairs ; and that poets in earlier times no less must
usually have seen something at first hand of adventure, political struggles, or war ; whereas poets now,
for the most part, live wholly private lives, and, like
the majority of their readers, are acquainted only
by report with anything of the kind? If Chaucer
had never been at Court, or seen service in the
French war, or gone on embassies abroad ; if
Spenser had not known Sidney and Raleigh and
been secretary to Lord Grey in Ireland ; if Milton
had spent his whole life at Horton ; would it have
made no difference to their poetry? Again, if we turn
to the drama and ask why the numerous tragedies
of the nineteenth century poets so rarely satisfy,
what is the answer? There are many reasons, and
among them the poet's ignorance of the stage will
doubtless count for much ; but must we not also
consider that he scarcely ever saw anything resembling the things he tried to portray? When we study
the history of the time in which the Elizabethan
dramas were composed, when we examine the portraits of the famous men, or read such a book as the
autobiography of Lord Herbert of Cherbury, we
realise that the violent actions and passions which
the dramatist depicted were like the things he saw.
Whatever Shakespeare's own disposition was, he
lived among these men, jested with the fellow-actor
who had borne arms abroad and killed his man in a
duel at home, conversed with nobles whose heads
perhaps were no great way from the block. But the
poet who strolls about the lanes or plods the London
streets with an umbrella for a sword, and who has

probably never seen a violent deed in his life, or
for a moment really longed to kill so much as a
critic, how is he to paint the vengeance of Hamlet
or the frenzy of Macbeth, and not merely to thrill
you with the emotions of his actors but to make
them *do* things that take your imagination by the
throat?

3.

Assuming, now, that (even if this last idea is
doubtful or unimportant) there is some truth in the
suggestion that the difficulties of the long poem
arise largely from the conditions described, and
especially from the nature of the intellectual atmosphere which the modern poet breathes, let us return
to Wordsworth's age in particular. In that age
these difficulties were aggravated in a quite exceptional way by special causes, causes responsible also
in part for the unusual originality and intensity of
the poetry. In it we find conditions removed to the
extremest distance from those of the poet who wrote,
in the midst of a generally accepted social order,
for an audience with which he shared traditional
ideas and beliefs and a more or less traditional
imaginative material. It was, in a word, a revolutionary age, in the electric atmosphere of which the
most potent intellectual influences were those of
Rousseau and (for the English poets) of Godwin.
Milton's time was not in the same sense revolutionary, much less Shakespeare's. The forces of the
great movement of mind in Shakespeare's day *we*
may formulate as 'ideas,' but they were not the
abstractly conceived ideas of Wordsworth's day.
Such theoretical ideas were potent in Milton's time,
but they were not ideas that made a total breach
with the past, rejecting as worthless, or worse, the
institutions, beliefs, and modes of life in which
human nature had endeavoured to realise itself, and
drawing airy pictures of a different human nature

on a new earth. Nor was the poetic mind of those
ages enraptured or dejected by the haunting many-
featured contrast of real and ideal. But the poetic
mind in Wordsworth's age breathed this atmosphere
of revolution, though it was not always sensitive to
the influence. Nor is it a question of the acceptance
or rejection of the 'ideas of the Revolution.' That
influence is clearly traceable in all the greater writers
except Scott and Jane Austen. It is equally obvious
in Wordsworth, who hungered for realities, recovered
from his theoretic malady, sought for good in life's
familiar face, yet remained a preacher; in Byron,
who was too shrewd, sceptical, and selfish to con-
tract that particular malady, but who suffered from
the sickness from which Goethe freed himself by
writing *Werther*,[1] and who punctuates his story in
Don Juan with bursts of laughter and tears; and
in Shelley, whose 'rapid spirit' was quickened, and
then clogged, by the abstractions of revolutionary
theory.

But doubtless Shelley is, in a sense, the typical
example of this influence and of its effects. From
the world of his imagination the shapes of the old
world had disappeared, and their place was taken
by a stream of radiant vapours, incessantly forming, shifting, and dissolving in the 'clear golden
dawn,' and hymning with the voices of seraphs, to
the music of the stars and the 'singing rain,' the
sublime ridiculous formulas of Godwin. In his
heart were emotions that responded to the vision,—
an aspiration or ecstasy, a dejection or despair, like
those of spirits rapt into Paradise or mourning over
its ruin. And he wrote, not, like Shakespeare or
Pope, for Londoners sitting in a theatre or a coffee-
house, intelligences vivid enough but definitely
embodied in a definite society; he wrote, or rather

---

[1] It is never to be forgotten, in comparing Goethe with the English
poets, that he was twenty years older than Wordsworth and Coleridge,
and forty years older than Byron and Shelley.

he sang, to his own soul, to other spirit-sparks of the fire of Liberty scattered over the dark earth, to spirits in the air, to the boundless spirit of Nature or Freedom or Love, his one place of rest and the one source of his vision, ecstasy, and sorrow. He sang *to* this, and he sang *of* it, and of the emotions it inspired, and of its world-wide contest with such shapes of darkness as Faith and Custom. And he made immortal music; now in melodies as exquisite and varied as the songs of Schubert, and now in symphonies where the crudest of Philosophies of History melted into golden harmony. But the songs were more perfect than the symphonies; and they could hardly fail to be so. For a single thought and mood, expressive of one aspect of things, suffices, with its melody, for a lyric, but not for a long poem. That requires a substance which implicitly contains a whole 'criticism' or interpretation of life. And although there was something always working in Shelley's mind, and issuing in those radiant vapours, that was far deeper and truer than his philosophic creed, its expression and even its development were constantly checked or distorted by the hard and narrow framework of that creed. And it was one which in effect condemned nine-tenths of the human nature that has formed the material of the world's great poems.[1]

The second and third quarters of the century were not in the same degree as the first a revolutionary time, and we feel this change in the

---

[1] The reader will remember that he must take these paragraphs as an exaggerated presentment of a single, though essential, aspect of the poetry of the time, and of Shelley's poetry in particular, and must supply the corrections and additions for himself. But I may beg him to observe that Godwin's formulas are called sublime as well as ridiculous. *Political Justice* would never have fascinated such young men as Wordsworth, Coleridge, and Shelley, unless a great truth had been falsified in it ; and the inspiration of this truth can be felt all through the preposterous logical structure reared on its misapprehension.

poetry. The fever-heat is gone, the rapture and the dejection moderate, the culture is wider, the thought more staid and considerate, the fascination of abstractions less potent, and the formative or plastic impulse, if not stronger, less impeded. Late in the period, with Morris, the born teller of tales re-appears. If, as we saw, the lyrical spirit continues to prevail, no one would deny to Browning the full and robust sympathy of the dramatist with all the variety of character and passion. Yet these changes and others are far from obliterating those features of the earlier generation on which we have dwelt. To describe the atmosphere of 'criticism' as that of a common faith or view of the world would be laughable. If not revolutionary, it was agitated, restless, and distressed by the conflict of theoretic ideas. To Arnold's mind it was indeed a most unhappy time for poetry, though the poetic impulse remained as yet, and even later, powerful. The past was dead, but he could share neither the soaring hope nor the passionate melancholy of the opening century. He was

> Wandering between two worlds, one dead,
> The other powerless to be born,
> With nowhere yet to rest his head.

And the two greatest poets, as well as he, still offer not only, as poets always must, an interpretation, but a definite theory of life, and, more insistently than ever before, of death. Confidence in the detail, at least, of such theories has diminished, and with the rapid advance of the critical sciences the poets may prophesy less than their predecessors; but they probe, and weigh, and deliberate more. And the strength of the 'inward' tendency, obvious in Tennyson and Arnold, may be clearly seen even in Browning, and not alone in such works as *Christmas Eve and Easter Day* or *La Saisiaz*.

Objective and dramatic as Browning is called
and by comparison is, he is surely most at home,
and succeeds most completely, in lyrics, and in
monologues divested of action and merely sugges-
tive of a story or suggested by one. He too must
begin, in *Pauline*, with the picture of a youthful
poet's soul. Dramatic the drama of *Paracelsus*
neither is nor tries to be : it consists of scenes in
the history of souls. Of the narrative *Sordello*
its author wrote : 'The historical decoration was
purposely of no more importance than a background requires ; and my stress lay on the incidents in the development of a soul : little else is
worth study.' Even if that is so, great narrative
poems are not written thus. And what Browning
says here applies more or less fully to most of his
works. In the end, if we set aside the short lyrics,
his best poems are all 'studies' of souls. 'Well,'
it may be answered, 'so are Shakespeare's tragedies
and tragi-comedies.' But the difference is great.
Shakespeare, doubtless, is little concerned with the
accuracy of the historical background,—much less
concerned than Browning. But his subject is not
a soul, nor even souls : it is the actions of souls,
or souls coming into action. It is more. It is that
clash of souls which exhibits not them alone, but
a whole of spiritual forces, appearing in them, but
spreading beyond them into the visible society to
which they essentially belong, and into invisible
regions which enclose it. The thing shown, therefore, is huge, multiform, ponderous, yet quivering
with an inward agitation which explodes into violent
bodily expression and speaks to the *eye* of imagination. What specially interests Browning is not
this. It is the soul moving in itself, often in its
most secret windings and recesses ; before action or
after it, where there is action at all ; and this soul
not essentially as in its society (that is 'background' or 'decoration'), but alone, or in relation

to another soul, or to God. He exhibits it best,
therefore, in monologue, musing, explaining, debat-
ing, pleading, overflowing into the expression of
feeling or passion, but not acting. The 'men and
women' that haunt the reader's imagination are not
so much men of action as lovers, artists, men of
religion. And when they act (as for example in
The Ring and the Book, or the dramas) what rivets
attention, and is first recalled to memory by their
names, is not the action, but its reflection in the
soul of the doer or spectator. Such, at least, is my
experience; and in the end a critic can only offer
to others his considered experience. But with
Homer and Shakespeare and Milton it is otherwise. Even with Dante it is otherwise. I see not
souls alone, but souls in visible attitudes, in outward movement, often in action. I see Paolo and
Francesca drifting on the wind : I see them sitting
and reading : I see them kiss : I *see* Dante's pity :

E caddi come corpo morto cade.

4.

I spoke of Tennyson and Browning in order to
point out that, although in their day the intellectual
atmosphere was no longer 'revolutionary,' it remained an atmosphere of highly reflective ideas
representing no common 'faith' or way of envisag-
ing the world, and that the inward tendency still
asserts itself in their poetry. We cannot pursue the
history further, but it does not appear that in the
last forty years culture has advanced much, or at all,
towards such a faith or way, or shows the working
of new semi-conscious creative ideas beneath the
surface of warring theories and opinions. Only the
younger among us can hope to see what Arnold
descried in the distance,

One mighty wave of thought and joy
Lifting mankind again.

And even when, for them or their descendants, that hope is realised, and with it the hope of a new great poetry, the atmosphere must assuredly still be one of 'criticism,' and Arnold's insistence on the necessity of the best criticism will still be as urgently required. It must indeed be more and more needed as the power of half-educated journalism grows. How poetry then will overcome the obstacles which, therefore, must in some measure still beset it, is a question for it, a question answerable not by the reflections of critics, but by the creative deeds of poets themselves. Accordingly, while one may safely prophesy that their long poems will differ from those of any past age, I have no idea of predicting the nature of this difference, and will refer in conclusion only to certain views which seem to me delusive.

It must surely be vain for the poet to seek an escape from modern difficulties by any attempt to withdraw himself from the atmosphere of free and scientific culture, to maintain by force simplicity of view and concreteness of imagination, to live in a past century or a sanctuary of esoteric art, whether secular or religious. Whatever of value such an attempt may yield—and that it may yield much I do not deny—it will never yield poems at once long and great.

Such poems, we may allow ourselves to hope, will sometimes deal with much of the common and painful and ugly stuff of life, and be in that sense more 'democratic' or universal than any poetry of the past. But it is vain to imagine that this can be done by a refusal to 'interpret' and an endeavour to photograph. Even in the most thorough-going prose 'realism' there is selection ; and, to go no further, selection itself is interpretation. And, as for poetry, the mirror which the least theoretical of great poets holds up to nature is his soul. And that, whether he likes it or not, is an activity

which divides, and sifts, and recombines into a
unity of its own, and by a method of its own, the
crude material which experience thrusts upon it.
This must be so; the only question is of the choice
of matter and the method of treatment. Nor can
the end to be achieved be anything but beauty,
though the meaning of that word may be extended
and deepened. And beauty in its essence is something that gives satisfaction, however much of pain,
repulsion, or horror that satisfaction may contain and
overcome.

'But, even so,' it may be said, 'why should the
poet trouble himself about figures, events, and
actions? That inward tendency in which you see
danger and difficulty is, on the contrary, simply
and solely what on one side you admit it to be, the
sign of our advance. What we really need is to
make our long poems *entirely* interior. We only
want to know how Dante felt; we do not *wish* to
see his pity felling him to the ground; and much
less do we wish to hear Othello say "and smote him
thus," or even to imagine the blow. We are not
children or savages.' We do not want, I agree,
attempts to repeat the Elizabethan drama. But
those who speak thus forget, perhaps, in how
many kinds of poem this inward tendency can
display its power without any injury or drawback.
They fail to ask themselves, perhaps, whether a
long poem so entirely 'interior' can possibly have
the clearness, variety, and solidity of effect that
the best long poems have possessed; whether it
can produce the same impression of a massive,
building, organising, 'architectonic' power of imagination; and whether all this and much else is of
little value. They can hardly have realised, one
must suspect, how much of life they wish to leave
unrepresented. They fail to consider, too, that
perhaps the business of art is not to ignore, but at
once to satisfy and to purify, the primitive instincts

from which it arises; and that, in the case of poetic
art, the love of a story, and of exceptional figures,
scenes, events, and actions, is one of those instincts,
and one that in the immense majority of men shows
no sign of decay. And finally, if they suppose that
the desire to see or imagine action, in particular, is
a symptom of mere sensationalism or a relic of
semi-barbarism, I am sure they are woefully mistaken. There is more virtue than their philosophy
dreams of in deeds, in 'the motion of a muscle
this way or that.' Doubtless it is the soul that
matters; but the soul that remains interior is not
the whole soul. If I suppose that mere self-scrutiny
can show me that, I deceive myself; and my deeds,
good and evil, will undeceive me.

A last delusion remains. 'There is,' we may be
told, 'a simple, final, and comfortable answer to all
these doubts and fears. The long poem is not
merely difficult, it is impossible. It is dead, and
should be publicly buried, and there is not the least
occasion to mourn it. It has become impossible
not because we cannot write it, but because we see
that we ought not. And, in truth, it never was
written. The thing called a long poem was really,
as any long poem must be, a number of short ones,
linked together by passages of prose. And these
passages *could* be nothing except prose; for poetry
is the language of a state of crisis, and a crisis is
brief. The long poem is an offence to art.' I
believe I have stated this theory fairly. It was,
unless I mistake, the invention of Poe, and it is
about as true as I conceive his story of the composition of *The Raven* to be. It became a gospel with
some representatives of the Symbolist movement in
France; and in fact it would condemn not only the
long poem, but the middle-sized one, and indeed all
sizes but the smallest. To reject this theory is to
imply no want of gratitude for the lyrics of some of
its adherents; but the theory itself seems strangely

thoughtless. Naturally, in any poem not quite short, there must be many variations and grades of poetic intensity ; but to represent the differences of these numerous grades as a simple antithesis between pure poetry and mere prose is like saying that, because the eyes are the most expressive part of the face, the rest of the face expresses nothing. To hold, again, that this variation of intensity is a defect is like holding that a face would be more beautiful if it were all eyes, a picture better if the illumination were equally intense all over it, a symphony better if it consisted of one movement, and if that were all crisis. And to speak as if a small poem could do all that a long one does, and do it much more completely, is to speak as though a humming-bird could have the same kind of beauty as an eagle, the rainbow in a fountain produce the same effect as the rainbow in the sky, or a moorland stream thunder like Niagara. A long poem, as we have seen, requires imaginative powers superfluous in a short one ; and it would be easy to show that it admits of strictly poetic effects of the highest value which the mere brevity of a short one excludes. That the long poem is doomed is a possible, however groundless, belief ; but it is futile to deny that, if it dies, something of inestimable worth will perish.[1]

[1] The theory criticised in this paragraph arises, I think, from a misapplication of the truth that the content of a genuine poem is fully expressible only in the words of that poem. It is seen that this is so in a lyric, and then it is assumed that it is *not* so in a narrative or drama. But the assumption is false. At first sight we may seem able to give a more adequate account of the long poem than of the short one ; but in reality you can no more convey the whole poetic content of the *Divine Comedy* in a form not its own than you can the content of a song.

The theory is connected in some minds with the view that 'music is the true type or measure of perfected art.' That view again rests on the idea that 'it is the art of music which most completely realises [the] artistic ideal, [the] perfect identification of form and matter,' and that accordingly 'the arts may be represented as continually struggling after the law or principle of music, to a condition which music alone completely realises' (Pater, *The Renaissance*, pp. 144, 145). I have by implication expressed dissent from this idea (p. 25); but, even if its truth is granted, what follows is that poetry should endeavour *in its own way* to achieve that perfect identification; but it does not in the least follow that it should endeavour to do so by reducing itself as nearly as possible to mere sound. Nor did Pater affirm this, or (so far as I see) imply it. But others have.

THE LETTERS OF KEATS

THE LETTERS OF KEATS

THERE is no lack of good criticism on the poetry of Keats. It has been discussed by the leading poets of three generations or semi-generations; by Matthew Arnold, by Mr. Swinburne, and, much more fully, by Mr. Bridges. Lord Houghton's *Life and Letters* and Mr. Colvin's biography both contain excellent criticisms or studies of the poems. And (to go no further) they have lately been edited by Mr. de Sélincourt in a volume invaluable to students of Keats, and reflecting honour not only on its author but on the Oxford School of English, to the strength of which he has contributed so much. My principal object is to consider Keats's attitude to poetry and his views about it, in connection with the ideas set forth in previous lectures on Shelley's views and on the age of Wordsworth. But I wish to preface my remarks on this subject, and to prepare for them, by an urgent appeal, addressed to any reader of the poems who may need it, to study the letters of Keats. If I may judge from my experience, such readers are still far too numerous; and I am sure that no one already familiar with the letters will be sorry to listen to quotations from them.[1]

[1] The Letters (except those to Miss Brawne, and a few others) have been edited by Colvin, and (without exception) by Forman (pub. Gowans & Gray). I refer to them by their numbers, followed by the initial of the editor's name. Both editions reproduce peculiarities of punctuation, etc.; but for my present purpose these are usually without interest, and I have consulted the convenience of the reader in making changes.

The best of Keats's poems, of course, can be fully
appreciated without extraneous help ; but the letters
throw light on all, and they are almost necessary
to the understanding of *Endymion* and of some
of the earlier or contemporaneous pieces. They
clearly reveal those changes in his mind and temper
which appear in his poetry. They dispose for ever
of the fictions once current of a puny Keats who
was 'snuffed out by an article,' a sensual Keats
who found his ideal in claret and 'slippery blisses,'
and a mere artist Keats who cared nothing for his
country and his fellow-creatures. Written in his
last four years by a man who died at twenty-five,
they contain abundant evidence of his immaturity
and his faults, but they disclose a nature and character which command on the whole not less respect
than affection, and they show not a little of that
general intellectual power which rarely fails to
accompany poetic genius.

Of Keats's character, as the letters manifest it,
Arnold has written. While speaking plainly and
decidedly of the weakness visible in those to Miss
Brawne, Arnold brought together the evidence which
proves that Keats 'had flint and iron in him,' 'had
virtue in the true and large sense of the word.'
And he selected passages, too, which illustrate the
'admirable wisdom and temper' and the 'strength
and clearness of judgment' shown by Keats, alike
in matters of friendship and in his criticisms of his
own productions, of the public, and of the literary
circles,—the 'jabberers about pictures and books,' as
Keats in a bitter mood once called them. We may
notice, in addition, two characteristics. In spite of
occasional despondency, and of feelings of awe at
the magnitude of his ambition, Keats, it is tolerably
plain from these letters, had a clear and habitual
consciousness of his genius. He never dreamed of
being a minor poet. He knew that he was a poet ;
sometimes he hoped to be a great one. I remember

no sign that he felt himself the inferior of any living
poet except Wordsworth. How he thought of
Byron, whom in boyhood he had admired, is obvious. When Shelley wrote, hinting a criticism, but
referring to himself as excelled by Keats in genius,
he returned the criticism without the compliment.
His few references to Coleridge are critical, and his
amusing description of Coleridge's talk is not more
reverential than Carlyle's. Something, indeed, of
the native pugnacity which his friends ascribe to
him seems to show itself in his allusions to contemporaries, including even Wordsworth. Yet with
all this, and with all his pride and his desire of fame,
no letters extant breathe a more simple and natural
modesty than these; and from end to end they
exhibit hardly a trace, if any trace, either of the
irritable vanity attributed to poets or of the sublime
egotism of Milton and Wordsworth. He was of
Shakespeare's tribe.

The other trait that I wish to refer to appears
in a particular series of letters—sometimes mere
notes—scattered through the collection. They are
addressed to Keats's school-girl sister Fanny, who
was eight years younger than he, and who died in
the same year as Browning.[1] Keats, as we see
him in 1817 and 1818, in the first half of Mr.
Colvin's collection, was absorbed by an enthusiasm
and ambition which his sister was too young to
understand. During his last two years he was,
besides, passionately and miserably in love, and,
latterly, ill and threatened with death. His soul
was full of bitterness. He shrank into himself,
avoided society, and rarely sought even intimate
friends. Yet, until he left England, he never ceased
to visit his sister when he could; and, when he
could not, he continued to write letters to her, full of
amusing nonsense, full of brotherly care for her,

[1] Keats himself, it is strange to think, was born in the same year as
Carlyle.

and of excellent advice offered as by an equal who happened to be her senior; letters quite free from thoughts of himself, and from the forced gaiety and the resentment against fate which in parts of his later correspondence with others betray his suffering. These letters to his sister are, in one sense, the least remarkable in the collection, yet it would lose much by their omission. They tell us next to nothing of his genius, but as we come upon them the light in our picture of him, if it had grown for a moment hard or troubled, becomes once more soft and bright.

To turn (with apologies for the distinction) from the character to the mind of Keats, if the reader has formed a notion of him as a youth with a genius for poetry and an exclusive interest in poetry, but otherwise not intellectually remarkable, this error will soon be dispelled by the letters. With Keats, no doubt, poetry and the hope of success in it were passions more glowing than we have reason to attribute to his contemporaries at the same time of life.[1] The letters remind us also that, compared with them, he was at a disadvantage in intellectual training and acquisitions, like the young Shakespeare among the University wits. They show, too —the earlier far more than the later—in certain literary mannerisms the unwholesome influence of Leigh Hunt and his circle. But everywhere we feel in them the presence of an intellectual nature, not merely sensitive and delicate, but open, daring, rich, and strong; exceedingly poetic and romantic, yet observant, acute, humorous, and sensible; intense without narrowness, and quite as various

---

[1] These passions were in his last two years overclouded at times, but they remained to the end. When, in the bitterness of his soul, he begged Severn to put on his tombstone no name, but only 'Here lies one whose name was writ in water,' he was thinking not merely of the reviewers who had robbed him of fame in his short life, but also of those unwritten poems, of which 'the faint conceptions' in happier days used to 'bring the blood into his forehead.'

both in its interests and its capacities as the mind
of Wordsworth or of Shelley.   Fundamentally, and
in spite of abundant high spirits and a love of nonsense, the mind of Keats was very serious and
thoughtful.   It was original, and not more imitative
than an original mind should be in youth ; an intelligence which now startles by flashes of sudden
beauty, and now is seen struggling with new and
deep thoughts, which labour into shape, with scanty
aid from theories, out of personal experience.
In quality—and I speak of nothing else—the mind
of Shakespeare at three and twenty may not have
been very different.

Short extracts can give but little idea of all this ;
but they may at least illustrate the variety of
Keats's mind, and the passages I am about to read
have been chosen mainly with this intention, and
not because the majority are among the most striking that might be found.   The earliest belong to
the September of 1817, and I take them partly for
their local interest.   Keats spent most of that
month here in Oxford, staying in the Magdalen
Hall of those days with his friend Bailey, a man
whose gentle and disinterested character he warmly
admired.   'We lead,' he writes to his sister, 'very
industrious lives—he in general studies, and I in
proceeding at a pretty good pace with a Poem
which I hope you will see early in the next year.'
It was *Endymion* : he wrote, it seems, the whole of
the Third Book in Bailey's rooms.   Unluckily the
hero in that Book is wandering at the bottom of the
sea ; but even in those regions, as Keats imagined
them, a diligent student may perhaps find some
traces of Oxford.   In the letters we hear of towers
and quadrangles, cloisters and groves ; of the deer
in Magdalen Park ; and how

> The mouldering arch,
> Shaded o'er by a larch,
> Lives next door to Wilson the hosier

(that should be discoverable). But we hear most of the clear streams—'more clear streams than ever I saw together.' ' I take a walk by the side of one of them every evening.' ' For these last five or six days,' he writes to Reynolds, 'we have had regularly a boat on the Isis, and explored all the streams about, which are more in number than your eyelashes. We sometimes skim into a bed of rushes, and there become naturalised river-folks. There is one particularly nice nest, which we have christened " Reynolds's Cove," in which we have read Wordsworth and talked as may be.' Of those talks over Wordsworth with the grave religious Bailey came perhaps the thoughts expressed later in the best-known of all the letters (it is too well known to quote), thoughts which take their origin from the *Lines written near Tintern Abbey*.[1]

About a year after this, Keats went with his friend Brown on a walking-tour to the Highlands; and I will quote two passages from the letters written during this tour, for the sake of the contrast they exhibit between the two strains in Keats's mind. The first is the later. The letter is dated ' Cairn-something July 17th ':

Steam-boats on Loch Lomond, and Barouches on its sides, take a little from the pleasure of such romantic chaps as Brown and I. The banks of the Clyde are extremely beautiful—the north end of Loch Lomond grand in excess—the entrance at the lower end to the narrow part is precious good—the evening was beautiful—nothing could surpass our fortune in the weather. Yet was I worldly enough to wish for a fleet of chivalry Barges with trumpets and banners, just to die away before me into that blue place among the mountains.[2]

Keats all over! Yes; but so is this, which was written a fortnight earlier from Carlisle :

After Skiddaw, we walked to Ireby, the oldest market town in Cumberland, where we were greatly amused by a country dancing-

[1] LII, C., LV, F. The quotations above are from XIV, XVI, C., XV, XVII, XVIII, F. The verses are a parody of Wordsworth's lines, ' The cock is crowing.'

[2] LXI, C., LXVI, F.

school holden at the Tun. It was indeed 'no new cotillion fresh from France.' No, they kickit and jumpit with mettle extraordinary, and whiskit, and friskit, and toed it and go'd it, and twirl'd it and whirl'd it, and stamped it, and sweated it, tattooing the floor like mad. The difference between our country dances and these Scottish figures is about the same as leisurely stirring a cup o' tea and beating up a batter-pudding. I was extremely gratified to think that, if I had pleasures they knew nothing of, they had also some into which I could not possibly enter. I hope I shall not return without having got the Highland fling. There was as fine a row of boys and girls as you ever saw; some beautiful faces, and one exquisite mouth. I never felt so near the glory of Patriotism, the glory of making by any means a country happier. This is what I like better than scenery.[1]

There is little enough here of the young poet who believes himself to care for nothing but 'Art'; and as little of the theoretic cosmopolitanism of some of Keats's friends.

Some three months later we find Keats writing from London to his brother and his sister-in-law in America; and he tells them of a young lady from India whom he has just met:

She is not a Cleopatra, but she is at least a Charmian. She has a rich Eastern look. When she comes into a room she makes an impression the same as the beauty of a leopardess. . . . You will by this time think I am in love with her; so before I go any further I will tell you I am not—she kept me awake one night as a tune of Mozart's might do. I speak of the thing as a pastime and an amusement, than which I can feel none deeper than a conversation with an imperial woman, the very 'yes' and 'no' of whose lips is to me a banquet. . . . I believe, though, she has faults—the same as Charmian and Cleopatra might have had. Yet she is a fine thing, speaking in a worldly way: for there are two distinct tempers of mind in which we judge of things,— the worldly, theatrical and pantomimical; and the unearthly, spiritual and ethereal. In the former, Buonaparte, Lord Byron, and this Charmian, hold the first place in our minds; in the latter, John Howard, Bishop Hooker rocking his child's cradle, and you, my dear sister, are the conquering feelings.[2]

I do not read this passage merely for its biographical interest, but a word may be ventured

---

[1] LVI, C., LXI, F.

[2] LXXIII, C., LXXXI, F. Mr. Hooker, I may remark, would not have thanked Keats for his bishopric.

on that.   The lady was not Miss Brawne ; but less
than a month later, on meeting Miss Brawne, he
immediately became her slave.   When we observe
the fact, and consider how very unlike the words I
have quoted are to anything in Keats's previous
letters, we can hardly help suspecting that he was
at this time in a peculiar condition and ripe for his
fate.   Then we remember that he had lately returned from his Scotch tour, which was broken
off because the Inverness doctor used the most
menacing language about the state of his throat ;
and further, that he was now, in the late autumn,
nursing his brother Tom, who died of consumption
before the year was out.   And an idea suggests
itself which, if exceedingly prosaic, has yet some
comfort in it.   How often have readers of Keats's
life cried out that, if only he had never met Miss
Brawne, he might have lived and prospered !   Does
it not seem at least as probable that, if Miss Brawne
had never existed, what happened would still have
happened, and even that the fever of passion which
helped to destroy him was itself a token of incipient
disease ?

I turn the leaf and come, in the same letter, to a
passage on politics.   The friends of Keats were, for
the most part, advanced liberals.   His own sympathies went that way.   A number of lines in the
poems of his boyhood show this, and so do many
remarks in the letters.   And his sympathies were
not mere sentiments.   ' I hope sincerely,' he wrote
in September, 1819, ' I shall be able to put a mite
of help to the liberal side of the question before
I die ' ; and a few days later, when he tells Brown
of his wish to act instead of dreaming, and to work
for his livelihood, composing deliberate poems only
when he can afford to, he says that he will write
as a journalist for whoever will pay him, but he
makes it a condition that he is to write ' on the
liberal side of the question.'   It is a mistake to

suppose that he had no political interests. But he cared nothing for the mere quarrels of Whig and Tory; a 'Radical' was for him the type of an 'obstinate and heady' man; and the perfectibility theories of friends like Shelley and Dilke slipped from his mind like water from a duck's back. We have seen the concrete shape his patriotism took. He always saw ideas embodied, and was 'convinced that small causes make great alterations.' I could easily find passages more characteristic than the following; but it is short, it shows that Keats thought for himself, and it has a curious interest just now (1905):[1]

Notwithstanding the part which the Liberals take in the cause of Napoleon, I cannot but think he has done more harm to the life of Liberty than anyone else could have done. Not that the divine right gentlemen have done, or intend to do, any good. No, they have taken a lesson of him, and will do all the further harm he would have done, without any of the good. The worst thing he has done is that he has taught them how to organise their monstrous armies. The Emperor Alexander, it is said, intends to divide his Empire as did Diocletian, creating two Czars beside himself, and continuing the supreme monarch of the whole. Should he do this, and they for a series of years keep peaceable among themselves, Russia may spread her conquest even to China. I think it a very likely thing that China itself may fall; Turkey certainly will. Meanwhile European North Russia will hold its horns against the rest of Europe, intriguing constantly with France.

Still aiming chiefly to show the variety there is in these letters, I may take next one or two passages which have an interest also from their bearing on Keats's poems. Here we have, for example, the unmistakable origin of the *Ode on Indolence*:

This morning I am in a sort of temper indolent and supremely careless. I long after a stanza or two of Thomson's *Castle of Indolence*. My passions are all asleep, from my having slumbered till nearly eleven and weakened the animal fibre all over me to a delightful sensation, about three degrees on this side of faintness. If I had teeth of pearl and the breath of lilies, I should call it

[1] From the letter last quoted. See also CXVI, CXVIII, CXIX, C., CXXXVII, CXXXIV, CXXXV F

languor, but as I am * I must call it laziness. In this state of
effeminacy the fibres of the brain are relaxed in common with the
rest of the body, and to such a happy degree that pleasure has
no show of enticement, and pain no unbearable power.[1] Neither
Poetry nor Ambition nor Love have any alertness of countenance
as they pass by me. They seem rather like figures on a Greek
vase—a man and two women whom no one but myself could
distinguish in their disguisement. This is the only happiness,
and is a rare instance of the advantage of the body overpowering
the mind.[2]

* Especially as I have a black eye.

'This is the only happiness'—the sentence will
surprise no one who has even dipped into Keats's
letters. It expresses a settled conviction. Happiness, he feels, belongs only to childhood and early
youth. A young man thinks he can keep it, but a
little experience shows him he must do without it.
The mere growth of the mind, if nothing else, is
fatal to it. To think is to be full of sorrow, because
it is to realise the sorrow of the world and to feel
the burden of the mystery. 'Health and spirits,'
he says, 'can only belong unalloyed to the selfish
man.'[3] Shelley might be speaking. 'To see an
entirely disinterested girl quite happy is the most
pleasant and extraordinary thing in the world. It
depends upon a thousand circumstances. On my
word it is extraordinary. Women must want
Imagination, and they may thank God for it : and
so may we, that a delicate being can feel happy
without any sense of crime.'[4] These passages,
taken alone, even when we observe his qualifications, would give a false impression of Keats ; but
they supply a curious commentary on the legend of
the sensuous Keats. We may connect with them
his feeling of the inferiority of poets (or rather of
such 'dreaming' poets as himself) to men of action.

In this same letter he copies out for his corre-
spondents several recently written poems, and

[1]   'Pain had no sting and pleasure's wreath no flower.'
[2] XCII, C., CVI, F.   [3] XIX, C., XXI, F.   [4] LIV, C., LIX, F.

among them the ballad *La Belle Dame Sans Merci*.
He copies it without a word of introduction. He
could not say, ' Here is the record of my love and
my despair,' for on this one subject he never opened
his heart to his brother. But when he has finished
the copy he adds a few lines referring to the stanza
(afterwards altered) :

> She took me to her elfin grot,
>   And there she wept and sighed full sore,
> And there I shut her wild wild eyes
>   With kisses four.

' Why four kisses, you will say, why four ? Because
I wish to restrain the headlong impetuosity of my
Muse. She would have fain said "score" without
hurting the rhyme : but we must temper the
Imagination, as the Critics say, with Judgment.
I was obliged to choose an even number that both
eyes might have fair play ; and, to speak truly, I
think two apiece quite sufficient. Suppose I had
said seven, there would have been three and a
half apiece—a very awkward affair, and well got
out of on my side.' This is not very like the
comments of Wordsworth on his best poems, but
I dare say the author of *Hamlet* made such jests
about it. Is it not strange, let me add, to think
that Keats and his friends were probably unconscious of the extraordinary merit of this poem ?
It was not published with the Odes in the volume
of 1820.

I will quote, finally, three passages to illustrate in
different ways Keats's insight into human nature.
It appears, on the whole, more decidedly in the
letters than in the poems, and it helps us to believe
that, so far as his gifts were concerned, his hope
of ultimate success in dramatic poetry was well
founded. The first is a piece of ' nonsense,' rattled
off on the spur of the moment to amuse his corre-
spondents, and worth quoting only for its last
sentence. He has been describing ' three witty

people, all distinct in their excellence'; and he goes on :

> I know three people of no wit at all, each distinct in his excellence—A, B, and C. A is the foolishest, B the sulkiest, C is a negative. A makes you yawn, B makes you hate, as for C you never see him at all though he were six feet high. I bear the first, I forbear the second, I am not certain that the third is. The first is gruel, the second ditch-water, the third is spilt—he ought to be wiped up.

C, who is spilt and ought to be wiped up, how often we have met and still shall meet him! Shakespeare, I think, would gladly have fathered the phrase that describes him, and the words that follow are not much out of the tune of Falstaff: 'C, they say, is not his mother's true child, but she bought him of the man who cries, Young lambs to sell.'[1]

In the second passage Keats is describing one of his friends :

> Dilke is a man who cannot feel he has a personal identity unless he has made up his mind about everything. The only means of strengthening one's intellect is to make up one's mind about nothing—to let the mind be a thoroughfare for all thoughts, not a select party. The genus is not scarce in population : all the stubborn arguers you meet are of the same brood. They never begin on a subject they have not pre-resolved on. They want to hammer their nail into you, and if you turn the point, still they think you wrong. Dilke will never come at a truth so long as he lives, because he is always trying at it. He is a Godwin Methodist.[2]

These lines illustrate the instinctive feeling of Keats that it is essential to the growth of the poetic mind to preserve its natural receptiveness and to welcome all the influences that stream in upon it. They illustrate also his dislike of the fixed theories held and preached by some members of his circle. We shall have to consider later the meaning of his occasional outbreaks against 'thought,' 'know-ledge,' 'philosophy.' It is important not to be

---

[1] CXXXI, C., CLII, F.

[2] CXVI, C., CXXXVII, F. The word 'turn' in the last sentence but two seems to be doubtful. Mr. Colvin reads 'have.'

misled by them, and not to forget the frequent
expressions of his feeling that what he lacks and
must strive to gain is this very 'knowledge' and
'philosophy.' Here I will only observe that his
polemics against them, though coloured by his
temperament, coincide to a large extent with
Wordsworth's dislike of 'a reasoning self-sufficing
thing,' his depreciation of mere book-knowledge, and
his praise of a wise passiveness. And, further, what
he objects to here is not the pursuit of truth, it is
the 'Methodism,' the stubborn argument, and the
habit of bringing to the argument and maintaining
throughout it a ready-made theory. He offers his
own thoughts and speculations freely enough to
Bailey and to his brother—men willing to probe
with him any serious idea—but not to Dilke. It is
clear that he neither liked nor rated high the confident assertions and negations of Shelley and his
other Godwinian friends and acquaintances. Probably from his ignorance of theories he felt at a
disadvantage in talking with them. But he did not
dismiss their theories as something of no interest to
a poet. He thought about them, convinced himself
that they were fundamentally unsound, and himself
philosophises in criticising them. The following
passage, from a letter to George and Georgiana
Keats, is the nearest approach to be found in his
writings to a theory of the world, a theology as he
jestingly calls it; and although it is long, I make no
apology for quoting it. He has been reading, he
says, Robertson's *History of America* and Voltaire's
Siècle de Louis XIV., and he observes that, though
the two civilisations described are so different, the
case of the great body of the people is equally
lamentable in both. And he goes on thus :

The whole appears to resolve into this—that man is originally a
poor forked creature, subject to the same mischances as the beasts
of the forest, destined to hardships and disquietude of some kind
or other. If he improves by degrees his bodily accommodations

and comforts, at each stage, at each ascent, there are waiting for him a fresh set of annoyances—he is mortal, and there is still a heaven with its stars above his head. The most interesting question that can come before us is, How far by the persevering endeavours of a seldom-appearing Socrates mankind may be made happy. I can imagine such happiness carried to an extreme, but what must it end in? Death—and who could in such a case bear with death? The whole troubles of life, which are now frittered away in a series of years, would then be accumulated for the last days of a being who, instead of hailing its approach, would leave this world as Eve left Paradise. But in truth I do not at all believe in this sort of perfectibility. The nature of the world will not admit of it—the inhabitants of the world will correspond to itself. Let the fish philosophise the ice away from the rivers in winter time, and they shall be at continual play in the tepid delight of summer. Look at the Poles, and at the sands of Africa —whirlpools and volcanoes. Let men exterminate them, and I will say that they may arrive at earthly happiness. The point at which man may arrive is as far as the parallel state in inanimate nature, and no further. For instance, suppose a rose to have sensation; it blooms on a beautiful morning; it enjoys itself; but then comes a cold wind, a hot sun. It cannot escape it, it cannot destroy its annoyances—they are as native to the world as itself. No more can man be happy in spite [?], the worldly elements will prey upon his nature.

The common cognomen of this world among the misguided and superstitious is 'a vale of tears,' from which we are to be redeemed by a certain arbitrary interposition of God and taken to Heaven. What a little circumscribed straitened notion! Call the world if you please 'The vale of Soul-making.' Then you will find out the use of the world (I am speaking now in the highest terms for human nature, admitting it to be immortal, which I will here take for granted for the purpose of showing a thought which has struck me concerning it). I say 'Soul-making' —Soul as distinguished from an Intelligence.[1] There may be intelligences or sparks of the divinity in millions, but they are not Souls till they acquire identities, till each one is personally itself. Intelligences are atoms of perception—they know and they see and they are pure; in short they are God. How then are souls to be made? How then are these sparks which are God to have identity given them—so as ever to possess a bliss peculiar to each one's individual existence? How but by the medium of a world like this? This point I sincerely wish to consider, because I think it a grander system of salvation than the Christian religion —or rather it is a system of Spirit-creation. This is effected by three grand materials acting the one upon the other for a series of

[1] Keats's use of the word is suggested, probably, by Milton's 'pure intelligence of heaven.'

years. These three materials are the *Intelligence*, the *human heart* (as distinguished from intelligence or mind), and the World or elemental space suited for the proper action of *Mind* and *Heart* on each other for the purpose of forming the *Soul* or *Intelligence destined to possess the sense of Identity*. I can scarcely express what I but dimly perceive—and yet I think I perceive it. That you may judge the more clearly I will put it in the most homely form possible. I will call the *world* a School instituted for the purpose of teaching little children to read. I will call the *human heart* the horn-book read in that School. And I will call the *Child able to read*, the *Soul* made from that School and its horn-book. Do you not see how necessary a world of pains and troubles is to school an Intelligence and make it a Soul? A place where the heart must feel and suffer in a thousand diverse ways. Not merely is the Heart a horn-book, it is the Mind's Bible, it is the mind's experience, it is the text from which the Mind or Intelligence sucks its identity. As various as the lives of men are, so various become their Souls; and thus does God make individual beings, Souls, identical Souls, of the sparks of his own essence. This appears to me a faint sketch of a system of Salvation which does not offend our reason and humanity.[1]

Surely, when Keats's education is considered, this, with all its crudity, is not a little remarkable. It would not be easy to find anything written at the same age by another poet of the time which shows more openness of mind, more knowledge of human nature, or more original power of thought.

About a fortnight after Keats wrote that description of A, B, and C, he received what he recognised at once for his death-warrant. He had yet fourteen months to endure, but at this point the development of his mind was arrested. During the three preceding years it had been very rapid, and is easy to trace; and it is all the more interesting because, in spite of its continuity, we are aware of a decided difference between the Keats of the earlier letters and the Keats of the later. The tour in Scotland in the summer of 1818 may be taken with sufficient accuracy as a dividing-line. The earlier Keats is the youth who had written the *Sonnet on first*

[1] XCII, C., CVI, F.

looking into Chapman's Homer, and *Sleep and Poetry*, and who was writing *Endymion*. He is thoughtful, often grave, sometimes despondent; but he is full of the enthusiasm of beauty, and of the joy and fear, the hope and the awe, that accompanied the sense of poetic power. He is the poet who looked, we are told, as though he had been gazing on some glorious sight; whose eyes shone and whose face worked with pleasure as he walked in the fields about Hampstead; who is described watching with rapture the billowing of the wind through the trees and over meadow-grasses and corn, and looking sometimes like a young eagle and sometimes like a wild fawn waiting for some cry from the forest depths. This is the Keats who wrote 'A thing of beauty is a joy for ever'; who found 'the Religion of Joy' in the monuments of the Greek spirit, in sculpture and vases, and mere translations and mere handbooks of mythology; who never ceased, he said, to wonder at all that incarnate delight, and would point out to Severn how essentially modern, how imperishable, the Greek spirit is—a joy for ever.

Yet, as we have seen already, he was aware, and we find him becoming more and more aware, that joy is not the only word. He had not read for nothing Wordsworth's great Ode, and *Tintern Abbey*, and the *Excursion*. We know it from *Endymion*, and the letter about the 'burden of the mystery' was written before the tour in Scotland. But after this we feel a more decided change, doubtless hastened by outward events. The Blackwood and Quarterly reviews of *Endymion* appeared—reviews not less inexcusable because we understand their origin. Then came his brother's death. A few weeks later he met Miss Brawne. Henceforth his youth has vanished. There are traces of morbid feeling in the change, painful traces; but they are connected, I think, solely with his passion. His

brother's death deepened his sympathies. The
reviews, so long as health remained to him, did him
nothing but good. He rated them at their true
value, but they gave him a salutary shock. They
quickened his perception, already growing keen, of
the weaknesses and mannerism of Hunt's verse and
his own. Through them he saw a false but useful
picture of himself, as a silly boy, dandled into self-
worship by foolish friends, and posturing as a man
of genius. He kept his faith in his genius, but he
felt that he must prove it. He became impatient of
dreaming. Poetry, he felt, is not mere luxury and
rapture, it is a deed. We trace at times a kind of
fierceness. He turns against his old self harshly.
Some of his friends, he says, think he has lost his
old poetic ardour, and perhaps they are right. He
speaks slightingly of wonders, even of scenery : the
human heart is something finer,—not its dreams, but
its actions and its anguish. His gaze is as intent as
ever,—more intent; but the glory he would see walks
in a fiery furnace, and to see it he must think and
learn. He is young, he says, writing at random,
straining his eyes at particles of light in the
midst of a great darkness. He knows at times
the 'agony' of ignorance. In one year he writes
six or seven of the best poems in the language, but
he is little satisfied. 'Thus far,' he says, 'I have
a consciousness of having been pretty dull and
heavy, both in subject and phrase.' Two months
later he ends a note to Haydon with the words, 'I
am afraid I shall pop off just when my mind is able
to run alone.' And so it was.

It is important to remember this change in Keats
in considering his ideas about poetry ; but we
have first to look at them in a more general
way. Many of the most interesting occur in
detached remarks or aphorisms, and these I must
pass by. The others I intended at first to deal with

in connection with Shelley's view of poetry; and, although that plan proved to be too large for a single lecture, I do not wish altogether to abandon it, because in the extracts which I have been reading the difference between the minds of the two poets has already appeared, and because it reappears both in their poetic practice and in their opinions about their art. Indeed, with so much difference, it might be thought unlikely that these opinions would show also a marked resemblance. For Keats, it may be said, was of all the great poets then alive the one least affected by the spirit of the time, or by that 'revolutionary' atmosphere of which I spoke in a previous lecture. He did not concern himself, we may be told, with the progress of humanity, or with Manchester Massacres or risings in Naples. He cared nothing for theories, abstractions, or ideals. He worshipped Beauty, not Liberty; and the beauty he worshipped was not 'intellectual,' but visible, audible, tangible. 'O for a life of sensations,' he cried, 'rather than of thoughts.' He was an artist, intent upon fashioning his material until the outward sensible form is perfectly expressive and delightful. In all this he was at the opposite pole to Shelley; and he himself felt it. He refused to visit Shelley, in order that he might keep his own unfettered scope; and he never speaks of Shelley cordially. He told him, too, that he might be more of an artist and load every rift of his subject with ore; and that, while many people regard the purpose of a work as the God, and the poetry as the Mammon, an artist must serve Mammon. And his practice, like his opinions, proves that, both in his strength and his limitations, he belongs to quite a different type.

In such a plea there would certainly be much truth; and yet it is not *the* truth, for it ignores other truths which must somehow be combined with it. There are great differences between the two poets, but then in Keats himself there are contending strains. Along with the differences, too, we find very close affinities. And these affinities with Shelley also show that Keats was deeply influenced by the spirit of his time. Let me illustrate these statements.

The poet who cried, 'O for a life of sensations,' was consoled, as his life withered away, by the remembrance that he 'had loved the principle of beauty in all things.' And this is not a chance expression; it repeats, for instance, a phrase used two years before, 'the mighty abstract idea I have of Beauty in all things.' If Shelley had used this language, it would be taken to prove his love of abstractions. How does it differ from the language of the *Hymn to Intellectual Beauty*?[1]

Again, we noticed in a previous lecture the likeness between *Alastor* and *Endymion*, each the first poem of any length in which the writer's genius decisively declared itself. Both tell the story of a young poet; of a dream in which his ideal appears in human form, and he knows the rapture of union with it; of the passion thus enkindled, and the search for its complete satisfaction. We may prefer to read *Endymion* simply as we read *Isabella*; but the question here is not of our preferences. If we examine the poem without regard to them, we shall be unable to doubt that to some extent the story symbolises or allegorises this pursuit of the principle of beauty by the poetic soul. This is one of the causes of its failure as a narrative. Keats had not in himself the experience required by parts of his design, and hence in them he had to write from mere

[1] CLXVI, F., LXXIII, C., LXXXI, F. In XLI, C., XLIV, F., occurs a passage ending with the words, 'they are able to "*consecrate whate'er they look upon.*"' Is not this a quotation from the *Hymn*:

> Spirit of BEAUTY that dost consecrate
> With thine own hues all thou dost shine upon?

If so, and if my memory serves me, this is the only quotation from Shelley's poetry in the letters of Keats. The *Hymn* had been published in Hunt's *Examiner*, Jan., 1817

imagination.   And the poem, besides, shows in a
flagrant degree the defect felt here and there in
Prometheus Unbound.   If we wish to read it as the
author meant it, we must ask for the significance of
the figures, events, and actions.   Yet it is clear
that not all of them are intended to have this further
significance, and we are perplexed by the question
where, and how far, we are to look for it.[1]

Take, again, some of the most famous of the
lyrical poems.   Is it true that Keats was untroubled
by that sense of contrast between ideal and real
which haunted Shelley and was so characteristic of
the time?   So far is this from being the case that a
critic might more plausibly object to his monoton-
ous insistence on that contrast.   Probably the best-
known lyrics of the two poets are the stanzas *To a
Skylark* and the *Ode to a Nightingale.*   Well, if
we summarise prosaically the subject of the one
poem we have summarised that of the other.   'Our
human life is all unrest and sorrow, an oscillation
between longing and satiety, a looking before and
after.   We are aware of a perfection that we cannot
attain, and that leaves us dissatisfied by everything
attainable.   And we die, and do not understand
death.   But the bird is beyond this division and
dissonance; it attains the ideal;

> Das Unzulängliche,
> Hier wird's Ereigniss.'

This is the burden of both poems.   In style, metre,
tone, atmosphere, they are far apart; the 'idea' is
identical.   And what else is the idea of the *Ode*

---

[1] The first critic, I believe, who seriously attempted to investigate
Keats's mind, and the ideas that were trying to take shape in
some of his poems, was F. M. Owen, whose *John Keats, a Study*
(1880) never attracted in her too brief life-time the attention it
deserved.   Mr. Bridges's treatment of these ideas is masterly.
To what is said above may be added that, although Keats was
dissatisfied with *Endymion* even before he had finished it, he did not
at any time criticise it on the ground that it tried to put too much
meaning into the myth.   On *Alastor* and *Endymion* see further the
Note appended to this lecture.

on a Grecian Urn, where a moment, arrested in its ideality by art and made eternal, is opposed to the change and decay of reality? And what else is the idea of the playful lines *To Fancy*,—Fancy who brings together the joys which in life are parted by distances of time and place, and who holds in sure possession what life wins only to lose? Even a poem so pictorial and narrative and free from symbolism as the *The Eve of St. Agnes* rests on the same feeling. The contrast, so exquisitely imagined and conveyed, between the cold, the storm, the old age, the empty pleasure and noisy enmity of the world outside Madeline's chamber, and the glow, the hush, the rich and dreamy bliss within it, is in effect the contrast which inspired the *Ode to a Nightingale*.

It would be easy to pursue this subject. It would be easy, too, to show that Keats was far from indifferent to the 'progress of humanity.' He conceived it in his own way, but it is as much the theme of *Hyperion* as of *Prometheus Unbound*. We are concerned however here not with the interpretation of his poems, but with his view of poetry, and especially with certain real or apparent inconsistencies in it. For in the letters he now praises 'sensation' and decries thought or knowledge, and now cries out for 'knowledge' as his greatest need; in one place declares that an artist must have self-concentration, perhaps selfishness, and in others insists that what he desires is to be of use to his fellow-men. We shall gain light on these matters and on his relation to Shelley if I try to reduce his general view to a precise and prosaic form.

That which the poet seeks is Beauty. Beauty is a 'principle'; it is One. All things beautiful manifest it, and so far therefore are one and the same. This idea of the unity of all beauty comes out in many crucial passages in the poems and letters I take a single example. The goddess Cynthia

in *Endymion* is the Principle of Beauty. In this
story she is also identified with the Moon. Accordingly the hero, gazing at the moon, declares that in
all that he ever loved he loved *her* :

> thou wast the deep glen—
> Thou wast the mountain-top—the sage's pen—
> The poet's harp—the voice of friends—the sun ;
> Thou wast the river—thou wast glory won ;
> Thou wast my clarion's blast—thou wast my steed—
> My goblet full of wine—my topmost deed :—
> Thou wast the charm of women, lovely Moon !
> O what a wild and harmonised tune
> My spirit struck from all the beautiful !

When he says this he does not yet understand that
the Moon and his strange visitant are one; he thinks
they are rivals.   So later, when he loves the Indian
maid, and is in despair because he fancies himself
therefore false to his goddess, he is in error ; for she
is only his goddess veiled, the shaded half of the
moon.

Still the mountain-top and the voice of friends
differ.   Indeed, the one Beauty is infinitely various.
But its manifestations, for Keats, tend to fall into
two main classes.   On the one hand there is the
kind of beauty that comes easily and is all sweetness
and pleasure.   In receiving it we seem to suppress
nothing in our nature.   Though it is not merely
sensuous, for the Principle of Beauty is in it, it
speaks to sense and delights us.   It is 'luxury.'
But the other kind is won through thought, and also
through pain.   And this second and more difficult
kind is also the higher, the fuller, the nearer to the
Principle.   That it is won through pain is doubly
true.   First, because the poet cannot reach it unless
he consents to suffer painful sympathies, which
disturb his enjoyment of the simpler and sweeter
beauty, and may even seem to lead him away from
beauty altogether.   Thus Endymion can attain
union with his goddess only by leaving the green
hill-sides where he met her first, and by wandering

unhappily in cold moonless regions inside the earth
and under the sea.   Here he feels for the woes of
other lovers, and to help them undertakes tasks
which seem to interrupt his search for Cynthia.
Returning to earth he becomes enamoured of a
maiden devoted to sorrow, and gains his goddess
just when he thinks he has resigned her. The
highest beauty, then, is reached through the poet's
pain ; and, in the second place, it has pain in itself,
or at least appears in objects that are painful.   In
his early poem *Sleep and Poetry* Keats asks himself
the question,

> And can I ever bid these joys farewell ?

And he answers :

> Yes, I must pass them for a nobler life,
> Where I may find the agonies, the strife
> Of human hearts.

He felt himself as yet unequal to this task.   He
never became equal to it, but the idea was realised
to some extent in *Isabella* and *Lamia* and *Hyperion*.
The first two of these are tales of passion, 'agony,'
and death.   The third, obviously, is on one side a
story of 'strife.'

Such, in its bare outline, is Keats's habitual view
of poetry. What, then, are the points where, in
spite of its evident resemblance to Shelley's, we feel
a marked difference ?   The most important seem to
be two.   In the first place Keats lays far the
heavier stress on the idea that beauty is manifested
in suffering and conflict.   The idea itself is to
be found in Shelley, but (as we saw in another
lecture) it is not congenial to him ; it appears
almost incidentally and is stated half-heartedly ;
and of the further idea that beauty is not only
manifested in this sphere, but is there manifested
most fully, we find, I believe, no trace.   And
this was inevitable ; for the whole tendency of
Shelley's mind was to regard suffering and conflict
with mere distress and horror as something senseless

and purely evil, and to look on the world as naturally
a paradise entirely free from them, but ruined by an
inexplicable failure on the part of man. To this
world of woe his Intellectual Beauty does not really
belong; it appears there only in flashes; its true
home is a place where no contradictions, not even
reconciled contradictions, exist. The idealism of
Keats is much more concrete. He has no belief
either in this natural paradise or in ' Godwinian
perfectibility.' Pain and conflict have a meaning
to him. Without them souls could not be made;
and the business of the world, he conjectures, is the
making of souls. They are not therefore simply
obstacles to the ideal. On the contrary, in this
world it manifests itself most fully in and through
them. For ' scenery is fine, but human nature is
finer ';[1] and the passions and actions of man are
finer than his enjoyments and dreams. In the same
way, the conflict in *Hyperion* is not one between
light and darkness, the ideal and mere might, as
in *Prometheus Unbound.* The Titans must yield
to the Olympians because, in a word, they are less
beautiful, and

> 'tis the eternal law
> That first in beauty should be first in might.

But the Titans, though less beautiful, *are* beautiful;
it is one and the same ' principle' that manifests
itself in them and more fully in their victors. Their
defeat therefore is not, in the end, defeat, but the
completion of their own being. This, it seems
probable, the hero in *Hyperion* would have come
to recognise, so that the poem, at least so far as
he is concerned, would have ended with a reconciliation born of strife.

Man is ' finer,' Keats says, and the Titans must
submit because they are less ' beautiful.' The

---

[1] A notable (but not isolated) remark, seeing that the poetic genius
of Keats showed itself soonest and perhaps most completely in the
rendering of Nature.

second point of difference between him and Shelley
lies in this emphasis on beauty. The ideal with
Shelley has many names, and one of them is beauty,
but we hardly feel it to be the name nearest to his
heart. The spirit of his worship is rather

> that sustaining Love
> Which, through the web of being blindly wove
> By man and beast and earth and air and sea,
> Burns bright or dim, as each are mirrors of
> The fire for which all thirst;

and 'love' is a word less distinctively aesthetic, if the
term must be used, than 'beauty.' But the ideal for
Keats is always and emphatically beauty or the
'principle of beauty.' When he sets the agonies
and strifes of human hearts above a painless or
luxurious loveliness, it is because they are the more
beautiful. He would not have said that the *Mid-
summer Night's Dream* is superior to *King Lear* in
beauty, but inferior to it in some other respect; it is
inferior in *beauty* to *King Lear*. Let art only be
'intense' enough, let the poet only look hard
enough and feel with force enough, so that the pain
in his object is seen truly as the vesture of great
passion and action, and all 'disagreeables' will
'evaporate,' and nothing will remain but beauty.[1]
Hence, though well aware how little he has as yet
of the great poet's power of vision, he is still
content when he can feel that a poem of his has
intensity, has (as he says of *Lamia*) 'that sort of
fire in it that must take hold of people some way.'[2]
And an earlier and inferior poem, *Isabella*, may
show his mind. The mere subject is exceedingly
painful, and Keats by no means suppresses the
painful incidents and details; but the poem can
hardly be called painful at all; for the final impression is that of beauty, almost as decidedly so as the
final impression left by the blissful story of *St. Agnes'
Eve*. And this is most characteristic of Keats. If

[1] XXIV, C., XXVI, F.   [2] CXVI, C., CXXXVII, F.

the word beauty is used in his sense, and not in
the common contracted sense, we may truly say
that he was, and must have remained, more than
any other poet of his time, a worshipper of Beauty.

When, then—to come to his apparent inconsistencies—he exalts sensation and decries thought or
knowledge, what he is crying out for is beauty.
The word 'sensation,' as a comparison of passages
would readily show, has not in his letters its usual
meaning. It stands for *poetic* sensation, and, indeed,
for much more. It is, to speak broadly, a name for
all poetic or imaginative experience ; and the contents of the speech of Oceanus are, in kind, just as
much 'sensation' as the eating of nectarines (which
may well be poetic to the poetic). This is, I repeat,
to speak broadly. For it is true that sometimes
in the earlier letters we find Keats false to his better
mind. Knowing that the more difficult beauty is
the fuller, he is yet, to our great advantage, so
entranced by the delight or glory of the easier, that
he rebels against everything that would disturb its
magic or trouble his 'exquisite sense of the luxurious.' And then he is tempted to see in thought
only that vexatious questioning that 'spoils the
singing of the nightingale,' and to forget that it is
necessary to the fuller and more difficult kind of
beauty. But these moods are occasional. He knew
that there was something wilful and weak about
them ; and they gradually disappear. On the
whole, the gist of his attitude to 'thought' or
'philosophy' may be stated as follows.

He was far from being indifferent to truth, or
from considering it unimportant for poetry. In an
early letter, when he criticises a poem of Wordsworth's, he ventures to say that 'if Wordsworth
had thought a little deeper at that moment he would
not have written it,' and that 'it is a kind of sketchy
intellectual landscape, not a search after truth.'[1]

[1] XIX, C., XXI, F.

He writes of a passage in *Endymion* : ' The whole
thing must, I think, have appeared to you, who are
a consecutive man, as a thing almost of mere words,
but I assure you that, when I wrote it, it was the
regular stepping of Imagination towards a truth.' [1]
And many passages show his conviction that for his
progress towards this truth 'thought,' 'knowledge,'
' philosophy,' are indispensable ; [2] that he must submit to the toil and the solitude that they involve,
just as he must undergo the pains of sympathy;
that 'there is but one way for him,' and that this
one ' road lies through application, study, and
thought.' [3] On the other hand he had, in the first
place, as we saw, a strong feeling that a man, and
especially a poet, must not be in a hurry to arrive
at results, and must not shut up his mind in the box
of his supposed results, but must be content with
half-knowledge, and capable of ' living in uncertain-
ties, mysteries, doubts, without any irritable reaching
after fact and reason.' And, in the second place,
a poet, he felt, will never be able to rest in thoughts
and reasonings which do not also satisfy imagination and give a truth which is also beauty; and
in so far as they fail to do this, in so far as they are
mere thoughts and reasonings, they are no more
than a means, though a necessary means, to an end,
which end is beauty,—that beauty which is also truth.
This alone is the poet's end, and therefore his law.
' With a great poet the sense of beauty overcomes
every other consideration, or rather obliterates all
consideration.' [4] Thought, knowledge, philosophy,
if they fall short of this, are nothing but a 'road'
to his goal. They bring matter for him to mould
to his purpose of beauty ; but he must not allow
them to impose *their* purpose on him, or to ask that
it shall appear in his product. These statements

[1] XXXII, C., XXXIV, F.
[2] He contemplates even the study of metaphysics, LI, C., LIV, F.
[3] I., C., LIII, F. [4] XXIV, C., XXVI, F.

formulate Keats's position more than he formulates it, but I believe that they represent it truly. He was led to it mainly by the poetic instinct in him, or because, while his mind had much general power, he was, more than Wordsworth or Coleridge or Shelley, a poet pure and simple.[1]

We can now deal more briefly with another apparent inconsistency. Keats says again and again that the poet must not live for himself, but must feel for others and try to help them ; that ' there is no worthy pursuit but the idea of doing some good for the world' ; that he is ambitious to do some good or to serve his country. Yet he writes to Shelley about the *Cenci* : ' There is only one part of it I am judge of—the poetry and dramatic effect, which by many spirits nowadays is considered the Mammon. A modern work, it is said, must have a purpose, which may be the God. An artist must serve Mammon ; he must have " self-concentration " —selfishness, perhaps.'[2] These are ungracious sentences, especially when we remember the letter to which Keats is replying ; and they are also unfair to Shelley, whose tragedy cannot justly be accused of having an ultra-poetic purpose, and whose Count Cenci shows much more dramatic imagination than any figure drawn by Keats. But it is ungracious too to criticise the irritability of a man condemned to death ; and in any case these sentences are perfectly consistent with Keats's expressed desire to do good. The poet is to do good ; yes, but by being a poet. He is to have a purpose of doing good by his poetry ; yes, but he is not to

[1] Cf. in addition to the letters already referred to, the obscure letter to Bailey, XXII, C., XXIV, F., which, however, is early, and not quite in agreement with later thoughts. I should observe perhaps that if Keats's position, as formulated above, is accepted, the question still remains whether a truth which is also beauty, or a beauty which is also truth, can be found by man ; and, if so, whether it can, in strictness, be called by either of those names.

[2] CLV, C., CCVI, F. See on these sentences the Note at the end of the lecture.

obtrude it in his poetry, or to show that he has a design upon us.[1] To make beauty is *his* philanthropy. He will not succeed in it best by making what is only in part beauty,—something like the *Excursion*, half poem and half lecture. He must be unselfish, no doubt, but perhaps by being selfish; by refusing, that is, to be diverted from his poetic way of helping by the desire to help in another way. This is the drift of Keats's thought. If we remember what he means by 'beauty' and 'poet,' and how he distinguishes the poet from the 'dreamer,'[2] we shall think it sound doctrine.

Keats was by nature both dreamer and poet, and his ambition was to become poet pure and simple. There was, in a further sense, a double strain in his nature. He had in him the poetic temper of his time, the ever-present sense of an infinite, the tendency to think of this as an ideal perfection manifesting itself in reality, and yet surpassing reality, and so capable of being contrasted with it. He was allied here especially to Wordsworth and to Shelley, by the former of whom he was greatly influenced. But there was also in him another tendency; and this, it would seem, was strengthening at the expense of the first, and would in time have dominated it. It was perhaps the deeper and more individual. It may be called the Shakespearean strain, and it works against any inclination to erect walls between ideal and real, or to magnify differences of grade into oppositions of kind. Keats had the impulse to interest himself in everything he saw or heard of, to be curious about a thing, accept it, identify himself with it, without first asking whether it is better or worse than another, or how far it is

[1] An expression used in reference to Wordsworth, XXXIV, C., XXXVI, F.

[2] I have not space to dwell on this distinction, but I must warn the reader that he will probably misunderstand the important passage in the revised *Hyperion*, 161 ff., unless he consults Mr. de Sélincourt's edition

from the ideal principle. It is this impulse that speaks in the words, 'If a sparrow come before my window, I take part in its existence and pick about the gravel';[1] and in the words, 'When she comes into a room she makes an impression the same as the beauty of a leopardess'; and in the feeling that she is fine, though Bishop Hooker is finer. It too is the source of his complaint that he has no personal identity, and of his description of the poetical character; 'It has no self; it is everything and nothing . . . It enjoys light and shade; it lives in gusto, be it foul or fair, high or low, rich or poor, mean or elevated. It has as much delight in conceiving an Iago as an Imogen. What shocks the virtuous philosopher delights the chameleon poet. It does no harm from its relish of the dark side of things, any more than from its taste for the bright one, because they both end in speculation.[2] A poet is the most unpoetical of anything in existence, because he has no identity. He is continually in, for, and filling some other body.'[3] That is not a description of Milton or Wordsworth or Shelley; neither does it apply very fully to Keats; but it describes something at least of the spirit of Shakespeare.

Now this spirit, it is obvious, tends in poetry, I do not say to a realistic, but to what may be called a concrete method of treatment; to the vivid presentment of scenes, individualities, actions, in preference to the expression of unembodied thoughts and feelings. The atmosphere of Wordsworth's age, as we have seen, was not, on the whole, favourable to it, and in various degrees it failed in strength, or it suffered, in all the greater poets.

[1] XXII, C., XXV, F.

[2] That is, in 'half-knowledge,' 'doubts,' 'mysteries' (see p. 235), while the philosopher is sometimes supposed by Keats to have a reasoned certainty about everything. It is curious to reflect that great metaphysicians, like Spinoza and Hegel, are often accused of the un-moral impartiality which Keats attributes to the poet.

[3] LXXVI, C., LXXX, F.

Scott had it in splendid abundance and vigour; but he had too little of the idealism or the metaphysical imagination which was common to those poets, and which Shakespeare united with his universal comprehension; nor was he, like Shakespeare and like some of them, a master of magic in language. But Keats had that magic in fuller measure, perhaps, than any of our poets since Milton; and, sharing the idealism of Wordsworth and Shelley, he possessed also wider sympathies, and, if not a more plastic or pictorial imagination than the latter, at least a greater freedom from the attraction of theoretic ideas. To what results might not this combination have led if his life had been as long as Wordsworth's or even as Byron's? It would be more than hazardous, I think, to say that he was the most highly endowed of all our poets in the nineteenth century, but he might well nave written its greatest long poems.

1905.

NOTE

I have pointed out certain marked resemblances between *Alastor* and *Endymion*, and it would be easy to extend the list. These resemblances are largely due to similarities in the minds of the two poets, and to the action of a common influence on both. But I believe that, in addition, Keats was affected by the reading of *Alastor*, which appeared in 1816, while his own poem was begun in the spring of 1817.

The common influence to which I refer was that of Wordsworth, and especially of the *Excursion*, published in 1814. There is a quotation, or rather a misquotation, from it in the Preface to *Alastor*. The *Excursion* is concerned in part with the danger of inactive and unsympathetic solitude; and this, treated of course in Shelley's own way, is the subject of *Alastor*, which also contains phrases reminiscent of Wordsworth's poem. Its Preface too reminds one immediately of the *Elegiac Stanzas on a Picture of Peele Castle*; of the main idea, and of the lines,

> Farewell, farewell, the heart that lives alone,
> Housed in a dream, at distance from the Kind.

As for Keats, the reader of his letters knows how much he was occupied in 1817 and 1818 with thoughts due to the reading of Wordsworth, and how great, though qualified, was his admiration of the *Excursion*. These thoughts concerned chiefly the poetic nature, its tendency to 'dream,' and the necessity that it should go beyond itself and feel for the sorrows of others. They may have been suggested *only* by Wordsworth; but we must remember that *Alastor* had been published, and that Keats would naturally read it. In comparing that poem with *Endymion* I am obliged to repeat remarks already made in the lecture.

Alastor, composed under the influence described, tells of the fate of a young poet, who is 'pure and tender-hearted,' but who, in his search for communion with the ideal influences of nature and of knowledge, keeps aloof from sympathies with his kind. 'So long as it is possible for his desires to point towards objects thus infinite and unmeasured, he is joyous and tranquil and self-possessed.' But a time comes when he thirsts for intercourse with an intelligence like himself. His ideal requirements are embodied in the form of a being who appears to him in a dream, and to whom he is united in passionate love. But his 'self-centred seclusion' now avenges itself. The 'spirit of sweet human love' vanishes as he wakes, and he wanders over the earth, vainly seeking the 'prototype' of the vision until he dies.

In *Endymion* the story of a dream-vision, of rapturous union with it, and of the consequent pursuit of it, re-appears, though the beginning and the end are different. The hero, before the coming of the vision, has of course a poetic soul, but he is not self-secluded, or inactive, or fragile, or philosophic; and his pursuit of the goddess leads not to extinction but to immortal union with her. It does lead, however, to adventures of which the main idea evidently is that the poetic soul can only reach complete union with the ideal (which union is immortality) by wandering in a world which seems to deprive him of it; by trying to mitigate the woes of others instead of seeking the ideal for himself; and by giving himself up to love for what seems to be a mere woman, but is found to be the goddess herself. It seems almost beyond doubt that the story of Cynthia and Endymion would not have taken this shape but for *Alastor*.

The reader will find this impression confirmed if he compares the descriptions in *Alastor* and *Endymion*, Book I., of the dreamer's feelings on awakening from his dream, of the disenchantment that has fallen on the landscape, and of his 'eager' pursuit of the lost vision. Everything is, in one sense, different, for the two poets differ greatly, and Keats, of course, was writing without any conscious recollection of the passage in *Alastor*; but the conception is the same.[1]

---

[1] The ultimate origin of the dream-passage in both poems may well be Adam's dream in *Paradise Lost*, Book viii. :

> She disappear'd, and left me dark : I waked
> To find her, or for ever to deplore
> Her loss, and other pleasures all abjure.

Keats alludes to this in XXII, C., XXIV, F.

Consider, again, the passage (near the beginning of *Endymion*, Book III.) quoted on p. 230 of the lecture. The hero is address-ing the moon; and he says, to put it baldly, that from his boyhood everything that was beautiful to him was associated with his love of the moon's beauty. The passage continues thus:

> On some bright essence could I lean, and lull
> Myself to immortality : I prest
> Nature's soft pillow in a wakeful rest.
> But, gentle Orb ! there came a nearer bliss —
> My strange love came—Felicity's abyss !
> She came, and thou didst fade, and fade away.

In spite of the dissimilarities, surely the 'wakeful rest' here corresponds to the condition of the poet in *Alastor* prior to the dream. 'So long as it is possible for his desires to point towards objects thus infinite and unmeasured, he is joyous and tranquil and self-possessed'; but when his 'strange love' comes these objects, like the objects of Endymion's earlier desires, no longer suffice him.

There is, however, further evidence, indeed positive proof, of the effect of *Alastor*, and especially of its Preface, on Keats's mind. In the revised version of *Hyperion*, Book I., the dreamer in the Temple wonders why he has been preserved from death. The Prophetess tells him the reason (I italicise certain words):

> 'None can usurp this height,' returned that shade,
> 'But those to whom the *miseries of the world*
> Are misery, and will not let them rest.
> *All else* who find a haven in the world,
> Where they may thoughtless sleep away their *days*,
> If by a chance into this fane they come,
> Rot on the pavement where thou rottedst half.'
> 'Are there not thousands in the world,' said I,
> Encouraged by the sooth voice of the shade,
> 'Who *love their fellows* even to the death,
> Who feel the giant agony of the world,
> And more, like slaves to poor humanity,
> Labour for mortal good?'

If the reader compares with this the following passage from the Preface to *Alastor*, and if he observes the words I have italicised in it, he will hardly doubt that some unconscious recollection of the Preface was at work in Keats's mind. Shelley is distinguishing the self-centred seclusion of his poet from that of common selfish souls :

'The picture is not barren of instruction to actual men. The Poet's self-centred seclusion was avenged by the furies of an irresistible passion pursuing him to speedy ruin. But that Power which strikes the luminaries of the world with sudden darkness and extinction, by awakening them to too exquisite a perception of its influences, dooms to a slow and poisonous decay those meaner spirits that dare to abjure its dominion. Their destiny is more abject and inglorious as their delinquency is more contemptible and pernicious. They who, deluded by no generous error, instigated by no sacred thirst of doubtful knowledge, duped by no illustrious superstition, loving nothing on this earth, and cherishing no hopes beyond, yet keep aloof from sympathies with their kind, rejoicing neither in human joy nor mourning with human grief; these, and such as they, have their apportioned curse. They languish, because none feel with them their common nature. They are morally dead. They are neither friends, nor lovers, nor fathers, nor citizens of the world, nor benefactors of their country. Among those who attempt to exist without human sympathy, the pure and tender-hearted perish through the intensity and passion of their search after its communities, when the vacancy of their spirit suddenly makes itself felt. *All else*, selfish, blind, and torpid, are those unforeseeing multitudes who constitute, together with their own, the lasting *misery* and loneliness *of the world*. Those who *love not their fellow-beings*, live unfruitful lives, and prepare for their old age a miserable grave.' [1]

---

[1] It is tempting to conjecture with Mr. Forman that the full-stop before the last sentence is a misprint, and that we should read ' the world,—those who,' etc., so that the last two clauses would be relative clauses co-ordinate with ' who love not their fellow-beings.' Not to speak of the run of the sentences, this conjecture is tempting because of the comma after ' fellow-beings,' and because the paragraph is followed by the quotation (' those ' should be ' they '),

The good die first,
And those whose hearts are dry as summer's dust
Burn to the socket.

The good who die first correspond with the ' pure and tender-hearted ' who perish and, as we naturally suppose, perish young, like the poet in *Alastor*. But, as the last sentence stands, these, as well as the torpid, live to old age. It is hard to believe that Shelley meant this ; but as he was in England when *Alastor* was printed, he probably revised the proofs, and it is perhaps easier to suppose that he wrote what is printed than that he passed unobserved the serious misprint supposed by Mr. Forman.

I have still a passage to refer to.   Let the reader turn to the quotation on p. 236 from Keats's reply to Shelley's letter of invitation to his home in Italy; and let him ask himself why Keats puts the word " self-concentration" in inverted commas.   He is not referring to anything in Shelley's letter, and he is not in the habit in the letters of using inverted commas except to mark a quotation.   Without doubt, I think, he is referring from memory to the Preface to *Alastor* and the phrase ' self-centred seclusion.' He has come to feel that this self-centred seclusion is *right* for a poet like himself, and that the direct pursuit of philanthropy in poetry (which he supposes Shelley to advocate) is wrong.   But this is another proof how much he had been influenced by Shelley's poem ; and it is perhaps not too rash to conjecture that his consciousness of this influence was one reason why he had earlier refused to visit Shelley, in order that he might ' have his own unfettered scope.' [1]

If it seems to anyone that these conclusions are derogatory to Keats, either as a man or a poet, I can only say that I differ from him entirely.   But I will add that there seems to me some reason to conjecture that Shelley had read the *Ode to a Nightingale* before he wrote the stanzas *To a Skylark.*

[1] XVIII, C., XX, F.

THE REJECTION OF FALSTAFF

THE REJECTION OF FALSTAFF[1]

OF the two persons principally concerned in the rejection of Falstaff, Henry, both as Prince and as King, has received, on the whole, full justice from readers and critics. Falstaff, on the other hand, has been in one respect the most unfortunate of Shakespeare's famous characters. All of them, in passing from the mind of their creator into other minds, suffer change; they tend to lose their harmony through the disproportionate attention bestowed on some one feature, or to lose their uniqueness by being conventionalised into types already familiar. But Falstaff was degraded by Shakespeare himself. The original character is to be found alive in the two parts of *Henry IV.*, dead in *Henry V.*, and nowhere else. But not very long after these plays were composed, Shakespeare wrote, and he afterwards revised, the very entertaining piece called *The Merry Wives of Windsor*. Perhaps his company wanted a new play on a sudden ; or perhaps, as one would rather believe, the tradition may be true that Queen Elizabeth, delighted with the Falstaff scenes of *Henry IV.*, expressed a wish to see the hero of them again, and to see him in love. Now it was no more possible for Shakespeare to show his

[1] In this lecture and the three that follow it I have mentioned the authors my obligations to whom I was conscious of in writing or have discovered since ; but other debts must doubtless remain, which from forgetfulness I am unable to acknowledge.

own Falstaff in love than to turn twice two into five. But he could write in haste—the tradition says, in a fortnight—a comedy or farce differing from all his other plays in this, that its scene is laid in English middle-class life, and that it is prosaic almost to the end. And among the characters he could introduce a disreputable fat old knight with attendants, and could call them Falstaff, Bardolph, Pistol, and Nym. And he could represent this knight assailing, for financial purposes, the virtue of two matrons, and in the event baffled, duped, treated like dirty linen, beaten, burnt, pricked, mocked, insulted, and, worst of all, repentant and didactic. It is horrible. It is almost enough to convince one that Shakespeare himself could sanction the parody of Ophelia in the *Two Noble Kinsmen*. But it no more touches the real Falstaff than Ophelia is degraded by that parody. To picture the real Falstaff befooled like the Falstaff of the *Merry Wives* is like imagining Iago the gull of Roderigo, or Becky Sharp the dupe of Amelia Osborne. Before he had been served the least of these tricks he would have had his brains taken out and buttered, and have given them to a dog for a New Year's gift. I quote the words of the impostor, for after all Shakespeare made him and gave to him a few sentences worthy of Falstaff himself. But they are only a few—one side of a sheet of notepaper would contain them. And yet critics have solemnly debated at what period in his life Sir John endured the gibes of Master Ford, and whether we should put this comedy between the two parts of *Henry IV.*, or between the second of them and *Henry V.* And the Falstaff of the general reader, it is to be feared, is an impossible conglomerate of two distinct characters, while the Falstaff of the mere playgoer is certainly much more like the impostor than the true man.

The separation of these two has long ago been effected by criticism, and is insisted on in almost all

competent estimates of the character of Falstaff.
I do not propose to attempt a full account either of
this character or of that of Prince Henry, but shall
connect the remarks I have to make on them with a
question which does not appear to have been satisfactorily discussed—the question of the rejection of
Falstaff by the Prince on his accession to the
throne. What do we feel, and what are we meant
to feel, as we witness this rejection? And what
does our feeling imply as to the characters of
Falstaff and the new King?

I.

Sir John, you remember, is in Gloucestershire,
engaged in borrowing a thousand pounds from
Justice Shallow; and here Pistol, riding helter-
skelter from London, brings him the great news
that the old King is as dead as nail in door, and
that Harry the Fifth is the man. Sir John, in
wild excitement, taking any man's horses, rushes to
London; and he carries Shallow with him, for he
longs to reward all his friends. We find him standing with his companions just outside Westminster
Abbey, in the crowd that is waiting for the King
to come out after his coronation. He himself is
stained with travel, and has had no time to spend
any of the thousand pounds in buying new liveries
for his men. But what of that? This poor show
only proves his earnestness of affection, his devotion,
how he could not deliberate or remember or have
patience to shift himself, but rode day and night,
thought of nothing else but to see Henry, and put
all affairs else in oblivion, as if there were nothing
else to be done but to see him. And now he stands
sweating with desire to see him, and repeating and
repeating this one desire of his heart—'to see him.'
The moment comes. There is a shout within the
Abbey like the roaring of the sea, and a clangour

of trumpets, and the doors open and the procession
streams out.

> Fal. God save thy grace, King Hal! my royal Hal!
> Pist. The heavens thee guard and keep, most royal
> imp of fame!
> Fal. God save thee, my sweet boy!
> King. My Lord Chief Justice, speak to that vain man.
> Ch. Just. Have you your wits? Know you what 'tis
> you speak?
> Fal. My King! my Jove! I speak to thee, my heart!
> King. I know thee not, old man: fall to thy prayers;
> How ill white hairs become a fool and jester!
> I have long dream'd of such a kind of man,
> So surfeit-swell'd, so old and so profane;
> But being awaked I do despise my dream.
> Make less thy body hence, and more thy grace;
> Leave gormandizing; know the grave doth gape
> For thee thrice wider than for other men.
> Reply not to me with a fool-born jest:
> Presume not that I am the thing I was;
> For God doth know, so shall the world perceive,
> That I have turn'd away my former self;
> So will I those that kept me company.
> When thou dost hear I am as I have been,
> Approach me, and thou shalt be as thou wast,
> The tutor and the feeder of my riots:
> Till then, I banish thee, on pain of death,
> As I have done the rest of my misleaders,
> Not to come near our person by ten mile.
> For competence of life I will allow you,
> That lack of means enforce you not to evil:
> And, as we hear you do reform yourselves,
> We will, according to your strengths and qualities,
> Give you advancement. Be it your charge, my lord,
> To see perform'd the tenour of our word.
> Set on.

The procession passes out of sight, but Falstaff
and his friends remain. He shows no resentment.
He comforts himself, or tries to comfort himself—
first, with the thought that he has Shallow's thousand
pounds, and then, more seriously, I believe, with
another thought. The King, he sees, must look
thus to the world; but he will be sent for in private
when night comes, and will yet make the fortunes

of his friends. But even as he speaks, the Chief
Justice, accompanied by Prince John, returns, and
gives the order to his officers :

> Go, carry Sir John Falstaff to the Fleet ;
> Take all his company along with him.

Falstaff breaks out, 'My lord, my lord,' but he is
cut short and hurried away ; and after a few words
between the Prince and the Chief Justice the scene
closes, and with it the drama.

What are our feelings during this scene? They
will depend on our feelings about Falstaff. If we
have not keenly enjoyed the Falstaff scenes of the
two plays, if we regard Sir John chiefly as an old
reprobate, not only a sensualist, a liar, and a coward,
but a cruel and dangerous ruffian, I suppose we
enjoy his discomfiture and consider that the King
has behaved magnificently. But if we *have* keenly
enjoyed the Falstaff scenes, if we have enjoyed
them as Shakespeare surely meant them to be
enjoyed, and if, accordingly, Falstaff is not to us
solely or even chiefly a reprobate and ruffian, we
feel, I think, during the King's speech, a good deal
of pain and some resentment ; and when, without
any further offence on Sir John's part, the Chief
Justice returns and sends him to prison, we stare in
astonishment. These, I believe, are, in greater or
less degree, the feelings of most of those who really
enjoy the Falstaff scenes (as many readers do not).
Nor are these feelings diminished when we remember the end of the whole story, as we find it in
Henry V., where we learn that Falstaff quickly
died, and, according to the testimony of persons not
very sentimental, died of a broken heart.[1] Suppose
this merely to mean that he sank under the shame
of his public disgrace, and it is pitiful enough : but
the words of Mrs. Quickly, 'The king has killed his

[1] See on this and other points Swinburne, *A Study of Shakespeare,*
p. 106 ff.

heart'; of Nym, 'The king hath run bad humours
on the knight; that's the even of it'; of Pistol,

> Nym, thou hast spoke the right,
> His heart is fracted and corroborate,

assuredly point to something more than wounded
pride; they point to wounded affection, and remind
us of Falstaff's own answer to Prince Hal's question,
'Sirrah, do I owe you a thousand pound?' 'A
thousand pound, Hal? a million: thy love is worth
a million: thou owest me thy love.'

Now why did Shakespeare end his drama with a
scene which, though undoubtedly striking, leaves an
impression so unpleasant? I will venture to put
aside without discussion the idea that he meant us
throughout the two plays to regard Falstaff with
disgust or indignation, so that we naturally feel
nothing but pleasure at his fall; for this idea implies
that kind of inability to understand Shakespeare
with which it is idle to argue. And there is another
and a much more ingenious suggestion which must
equally be rejected as impossible. According to it,
Falstaff, having listened to the King's speech, did
not seriously hope to be sent for by him in private;
he fully realised the situation at once, and was only
making game of Shallow; and in his immediate
turn upon Shallow when the King goes out, 'Master
Shallow, I owe you a thousand pound,' we are meant
to see his humorous superiority to any rebuff, so that
we end the play with the delightful feeling that,
while Henry has done the right thing, Falstaff, in
his outward overthrow, has still proved himself
inwardly invincible. This suggestion comes from a
critic who understands Falstaff, and in the suggestion itself shows that he understands him.[1] But it
provides no solution, because it wholly ignores, and
could not account for, that which follows the short
conversation with Shallow. Falstaff's dismissal to

---

[1] Rötscher, *Shakespeare in seinen höchsten Charaktergebilden*, 1864.

the Fleet, and his subsequent death, prove beyond doubt that his rejection was meant by Shakespeare to be taken as a catastrophe which not even his humour could enable him to surmount.

Moreover, these interpretations, even if otherwise admissible, would still leave our problem only partly solved. For what troubles us is not only the disappointment of Falstaff, it is the conduct of Henry. It was inevitable that on his accession he should separate himself from Sir John, and we wish nothing else. It is satisfactory that Sir John should have a competence, with the hope of promotion in the highly improbable case of his reforming himself. And if Henry could not trust himself within ten miles of so fascinating a companion, by all means let him be banished that distance : we do not complain. These arrangements would not have prevented a satisfactory ending : the King could have communicated his decision, and Falstaff could have accepted it, in a private interview rich in humour and merely touched with pathos. But Shakespeare has so contrived matters that Henry could not send a private warning to Falstaff even if he wished to, and in their public meeting Falstaff is made to behave in so infatuated and outrageous a manner that great sternness on the King's part was unavoidable. And the curious thing is that Shakespeare did not stop here. If this had been all we should have felt pain for Falstaff, but not, perhaps, resentment against Henry. But two things we do resent. Why, when this painful incident seems to be over, should the Chief Justice return and send Falstaff to prison ? Can this possibly be meant for an act of private vengeance on the part of the Chief Justice, unknown to the King ? No ; for in that case Shakespeare would have shown at once that the King disapproved and cancelled it. It must have been the King's own act. This is one thing we resent ; the other is the King's sermon. He had a right to turn away his former self, and his old companions with it, but he had no right to talk all of a sudden like a clergyman ; and surely it was both ungenerous and insincere to speak of them as his 'misleaders,' as though in the days of Eastcheap and Gadshill he had been a weak and silly lad. We have seen his former self, and we know that it was nothing of the kind. He had shown himself, for all his follies, a very strong and independent young man, deliberately amusing himself among men over whom he had just as much ascendency as he chose to exert. Nay, he amused himself not only among them, but at their expense. In his first soliloquy—and first soliloquies are usually significant—he declares that he associates with them in order that, when at some future time he shows his true character, he may be the more wondered at for his previous aberrations. You may think he deceives himself here ; you may believe that he frequented Sir John's company out of delight in it and not merely with this cold-blooded design ; but at any rate he *thought* the design was his one motive. And, that being so, two results follow. He ought in honour long ago to have given Sir John clearly to understand that they must say good-bye on the day of his accession. And, having neglected to do this, he ought not to have lectured him as his misleader. It was not only ungenerous, it was dishonest. It looks disagreeably like an attempt to buy the praise of the respectable at the cost of honour and truth. And it succeeded. Henry *always* succeeded.

You will see what I am suggesting, for the moment, as a solution of our problem. I am suggesting that our fault lies not in our resentment at Henry's conduct, but in our surprise at it ; that if we had read his character truly in the light that Shakespeare gave us, we should have been prepared for a display both of hardness and of policy at this point in his career. And although this suggestion does not suffice to solve the problem before us, I am convinced that in itself it is true. Nor is it rendered at all improbable by the fact that Shakespeare has made Henry, on the whole, a fine and very attractive character, and that here he makes no one express any disapprobation of the treatment of Falstaff. For in similar cases Shakespeare is constantly misunderstood. His readers expect him to mark in some distinct way his approval or disapproval of that which he represents; and hence where *they* disapprove and *he* says nothing, they fancy that he does *not* disapprove, and they blame his indifference, like Dr. Johnson, or at the least are puzzled. But the truth is that he shows the fact and leaves the judgment to them. And again, when he makes us like a character we expect the character to have no faults that are not expressly pointed out, and when other faults appear we either ignore them or try to explain them away. This is one of our methods of conventionalising Shakespeare. We want the world's population to be neatly divided into sheep and goats, and we want an angel by us to say, ' Look, that is a goat and this is a sheep,' and we try to turn Shakespeare into this angel. His impartiality makes us uncomfortable : we cannot bear to see him, like the sun, lighting up everything and judging nothing. And this is perhaps especially the case in his historical plays, where we are always trying to turn him into a partisan. He shows us that Richard II. was unworthy to be king, and we at once conclude that he thought Bolingbroke's usurpation justified; whereas he shows merely, what under the conditions was bound to exist, an inextricable tangle of right and unright. Or, Bolingbroke being evidently wronged, we suppose Bolingbroke's statements to be true, and are quite surprised when, after attaining his end through them, he mentions casually on his death-bed that they were lies. Shakespeare makes us admire Hotspur heartily; and accordingly, when we see Hotspur discussing with others how large his particular slice of his mother-country is to be, we either fail to recognise the monstrosity of the proceeding, or, recognising it, we complain that Shakespeare is inconsistent. Prince John breaks a tottering rebellion by practising a detestable fraud on the rebels. We are against the rebels, and have heard high praise of Prince John, but we cannot help seeing that his fraud is detestable; so we say indignantly to Shakespeare, 'Why, you told us he was a sheep'; whereas, in fact, if we had used our eyes we should have known beforehand that he was the brave, determined, loyal, cold-blooded, pitiless, unscrupulous son of a usurper whose throne was in danger.

To come, then, to Henry. Both as prince and as king he is deservedly a favourite, and particularly so with English readers, being, as he is, perhaps the most distinctively English of all Shakespeare's men. In *Henry V.* he is treated as a national hero. In this play he has lost much of the wit which in him seems to have depended on contact with Falstaff, but he has also laid aside the most serious faults of his youth. He inspires in a high degree fear, enthusiasm, and affection; thanks to his beautiful modesty he has the charm which is lacking to another mighty warrior, Coriolanus; his youthful escapades have given him an understanding of simple folk, and sympathy with them; he is the author of the saying, 'There is some soul of goodness in things evil'; and he is much more obviously religious than most of Shakespeare's heroes. Having these and other fine qualities, and being without certain dangerous tendencies which mark the tragic heroes, he is, perhaps, the most *efficient* character drawn by Shakespeare, unless Ulysses, in *Troilus and Cressida*, is his equal. And so he has been described as Shakespeare's ideal man of action;

nay, it has even been declared that here for once Shakespeare plainly disclosed his own ethical creed, and showed us his ideal, not simply of a man of action, but of a man.

But Henry is neither of these. The poet who drew Hamlet and Othello can never have thought that even the ideal man of action would lack that light upon the brow which at once transfigures them and marks their doom. It is as easy to believe that, because the lunatic, the lover, and the poet are not far apart, Shakespeare would have chosen never to have loved and sung. Even poor Timon, the most inefficient of the tragic heroes, has something in him that Henry never shows. Nor is it merely that his nature is limited: if we follow Shakespeare and look closely at Henry, we shall discover with the many fine traits a few less pleasing. Henry IV. describes him as the noble image of his own youth; and, for all his superiority to his father, he is still his father's son, the son of the man whom Hotspur called a 'vile politician.' Henry's religion, for example, is genuine, it is rooted in his modesty; but it is also superstitious—an attempt to buy off supernatural vengeance for Richard's blood; and it is also in part political, like his father's projected crusade. Just as he went to war chiefly because, as his father told him, it was the way to keep factious nobles quiet and unite the nation, so when he adjures the Archbishop to satisfy him as to his right to the French throne, he knows very well that the Archbishop *wants* the war, because it will defer and perhaps prevent what he considers the spoliation of the Church. This same strain of policy is what Shakespeare marks in the first soliloquy in *Henry IV.*, where the prince describes his riotous life as a mere scheme to win him glory later. It implies that readiness to use other people as means to his own ends which is a conspicuous feature in his father; and it reminds us of his father's plan of keeping himself out of the people's sight while Richard was making himself cheap by his incessant public appearances. And if I am not mistaken there is a further likeness. Henry is kindly and pleasant to every one as Prince, to every one deserving as King; and he is so not merely out of policy: but there is no sign in him of a strong affection for any one, such an affection as we recognise at a glance in Hamlet and Horatio, Brutus and Cassius, and many more. We do not find this in *Henry V.*, not even in the noble address to Lord Scroop, and in *Henry IV.* we find, I think, a liking for Falstaff and Poins, but no more: there is no more than a liking, for instance, in his soliloquy over the supposed corpse of his fat friend, and he never speaks of Falstaff to Poins with any affection. The truth is, that the members of the family of Henry IV. have love for one another, but they cannot spare love for any one outside their family, which stands firmly united, defending its royal position against attack and instinctively isolating itself from outside influence.

Thus I would suggest that Henry's conduct in his rejection of Falstaff is in perfect keeping with his character on its unpleasant side as well as on its finer; and that, so far as Henry is concerned, we ought not to feel surprise at it. And on this view we may even explain the strange incident of the Chief Justice being sent back to order Falstaff to prison (for there is no sign of any such uncertainty in the text as might suggest an interpolation by the players). Remembering his father's words about Henry, 'Being incensed, he's flint,' and remembering in *Henry V.* his ruthlessness about killing the prisoners when he is incensed, we may imagine that, after he had left Falstaff and was no longer influenced by the face of his old companion, he gave way to anger at the indecent familiarity which had provoked a compromising scene on the most cere-

monial of occasions and in the presence alike of
court and crowd, and that he sent the Chief Justice
back to take vengeance.   And this is consistent with
the fact that in the next play we find Falstaff shortly
afterwards not only freed from prison, but unmolested
in his old haunt in Eastcheap, well within ten miles
of Henry's person.   His anger had soon passed,
and he knew that the requisite effect had been produced both on Falstaff and on the world.

But all this, however true, will not solve our
problem.   It seems, on the contrary, to increase
its difficulty.   For the natural conclusion is that
Shakespeare *intended* us to feel resentment against
Henry.   And yet that cannot be, for it implies that
he meant the play to end disagreeably ; and no one
who understands Shakespeare at all will consider
that supposition for a moment credible.   No ; he
must have meant the play to end pleasantly, although
he made Henry's action consistent.   And hence it
follows that he must have intended our sympathy
with Falstaff to be so far weakened when the re-
jection-scene arrives that his discomfiture should be
satisfactory to us ; that we should enjoy this sudden
reverse of enormous hopes (a thing always ludicrous
if sympathy is absent) ; that we should approve the
moral judgment that falls on him ; and so should
pass lightly over that disclosure of unpleasant traits
in the King's character which Shakespeare was too
true an artist to suppress.   Thus our pain and resentment, if we feel them, are wrong, in the sense that
they do not answer to the dramatist's intention.   But
it does not follow that they are wrong in a further
sense.   They may be right, because the dramatist
has missed what he aimed at.   And this, though
the dramatist was Shakespeare, is what I would
suggest.   In the Falstaff scenes he overshot his
mark.   He created so extraordinary a being, and
fixed him so firmly on his intellectual throne, that
when he sought to dethrone him he could not.   The

moment comes when we are to look at Falstaff in a serious light, and the comic hero is to figure as a baffled schemer; but we cannot make the required change, either in our attitude or in our sympathies. We wish Henry a glorious reign and much joy of his crew of hypocritical politicians, lay and clerical; but our hearts go with Falstaff to the Fleet, or, if necessary, to Arthur's bosom or wheresomever he is.[1]

In the remainder of the lecture I will try to make this view clear. And to that end we must go back to the Falstaff of the body of the two plays, the immortal Falstaff, a character almost purely humorous, and therefore no subject for moral judgments I can but draw an outline, and in describing one aspect of this character must be content to hold another in reserve.

2.

Up to a certain point Falstaff is ludicrous in the same way as many other figures, his distinction lying, so far, chiefly in the mere abundance of ludicrous traits. *Why* we should laugh at a man with a huge belly and corresponding appetites; at the inconveniences he suffers on a hot day, or in playing the footpad, or when he falls down and there are no levers at hand to lift him up again; at the incongruity of his unwieldy bulk and the nimbleness of his spirit, the infirmities of his age and his youthful lightness of heart; at the enormity of his lies and wiles, and the suddenness of their exposure and frustration; at the contrast between his reputation and his real character, seen most absurdly when, at the mere mention of his name, a redoubted rebel surrenders to him—*why*, I say, we should laugh at

[1] That from the beginning Shakespeare intended Henry's accession to be Falstaff's catastrophe is clear from the fact that, when the two characters first appear, Falstaff is made to betray at once the hopes with which he looks forward to Henry's reign. See the First Part of *Henry IV.*, Act I., Scene ii.

these and many such things, this is no place to inquire; but unquestionably we do. Here we have them poured out in endless profusion and with that air of careless ease which is so fascinating in Shakespeare; and with the enjoyment of them I believe many readers stop. But while they are quite essential to the character, there is in it much more. For these things by themselves do not explain why, beside laughing at Falstaff, we are made happy by him and laugh *with* him. He is not, like Parolles, a mere *object* of mirth.

The main reason why he makes us so happy and puts us so entirely at our ease is that he himself is happy and entirely at his ease. ' Happy ' is too weak a word; he is in bliss, and we share his glory. Enjoyment—no fitful pleasure crossing a dull life, nor any vacant convulsive mirth—but a rich deep-toned chuckling enjoyment circulates continually through all his being. If you ask *what* he enjoys, no doubt the answer is, in the first place, eating and drinking, taking his ease at his inn, and the company of other merry souls. Compared with these things, what we count the graver interests of life are nothing to him. But then, while we are under his spell, it is impossible to consider these graver interests; gravity is to us, as to him, inferior to gravy; and what he does enjoy he enjoys with such a luscious and good-humoured zest that we sympathise and he makes us happy. And if any one objected, we should answer with Sir Toby Belch, ' Dost thou think, because thou art virtuous, there shall be no more cakes and ale ? '

But this, again, is far from all. Falstaff's ease and enjoyment are not simply those of the happy man of appetite;[1] they are those of the humorist, and the humorist of genius. Instead of being comic to you and serious to himself, he is more ludicrous to himself than to you; and he makes himself out

[1] Cf. Hazlitt, *Characters of Shakespear's Plays.*

more ludicrous than he is, in order that he and others may laugh. Prince Hal never made such sport of Falstaff's person as he himself did. It is *he* who says that his skin hangs about him like an old lady's loose gown, and that he walks before his page like a sow that hath o'erwhelmed all her litter but one. And he jests at himself when he is alone just as much as when others are by. It is the same with his appetites. The direct enjoyment they bring him is scarcely so great as the enjoyment of laughing at this enjoyment; and for all his addiction to sack you never see him for an instant with a brain dulled by it, or a temper turned solemn, silly, quarrelsome, or pious. The virtue it instils into him, of filling his brain with nimble, fiery, and delectable shapes—this, and his humorous attitude towards it, free him, in a manner, from slavery to it; and it is this freedom, and no secret longing for better things (those who attribute such a longing to him are far astray), that makes his enjoyment contagious and prevents our sympathy with it from being disturbed.

The bliss of freedom gained in humour is the essence of Falstaff. His humour is not directed only or chiefly against obvious absurdities; he is the enemy of everything that would interfere with his ease, and therefore of anything serious, and especially of everything respectable and moral. For these things impose limits and obligations, and make us the subjects of old father antic the law, and the categorical imperative, and our station and its duties, and conscience, and reputation, and other people's opinions, and all sorts of nuisances. I say he is therefore their enemy; but I do him wrong; to say that he is their enemy implies that he regards them as serious and recognises their power, when in truth he refuses to recognise them at all. They are to him absurd; and to reduce a thing *ad absurdum* is to reduce it to nothing and to walk about free and rejoicing. This is what Falstaff does with all the would-be serious things of life, sometimes only by his words, sometimes by his actions too. He will make truth appear absurd by solemn statements, which he utters with perfect gravity and which he expects nobody to believe; and honour, by demonstrating that it cannot set a leg, and that neither the living nor the dead can possess it; and law, by evading all the attacks of its highest representative and almost forcing him to laugh at his own defeat; and patriotism, by filling his pockets with the bribes offered by competent soldiers who want to escape service, while he takes in their stead the halt and maimed and the gaol-birds; and duty, by showing how he labours in his vocation—of thieving; and courage, alike by mocking at his own capture of Colvile and gravely claiming to have killed Hotspur; and war, by offering the Prince his bottle of sack when he is asked for a sword; and religion, by amusing himself with remorse at odd times when he has nothing else to do; and the fear of death, by maintaining perfectly untouched, in the face of imminent peril and even while he *feels* the fear of death, the very same power of dissolving it in persiflage that he shows when he sits at ease in his inn. These are the wonderful achievements which he performs, not with the sourness of a cynic, but with the gaiety of a boy. And, therefore, we praise him, we laud him, for he offends none but the virtuous, and denies that life is real or life is earnest, and delivers us from the oppression of such nightmares, and lifts us into the atmosphere of perfect freedom.

No one in the play understands Falstaff fully, any more than Hamlet was understood by the persons round him. They are both men of genius. Mrs. Quickly and Bardolph are his slaves, but they know not why. 'Well, fare thee well,' says the hostess whom he has pillaged and forgiven; 'I have known thee these twenty-nine years, come peas-cod time, but an honester and truer-hearted man—well, fare thee well.' Poins and the Prince delight in him; they get him into corners for the pleasure of seeing him escape in ways they cannot imagine; but they often take him much too seriously. Poins, for instance, rarely sees, the Prince does not always see, and moralising critics never see, that when Falstaff speaks ill of a companion behind his back, or writes to the Prince that Poins spreads it abroad that the Prince is to marry his sister, he knows quite well that what he says will be repeated, or rather, perhaps, is absolutely indifferent whether it be repeated or not, being certain that it can only give him an opportunity for humour. It is the same with his lying, and almost the same with his cowardice, the two main vices laid to his charge even by sympathisers. Falstaff is neither a liar nor a coward in the usual sense, like the typical cowardly boaster of comedy. He tells his lies either for their own humour, or on purpose to get himself into a difficulty. He rarely expects to be believed, perhaps never. He abandons a statement or contradicts it the moment it is made. There is scarcely more intent in his lying than in the humorous exaggerations which he pours out in soliloquy just as much as when others are by. Poins and the Prince understand this in part. You see them waiting eagerly to convict him, not that they may really put him to shame, but in order to enjoy the greater lie that will swallow up the less. But their sense of humour lags behind his. Even the Prince seems to accept as half-serious that remorse of his which passes so suddenly into glee at the idea of taking a purse, and his request to his friend to bestride him if he should see him down in the battle. Bestride Falstaff! 'Hence! Wilt thou lift up Olympus?'

Again, the attack of the Prince and Poins on Falstaff and the other thieves on Gadshill is con-

trived, we know, with a view to the incomprehensible
lies it will induce him to tell. But when, more than
rising to the occasion, he turns two men in buckram
into four, and then seven, and then nine, and then
eleven, almost in a breath, I believe they partly
misunderstand his intention, and too many of his
critics misunderstand it altogether. Shakespeare
was not writing a mere farce. It is preposterous to
suppose that a man of Falstaff's intelligence would
utter these gross, palpable, open lies with the serious
intention to deceive, or forget that, if it was too
dark for him to see his own hand, he could hardly
see that the three misbegotten knaves were wearing
Kendal green. No doubt, if he *had* been believed,
he would have been hugely tickled at it, but he no
more expected to be believed than when he claimed
to have killed Hotspur. Yet he is supposed to be
serious even then. Such interpretations would destroy the poet's whole conception ; and of those who
adopt them one might ask this out of some twenty
similar questions :—When Falstaff, in the men in
buckram scene, begins by calling twice at short
intervals for sack, and then a little later calls for
more and says, 'I am a rogue if I drunk to-day,'
and the Prince answers, 'O villain, thy lips are
scarce wiped since thou drunk'st last,' do they think
that *that* lie was meant to deceive? And if not,
why do they take it for granted that the others
were? I suppose they consider that Falstaff was in
earnest when, wanting to get twenty-two yards of
satin on trust from Master Dombledon the silk-
mercer, he offered Bardolph as security ; or when
he said to the Chief Justice about Mrs. Quickly,
who accused him of breaking his promise to marry
her, 'My lord, this is a poor mad soul, and she says
up and down the town that her eldest son is like
you'; or when he explained his enormous bulk by
exclaiming, 'A plague of sighing and grief! It
blows a man up like a bladder'; or when he

accounted for his voice being cracked by declaring that he had 'lost it with singing of anthems'; or even when he sold his soul on Good-Friday to the devil for a cup of Madeira and a cold capon's leg. Falstaff's lies about Hotspur and the men in buck- ram do not essentially differ from these statements. There is nothing serious in any of them except the refusal to take anything seriously.

This is also the explanation of Falstaff's cow- ardice, a subject on which I should say nothing if Maurice Morgann's essay,[1] now more than a century old, were better known. That Falstaff sometimes behaves in what we should generally call a cowardly way is certain ; but that does not show that he was a coward ; and if the word means a person who feels painful fear in the presence of danger, and yields to that fear in spite of his better feelings and con- victions, then assuredly Falstaff was no coward. The stock bully and boaster of comedy is one, but not Falstaff. It is perfectly clear in the first place that, though he had unfortunately a reputation for stabbing and caring not what mischief he did if his weapon were out, he had not a reputation for cowardice. Shallow remembered him five-and-fifty years ago breaking Scogan's head at the court-gate when he was a crack not thus high ; and Shallow knew him later a good back-swordsman. Then we lose sight of him till about twenty years after, when his association with Bardolph began ; and that association implies that by the time he was thirty- five or forty he had sunk into the mode of life we witness in the plays. Yet, even as we see him there, he remains a person of consideration in the army. Twelve captains hurry about London search- ing for him. He is present at the Council of War in the King's tent at Shrewsbury, where the only other persons are the King, the two princes, a noble- man and Sir Walter Blunt. The messenger who

[1] See Note at end of lecture.

brings the false report of the battle to Northumber-
land mentions, as one of the important incidents, the
death of Sir John Falstaff. Colvile, expressly described as a famous rebel, surrenders to him as soon
as he hears his name. And if his own wish that his
name were not so terrible to the enemy, and his own
boast of his European reputation, are not evidence
of the first rank, they must not be entirely ignored
in presence of these other facts. What do these
facts mean? Does Shakespeare put them all in with
no purpose at all, or in defiance of his own intentions? It is not credible.

And when, in the second place, we look at
Falstaff's actions, what do we find? He boldly con-
fronted Colvile, he was quite ready to fight with
him, however pleased that Colvile, like a kind fellow,
gave himself away. When he saw Henry and Hotspur fighting, Falstaff, instead of making off in a
panic, stayed to take his chance if Hotspur should
be the victor. He *led* his hundred and fifty raga-
muffins where they were peppered, he did not *send*
them. To draw upon Pistol and force him down-
stairs and wound him in the shoulder was no great
feat, perhaps, but the stock coward would have
shrunk from it. When the Sheriff came to the inn
to arrest him for an offence whose penalty was
death, Falstaff, who was hidden behind the arras,
did not stand there quaking for fear, he immediately
fell asleep and snored. When he stood in the battle
reflecting on what would happen if the weight of his
paunch should be increased by that of a bullet, he
cannot have been in a tremor of craven fear. He
never shows such fear; and surely the man who, in
danger of his life, and with no one by to hear him,
meditates thus: ' I like not such grinning honour as
Sir Walter hath. Give me life: which if I can save,
so; if not, honour comes unlooked-for, and there's
an end,' is not what we commonly call a coward.

' Well,' it will be answered, ' but he ran away on

Gadshill; and when Douglas attacked him he fell down and shammed dead.' Yes, I am thankful to say, he did. For of course he did not want to be dead. He wanted to live and be merry. And as he had reduced the idea of honour *ad absurdum*, had scarcely any self-respect, and only a respect for reputation as a means of life, naturally he avoided death when he could do so without a ruinous loss of reputation, and (observe) with the satisfaction of playing a colossal practical joke. For *that* after all was his first object. If his one thought had been to avoid death he would not have faced Douglas at all, but would have run away as fast as his legs could carry him; and unless Douglas had been one of those exceptional Scotchmen who have no sense of humour, he would never have thought of pursuing so ridiculous an object as Falstaff running. So that, as Mr. Swinburne remarks, Poins is right when he thus distinguishes Falstaff from his companions in robbery: 'For two of them, I know them to be as true-bred cowards as ever turned back; and for the third, if he fight longer than he sees reason, I'll forswear arms.' And the event justifies this distinction. For it is exactly thus that, according to the original stage-direction, Falstaff behaves when Henry and Poins attack him and the others. The rest run away at once; Falstaff, here as afterwards with Douglas, fights for a blow or two, but, finding himself deserted and outmatched, runs away also. Of course. He saw no reason to stay. *Any* man who had risen superior to all serious motives would have run away. But it does not follow that he would run from mere fear, or be, in the ordinary sense, a coward.[1]

---

[1] It is to be regretted, however, that in carrying his guts away so nimbly he 'roared for mercy'; for I fear we have no ground for rejecting Henry's statement to that effect, and I do not see my way to adopt the suggestion (I forget whose it is) that Falstaff spoke the truth when he swore that he knew Henry and Poins as well as he that made them.

3.

The main source, then, of our sympathetic delight in Falstaff is his humorous superiority to everything serious, and the freedom of soul enjoyed in it. But, of course, this is not the whole of his character. Shakespeare knew well enough that perfect freedom is not to be gained in this manner ; we are ourselves aware of it even while we are sympathising with Falstaff ; and as soon as we regard him seriously it becomes obvious. His freedom is limited in two main ways. For one thing he cannot rid himself entirely of respect for all that he professes to ridicule. He shows a certain pride in his rank : unlike the Prince, he is haughty to the drawers, who call him a proud Jack. He is not really quite indifferent to reputation. When the Chief Justice bids him pay his debt to Mrs. Quickly for his reputation's sake, I think he feels a twinge, though to be sure he proceeds to pay her by borrowing from her. He is also stung by any thoroughly serious imputation on his courage, and winces at the recollection of his running away on Gadshill ; he knows that his behaviour there certainly looked cowardly, and perhaps he remembers that he would not have behaved so once. It is, further, very significant that, for all his dissolute talk, he has never yet allowed the Prince and Poins to *see* him as they saw him afterwards with Doll Tearsheet ; not, of course, that he has any moral shame in the matter, but he knows that in such a situation he, in his old age, must appear contemptible—not a humorist but a mere object of mirth. And, finally, he has affection in him—affection, I think, for Poins and Bardolph, and certainly for the Prince ; and that is a thing which he cannot jest out of existence. Hence, as the effect of his rejection shows, he is not really invulnerable. And then, in the second place, since he is in the flesh, his godlike freedom has conse-

quences and conditions; consequences, for there is
something painfully wrong with his great toe; conditions, for he cannot eat and drink for ever without
money, and his purse suffers from consumption, a
disease for which he can find no remedy.[1] As
the Chief Justice tells him, his means are very
slender and his waste great; and his answer, 'I
would it were otherwise; I would my means were
greater and my waist slenderer,' though worth
much money, brings none in. And so he is driven
to evil deeds; not only to cheating his tailor like
a gentleman, but to fleecing Justice Shallow, and
to highway robbery, and to cruel depredations on
the poor woman whose affection he has secured.
All this is perfectly consistent with the other side
of his character, but by itself it makes an ugly
picture.

Yes, it makes an ugly picture when you look at it
seriously. But then, surely, so long as the humorous
atmosphere is preserved and the humorous attitude
maintained, you do not look at it so. You no more
regard Falstaff's misdeeds morally than you do the
much more atrocious misdeeds of Punch or Reynard
the Fox. You do not exactly ignore them, but you
attend only to their comic aspect. This is the very
spirit of comedy, and certainly of Shakespeare's
comic world, which is one of make-believe, not
merely as his tragic world is, but in a further sense
—a world in which gross improbabilities are accepted
with a smile, and many things are welcomed as
merely laughable which, regarded gravely, would
excite anger and disgust. The intervention of a
serious spirit breaks up such a world, and would
destroy our pleasure in Falstaff's company. Accordingly through the greater part of these dramas
Shakespeare carefully confines this spirit to the

---

[1] Panurge too was 'naturally subject to a kind of disease which at
that time they called lack of money'; it was a 'flux in his purse'
(Rabelais, Book II., chapters xvi., xvii.).

scenes of war and policy, and dismisses it entirely
in the humorous parts. Hence, if *Henry IV.* had
been a comedy like *Twelfth Night*, I am sure that
he would no more have ended it with the painful
disgrace of Falstaff than he ended *Twelfth Night*
by disgracing Sir Toby Belch.[1]

But *Henry IV.* was to be in the main a historical
play, and its chief hero Prince Henry. In the
course of it his greater and finer qualities were to be
gradually revealed, and it was to end with beautiful
scenes of reconciliation and affection between his
father and him, and a final emergence of the wild
Prince as a just, wise, stern, and glorious King.
Hence, no doubt, it seemed to Shakespeare that
Falstaff at last must be disgraced, and must therefore appear no longer as the invincible humorist, but
as an object of ridicule and even of aversion.   And
probably also his poet's insight showed him that
Henry, as he conceived him, *would* behave harshly
to Falstaff in order to impress the world, especially
when his mind had been wrought to a high pitch by
the scene with his dying father and the impression
of his own solemn consecration to great duties.

This conception was a natural and a fine one;
and if the execution was not an entire success, it is
yet full of interest.   Shakespeare's purpose being to
work a gradual change in our feelings towards
Falstaff, and to tinge the humorous atmosphere
more and more deeply with seriousness, we see him
carrying out this purpose in the Second Part of
Henry IV. Here he separates the Prince from
Falstaff as much as he can, thus withdrawing him
from Falstaff's influence, and weakening in our minds
the connection between the two.   In the First Part
we constantly see them together ; in the Second (it
is a remarkable fact) only once before the rejection.
Further, in the scenes where Henry appears apart

---

[1] I seem to remember that, according to Gervinus, Shakespeare did
disgrace Sir Toby—by marrying him to Maria !

from Falstaff, we watch him growing more and more grave, and awakening more and more poetic interest ; while Falstaff, though his humour scarcely flags to the end, exhibits more and more of his seamy side. This is nowhere turned to the full light in Part I. ; but in Part II. we see him as the heartless destroyer of Mrs. Quickly, as a ruffian seriously defying the Chief Justice because his position as an officer on service gives him power to do wrong, as the pike preparing to snap up the poor old dace Shallow, and (this is the one scene where Henry and he meet) as the worn-out lecher, not laughing at his servitude to the flesh but sunk in it. Finally, immediately before the rejection, the world where he is king is exposed in all its sordid criminality when we find Mrs. Quickly and Doll arrested for being concerned in the death of one man, if not more, beaten to death by their bullies ; and the dangerousness of Falstaff is emphasised in his last words as he hurries from Shallow's house to London, words at first touched with humour but at bottom only too seriously meant : ' Let us take any man's horses ; the laws of England are at my commandment. Happy are they which have been my friends, and woe unto my Lord Chief Justice.' His dismissal to the Fleet by the Chief Justice is the dramatic vengeance for that threat.

Yet all these excellent devices fail. They cause us momentary embarrassment at times when repellent traits in Falstaff's character are disclosed ; but they fail to change our attitude of humour into one of seriousness, and our sympathy into repulsion. And they were bound to fail, because Shakespeare shrank from adding to them the one device which would have ensured success. If, as the Second Part of *Henry IV.* advanced, he had clouded over Falstaff's humour so heavily that the man of genius turned into the Falstaff of the *Merry Wives*, we should have witnessed his rejection without a pang.

This Shakespeare was too much of an artist to do—
though even in this way he did something—and
without this device he could not succeed. As I
said, in the creation of Falstaff he overreached himself. He was caught up on the wind of his own
genius, and carried so far that he could not descend
to earth at the selected spot. It is not a misfortune
that happens to many authors, nor is it one we can
regret, for it costs us but a trifling inconvenience in
one scene, while we owe to it perhaps the greatest
comic character in literature. For it is in this
character, and not in the judgment he brings
upon Falstaff's head, that Shakespeare asserts his
supremacy. To show that Falstaff's freedom of soul
was in part illusory, and that the realities of life
refused to be conjured away by his humour—this
was what we might expect from Shakespeare's un-
failing sanity, but it was surely no achievement
beyond the power of lesser men. The achievement
was Falstaff himself, and the conception of that
freedom of soul, a freedom illusory only in part, and
attainable only by a mind which had received from
Shakespeare's own the inexplicable touch of infinity
which he bestowed on Hamlet and Macbeth and
Cleopatra, but denied to Henry the Fifth.

1902.

NOTE

For the benefit of readers unacquainted with Morgann's Essay I reproduce here, with additions, some remarks omitted from the lecture for want of time. 'Maurice Morgann, Esq. the ingenious writer of this work, descended from an antient and respectable family in Wales; he filled the office of under Secretary of State to the late Marquis of Lansdown, during his first administration; and was afterwards Secretary to the Embassy for ratifying the peace with America, in 1783. He died at his house in Knightsbridge, in the seventy-seventh year of his age, on the 28th March, 1802' (Preface to the edition of 1825). He was a remarkable and original man, who seems to have written a good deal, but, beyond. this essay and some pamphlets on public affairs, all or nearly all anonymous, he published nothing, and at his death he left orders that all his papers should be destroyed. The *Essay on the Dramatic Character of Sir John Falstaff* was first published in 1777. It arose out of a conversation in which Morgann expressed his belief that Shakespeare never meant Falstaff for a coward. He was challenged to explain and support in print what was considered an extraordinary paradox, and his essay bears on its title-page the quotation, 'I am not John of Gaunt, your grandfather: but yet no coward, Hal'—one of Falstaff's few serious sentences. But Morgann did not confine himself to the question of Falstaff's cowardice; he analysed the whole character, and incidentally touched on many points in Shakespearean criticism. 'The reader,' he observes, 'will not need to be told that this inquiry will resolve itself of course into a critique on the genius, the arts, and the conduct, of Shakespeare: for what is Falstaff, what Lear, what Hamlet, or Othello, but different modifications of Shakespeare's thought?

It is true that this inquiry is narrowed almost to a single point; but general criticism is as uninstructive as it is easy : Shakespeare deserves to be considered in detail ;—a task hitherto unattempted.' The last words are significant. Morgann was conscious that he was striking out a new line. The Eighteenth Century critics had done much for Shakespeare in the way of scholarship; some of them had praised him well and blamed him well; but they had done little to interpret the process of his imagination from within. This was what Morgann attempted. His attitude towards Shakespeare is that of Goethe, Coleridge, Lamb, Hazlitt. The dangers of his method might be illustrated from the Essay, but in his hands it yielded most valuable results. And though he did not attempt the eloquence of some of his successors, but wrote like a cultivated ironical man of the world, he wrote delightfully; so that in all respects his Essay, which has long been out of print, deserves to be republished and better known. [It was republished in Mr. Nichol Smith's excellent *Eighteenth Century Essays on Shakespeare*, 1903; and, in 1912, by itself, with an introduction by W. A. Gill.]

Readers of Boswell (under the year 1783) will remember that Morgann, who once met Johnson, favoured his biographer with two most characteristic anecdotes. Boswell also records Johnson's judgment of Morgann's Essay, which, says Mr. Swinburne, elicited from him 'as good a jest and as bad a criticism as might have been expected.' Johnson, we are told, being asked his opinion of the Essay, answered : 'Why, Sir, we shall have the man come forth again; and as he has proved Falstaff to be no coward, he may prove Iago to be a very good character.' The following passage from Morgann's *Essay* (p. 66 of the 1825 edition, p. 248 of Mr. Nichol Smith's book) gives, I presume, his opinion ot Johnson. Having referred to Warburton, he adds : 'Another has since undertaken the custody of our author, whom he seems to consider as a sort of wild Proteus or madman, and accordingly knocks him down with the butt-end of his critical staff, as often as he exceeds that line of sober discretion, which this learned Editor appears to have chalked out for him : yet is this Editor, notwithstanding, "a man, take him for all in all," very highly respectable for his genius and his learning.'

SHAKESPEARE'S *ANTONY AND
CLEOPATRA*

SHAKESPEARE'S *ANTONY AND CLEOPATRA*[1]

COLERIDGE'S one page of general criticism on *Antony and Cleopatra* contains some notable remarks. 'Of all Shakespeare's historical plays,' he writes, '*Antony and Cleopatra* is by far the most wonderful. There is not one in which he has followed history so minutely, and yet there are few in which he impresses the notion of angelic strength so much— perhaps none in which he impresses it more strongly. This is greatly owing to the manner in which the fiery force is sustained throughout.' In a later sentence he refers to the play as 'this astonishing drama.' In another he describes the style : '*feliciter audax* is the motto for its style comparatively with that of Shakespeare's other works.' And he translates this motto in the phrase 'happy valiancy of style.'

Coleridge's assertion that in *Antony and Cleopatra* Shakespeare followed history more minutely than in any other play might well be disputed; and his statement about the style of this drama requires some qualification in view of the results of later criticism as to the order of Shakespeare's works. The style is less individual than he imagined. On

---

[1] As this lecture was composed after the publication of my *Shakespearean Tragedy* I ignored in it, as far as possible, such aspects of the play as were noticed in that book, to the Index of which I may refer the reader.

the whole it is common to the six or seven dramas
subsequent to *Macbeth*, though in *Antony and Cleopatra*, probably the earliest of them, its development
is not yet complete. And we must add that this
style has certain special defects, unmentioned by
Coleridge, as well as the quality which he points out
in it. But it is true that here that quality is almost
continuously present ; and in the phrase by which he
describes it, as in his other phrases, he has signalised
once for all some of the most salient features of the
drama.

It is curious to notice, for example, alike in books
and in conversation, how often the first epithets
used in reference to *Antony and Cleopatra* are
'wonderful' and 'astonishing.' And the main
source of the feeling thus expressed seems to be
the 'angelic strength' or 'fiery force' of which
Coleridge wrote. The first of these two phrases is,
I think, the more entirely happy. Except perhaps
towards the close, one is not so conscious of fiery
force as in certain other tragedies ; but one is
astonished at the apparent ease with which extraordinary effects are produced, the ease, if I may
paraphrase Coleridge, of an angel moving with a
wave of the hand that heavy matter which men find
so intractable. We feel this sovereign ease in con-
templating Shakespeare's picture of the world—a
vast canvas, crowded with figures, glowing with
colour and a superb animation, reminding one
spectator of Paul Veronese and another of Rubens.
We feel it again when we observe (as we can even
without consulting Plutarch) the nature of the
material ; how bulky it was, and, in some respects,
how undramatic ; and how the artist, though he
could not treat history like legend or fiction, seems
to push whole masses aside, and to shift and
refashion the remainder, almost with the air of an
architect playing (at times rather carelessly) with a
child's bricks.

Something similar is felt even in the portrait of Cleopatra. Marvellous as it is, the drawing of it suggests not so much the passionate concentration or fiery force of *Macbeth*, as that sense of effortless and exultant mastery which we feel in the portraits of Mercutio and Falstaff. And surely it is a total mistake to find in this portrait any trace of the distempered mood which disturbs our pleasure in *Troilus and Cressida*. If the sonnets about the dark lady were, as need not be doubted, in some degree autobiographical, Shakespeare may well have used his personal experience both when he drew Cressida and when he drew Cleopatra. And, if he did, the story in the later play was the nearer to his own ; for Antony might well have said what Troilus could never say,

> When my love swears that she is made of truth,
> I do believe her, though I know she lies.

But in the later play, not only is the poets vision unclouded, but his whole nature, emotional as well as intellectual, is free. The subject no more embitters or seduces him than the ambition of Macbeth. So that here too we feel the angelic strength of which Coleridge speaks. If we quarrelled with the phrase at all, it would be because we fancied we could trace in Shakespeare's attitude something of the irony of superiority; and this may not altogether suit our conception of an angel.

I have still another sentence to quote from Coleridge : ' The highest praise, or rather form of praise, of this play which I can offer in my own mind, is the doubt which the perusal always occasions in me, whether the " Antony and Cleopatra " is not, in all exhibitions of a giant power in its strength and vigour of maturity, a formidable rival of " Macbeth," " Lear," " Hamlet," and " Othello." ' Now, unless the clause here about the 'giant power' may be taken to restrict the rivalry to the quality of

angelic strength, Coleridge's doubt seems to show a
lapse in critical judgment. To regard this tragedy
as a rival of the famous four, whether on the stage
or in the study, is surely an error. The world
certainly has not so regarded it; and, though the
world's reasons for its verdicts on works of art may
be worth little, its mere verdict is worth much.
Here, it seems to me, that verdict must be accepted.
One may notice that, in calling *Antony and Cleopatra* wonderful or astonishing, we appear to be
thinking first of the artist and his activity, while in
the case of the four famous tragedies it is the
product of this activity, the thing presented, that
first engrosses us. I know that I am stating this
difference too sharply, but I believe that it is often
felt; and, if this is so, the fact is significant. It
implies that, although *Antony and Cleopatra* may
be for us as wonderful an achievement as the
greatest of Shakespeare's plays, it has not an equal
value. Besides, in the attempt to rank it with them
there is involved something more, and more important, than an error in valuation. There is a
failure to discriminate the peculiar marks of *Antony
and Cleopatra* itself, marks which, whether or no it
be the equal of the earlier tragedies, make it
decidedly different. If I speak first of some of
these differences it is because they thus contribute
to the individuality of the play, and because they
seem often not to be distinctly apprehended in
criticism.

I.

Why, let us begin by asking, is *Antony and
Cleopatra*, though so wonderful an achievement, a
play rarely acted? For a tragedy, it is not painful.
Though unfit for children, it cannot be called indecent; some slight omissions, and such a flattening
of the heroine's part as might confidently be expected,
would leave it perfectly presentable. It is, no doubt,

in the third and fourth Acts, very defective in construction. Even on the Elizabethan stage, where
scene followed scene without a pause, this must
have been felt; and in our theatres it would be felt
much more. There, in fact, these two and forty
scenes could not possibly be acted as they stand.
But defective construction would not distress the
bulk of an audience, if the matter presented were
that of *Hamlet* or *Othello*, of *Lear* or *Macbeth*.
The matter, then, must lack something which is
present in those tragedies; and it is mainly owing
to this difference in substance that *Antony and Cleopatra* has never attained their popularity either on
the stage or off it.

Most of Shakespeare's tragedies are dramatic, in
a special sense of the word as well as in its general
sense, from beginning to end. The story is not
merely exciting and impressive from the movement
of conflicting forces towards a terrible issue, but
from time to time there come situations and events
which, even apart from their bearing on this issue,
appeal most powerfully to the dramatic feelings—
scenes of action or passion which agitate the
audience with alarm, horror, painful expectation, or
absorbing sympathies and antipathies. Think of
the street fights in *Romeo and Juliet*, the killing of
Mercutio and Tybalt, the rapture of the lovers, and
their despair when Romeo is banished. Think of
the ghost-scenes in the first Act of *Hamlet*, the
passion of the early soliloquies, the scene between
Hamlet and Ophelia, the play-scene, the sparing
of the King at prayer, the killing of Polonius. Is
not *Hamlet*, if you choose so to regard it, the best
melodrama in the world? Think at your leisure of
Othello, *Lear*, and *Macbeth* from the same point of
view; but consider here and now even the two
tragedies which, as dealing with Roman history, are
companions of *Antony and Cleopatra*. Recall in
Julius Cæsar the first suggestion of the murder, the

preparation for it in a 'tempest dropping fire,' the murder itself, the speech of Antony over the corpse, and the tumult of the furious crowd; in *Coriolanus* the bloody battles on the stage, the scene in which the hero attains the consulship, the scene of rage in which he is banished. And remember that in each of these seven tragedies the matter referred to is contained in the first three Acts.

In the first three Acts of our play what is there resembling this? Almost nothing. People converse, discuss, accuse one another, excuse themselves, mock, describe, drink together, arrange a marriage, meet and part; but they do not kill, do not even tremble or weep. We see hardly one violent movement; until the battle of Actium is over we witness scarcely any vehement passion; and that battle, as it is a naval action, we do not see. Even later, Enobarbus, when he dies, simply dies; he does not kill himself.[1] We hear wonderful talk; but it is not talk, like that of Macbeth and Lady Macbeth, or that of Othello and Iago, at which we hold our breath. The scenes that we remember first are those that portray Cleopatra; Cleopatra coquetting, tormenting, beguiling her lover to stay; Cleopatra left with her women and longing for him; Cleopatra receiving the news of his marriage; Cleopatra questioning the messenger about Octavia's personal appearance. But this is to say that the scenes we remember first are the least indispensable to the plot. One at least is not essential to it at all. And this, the astonishing scene where she storms at the messenger, strikes him, and draws her dagger on him, is the one passage in the first half of the drama that contains either an explosion of passion or an exciting bodily action. Nor is this all. The first half of the play, though it forebodes tragedy, is not decisively tragic in tone. Certainly the Cleopatra scenes are not so.

[1] See Note A.

We read them, and we should witness them, in delighted wonder and even with amusement. The only scene that can vie with them, that of the revel on Pompey's ship, though full of menace, is in great part humorous. Enobarbus, in this part of the play, is always humorous. Even later, when the tragic tone is deepening, the whipping of Thyreus, in spite of Antony's rage, moves mirth. A play of which all this can truly be said may well be as masterly as *Othello* or *Macbeth*, and more delightful; but, in the greater part of its course, it cannot possibly excite the same emotions. It makes no attempt to do so; and to regard it as though it made this attempt is to miss its specific character and the intention of its author.

That character depends only in part on Shakespeare's fidelity to his historical authority, a fidelity which, I may remark, is often greatly exaggerated. For Shakespeare did not merely present the story of ten years as though it occupied perhaps one fifth of that time, nor did he merely invent freely, but in critical places he effected startling changes in the order and combination of events. Still it may be said that, dealing with a history so famous, he could not well make the first half of his play very exciting, moving, or tragic. And this is true so far as mere situations and events are concerned. But, if he had chosen, he might easily have heightened the tone and tension in another way. He might have made the story of Antony's attempt to break his bondage, and the story of his relapse, extremely exciting, by portraying with all his force the severity of the struggle and the magnitude of the fatal step.

And the structure of the play might seem at first to suggest this intention. At the opening, Antony is shown almost in the beginning of his infatuation; for Cleopatra is not sure of her power over him, exerts all her fascination to detain him, and plays the part of the innocent victim who has yielded to

passion and must now expect to be deserted by
her seducer. Alarmed and ashamed at the news
of the results of his inaction, he rouses himself,
tears himself away, and speeds to Italy. His very
coming is enough to frighten Pompey into peace.
He reconciles himself with Octavius, and, by his
marriage with the good and beautiful Octavia, seems
to have knit a bond of lasting amity with her
brother, and to have guarded himself against the
passion that threatened him with ruin. At this
point his power, the world's peace, and his own
peace, appear to be secured ; his fortune has
mounted to its apex. But soon (very much sooner
than in Plutarch's story) comes the downward turn
or counter-stroke. New causes of offence arise
between the brothers-in-law. To remove them
Octavia leaves her husband in Athens and hurries
to Rome. Immediately Antony returns to Cleopatra and, surrendering himself at once and wholly
to her enchantment is quickly driven to his doom.

Now Shakespeare, I say, with his matchless power
of depicting an inward struggle, might have made
this story, even where it could not furnish him with
thrilling incidents, the source of powerful tragic
emotions ; and, in doing so, he would have departed
from his authority merely in his conception of the
hero's character. But he does no such thing till
the catastrophe is near. Antony breaks away from
Cleopatra without any strenuous conflict. No
serious doubt of his return is permitted to agitate
us. We are almost assured of it through the impression made on us by Octavius, through occasional
glimpses into Antony's mind, through the absence
of any doubt in Enobarbus, through scenes in
Alexandria which display Cleopatra and display her
irresistible. And, finally, the downward turn itself,
the fatal step of Antony's return, is shown without
the slightest emphasis. Nay, it is not shown, it is
only reported ; and not a line portrays any inward

struggle preceding it.   On this side also, then, the
drama makes no attempt to rival the other tragedies;
and it was essential to its own peculiar character and
its most transcendent effects that this attempt should
not be made, but that Antony's passion should be
represented as a force which he could hardly even
desire to resist.   By the very scheme of the work,
therefore, tragic impressions of any great volume or
depth were reserved for the last stage of the conflict; while the main interest, down to the battle of
Actium, was directed to matters exceedingly interesting and even, in the wider sense, dramatic, but not
overtly either terrible or piteous : on the one hand,
to the political aspect of the story ; on the other, to
the personal causes which helped to make the issue
inevitable.

2.

The political situation and its development are
simple.   The story is taken up almost where it was
left, years before, in *Julius Cæsar*.   There Brutus
and Cassius, to prevent the rule of one man, assas-
sinate Cæsar.   Their purpose is condemned to
failure, not merely because they make mistakes, but
because that political necessity which Napoleon
identified with destiny requires the rule of one man.
They spill Cæsar's blood, but his spirit walks abroad
and turns their swords against their own breasts;
and the world is left divided among three men, his
friends and his heir.   Here *Antony and Cleopatra*
takes up the tale ; and its business, from this point
of view, is to show the reduction of these three to
one.   That Lepidus will not be this one was clear
already in *Julius Cæsar*; it must be Octavius or
Antony.   Both ambitious, they are also men of such
opposite tempers that they would scarcely long agree
even if they wished to, and even if destiny were not
stronger than they.   As it is, one of them has fixed
his eyes on the end, sacrifices everything for it, uses

everything as a means to it.   The other, though far
the greater soldier and worshipped by his followers,
has no such singleness of aim ; nor yet is power,
however desirable to him, the most desirable thing
in the world.   At the beginning he is risking it for
love ; at the end he has lost his half of the world,
and lost his life, and Octavius rules alone.   Whether
Shakespeare had this clearly in his mind is a question
neither answerable nor important ; this is what came
out of his mind.

Shakespeare, I think, took little interest in the
character of Octavius, and he has not made it
wholly clear.   It is not distinct in Plutarch's ' Life
of Antony ' ; and I have not found traces that the
poet studied closely the ' Life of Octavius ' included
in North's volume.   To Shakespeare he is one of
those men, like Bolingbroke and Ulysses, who have
plenty of ' judgment ' and not much ' blood.'   Victory
in the world, according to the poet, almost always
goes to such men ; and he makes us respect, fear,
and dislike them.   His Octavius is very formidable.
His cold determination half paralyses Antony ; it is
so even in *Julius Cæsar.*   In *Antony and Cleopatra*
Octavius is more than once in the wrong ; but he
never admits it ; he silently pushes his rival a step
backward ; and, when he ceases to fear, he shows
contempt.   He neither enjoys war nor is great in it ;
at first, therefore, he is anxious about the power of
Pompey, and stands in need of Antony.   As soon
as Antony's presence has served his turn, and he
has patched up a union with him and seen him safely
off to Athens, he destroys first Pompey and next
Lepidus.   Then, dexterously using Antony's faithlessness to Octavia and excesses in the East in
order to put himself in the right, he makes for his
victim with admirable celerity while he is still drunk
with the joy of reunion with Cleopatra.   For his
ends Octavius is perfectly efficient, but he is so
partly from his limitations.   One phrase of his is

exceedingly characteristic. When Antony in rage
and desperation challenges him to single combat,
Octavius calls him 'the old ruffian.' There is a
horrid aptness in the phrase, but it disgusts us. It
is shameful in this boy, as hard and smooth as
polished steel, to feel at such a time nothing of the
greatness of his victim and the tragedy of his victim's
fall. Though the challenge of Antony is absurd,
we would give much to see them sword to sword.
And when Cleopatra by her death cheats the conqueror of his prize, we feel unmixed delight.

The doubtful point in the character is this. Plutarch says that Octavius was reported to love his
sister dearly; and Shakespeare's Octavius several
times expresses such love. When, then, he proposed the marriage with Antony (for of course it
was he who spoke through Agrippa), was he honest,
or was he laying a trap and, in doing so, sacrificing
his sister? Did he hope the marriage would really
unite him with his brother-in-law; or did he merely
mean it to be a source of future differences; or did
he calculate that, whether it secured peace or dis-
sension, it would in either case bring him great
advantage? Shakespeare, who was quite as intelligent as his readers, must have asked himself some
such question; but he may not have cared to
answer it even to himself; and, in any case, he has
left the actor (at least the actor in days later than
his own) to choose an answer. If I were forced to
choose, I should take the view that Octavius was,
at any rate, not wholly honest; partly because I
think it best suits Shakespeare's usual way of conceiving a character of the kind; partly because
Plutarch construed in this manner Octavius's behaviour in regard to his sister at a later time, and
this hint might naturally influence the poet's way of
imagining his earlier action.[1]

---

[1] 'Now whilest Antonius was busie in this preparation, Octavia his
wife, whom he had left at Rome, would needs take sea to come unto

Though the character of Octavius is neither attractive nor wholly clear, his figure is invested with a certain tragic dignity, because he is felt to be the Man of Destiny, the agent of forces against which the intentions of an individual would avail nothing. He is represented as having himself some feeling of this sort. His lament over Antony, his grief that their stars were irreconcilable, may well be genuine, though we should be surer if it were uttered in soliloquy. His austere words to Octavia again probably speak his true mind :

> Be you not troubled with the time, which drives
> O'er your content these strong necessities;
> But let determined things to destiny
> Hold unbewailed their way.

In any case the feeling of fate comes through to us. It is aided by slight touches of supernatural effect ; first in the Soothsayer's warning to Antony that his genius or angel is overpowered whenever he is near Octavius; then in the strangely effective scene where Antony's soldiers, in the night before his last battle, hear music in the air or under the earth :

> 'Tis the god Hercules, whom Antony loved,
> Now leaves him.

And to the influence of this feeling in giving impressiveness to the story is added that of the immense scale and world-wide issue of the conflict. Even the distances traversed by fleets and armies enhance this effect.

And yet there seems to be something half-hearted in Shakespeare's appeal here, something even ironical in his presentation of this conflict. Its external magnitude, like Antony's magnificence in lavishing realms and gathering the kings of the East in his

him. Her brother Octauius Cæsar was willing vnto it, not for his respect at all (as most authors do report) as for that he might haue an honest colour to make warre with Antonius if he did misuse her, and not esteeme of her as she ought to be.'—*Life of Antony* (North's Translation), sect. 29. The view I take does not, of course, imply that Octavius had no love for his sister.

support, fails to uplift or dilate the imagination. The struggle in Lear's little island seems to us to have an infinitely wider scope. It is here that we are sometimes reminded of *Troilus and Cressida*, and the cold and disenchanting light that is there cast on the Trojan War. The spectacle which he portrays leaves Shakespeare quite undazzled ; he even makes it appear inwardly small. The lordship of the world, we ask ourselves, what is it worth, and in what spirit do these 'world-sharers' contend for it? They are no champions of their country like Henry V. The conqueror knows not even the glory of battle. Their aims, for all we see, are as personal as if they were captains of banditti ; and they are followed merely from self-interest or private attachment. The scene on Pompey's galley is full of this irony. One 'third part of the world' is carried drunk to bed. In the midst of this mock boon-companionship the pirate whispers to his leader to cut first the cable of his ship and then the throats of the two other Emperors ; and at the moment we should not greatly care if Pompey took the advice. Later, a short scene, totally useless to the plot and purely satiric in its purport, is slipped in to show how Ventidius fears to pursue his Parthian conquests because it is not safe for Antony's lieutenant to outdo his master.[1] A painful sense of hollowness oppresses us. We know too well what must happen in a world so splendid, so false, and so petty. We turn for relief from the political game to those who are sure to lose it ; to those who love some human being better than a prize, to Eros and Charmian and Iras ; to Enobarbus, whom the world corrupts, but who has a heart that can break with shame ; to the lovers, who seem to us to find in death something better than their victor's life.

This presentation of the outward conflict has two results. First, it blunts our feeling of the greatness

[1] See Note B.

of Antony's fall from prosperity. Indeed this feeling, which we might expect to be unusually acute, is
hardly so ; it is less acute, for example, than the like
feeling in the case of Richard II., who loses so much
smaller a realm. Our deeper sympathies are focussed
rather on Antony's heart, on the inward fall to
which the enchantment of passion leads him, and
the inward recovery which succeeds it. And the
second result is this. The greatness of Antony and
Cleopatra in their fall is so much heightened by
contrast with the world they lose and the conqueror
who wins it, that the positive element in the final
tragic impression, the element of reconciliation, is
strongly emphasised. The peculiar effect of the
drama depends partly, as we have seen, on the
absence of decidedly tragic scenes and events in its
first half ; but it depends quite as much on this
emphasis. In any Shakespearean tragedy we watch
some elect spirit colliding, partly through its error
and defect, with a superhuman power which bears it
down ; and yet we feel that this spirit, even in the
error and defect, rises by its greatness into ideal
union with the power that overwhelms it. In some
tragedies this latter feeling is relatively weak. In
Antony and Cleopatra it is unusually strong ; stronger,
with some readers at least, than the fear and grief
and pity with which they contemplate the tragic
error and the advance of doom.

3.

The two aspects of the tragedy are presented
together in the opening scene. Here is the first.
In Cleopatra's palace one friend of Antony is
describing to another, just arrived from Rome, the
dotage of their great general ; and, as the lovers
enter, he exclaims :

> Look, where they come :
> Take but good note, and you shall see in him
> The triple pillar of the world transformed
> Into a strumpet's fool : behold and see.

With the next words the other aspect appears :

> CLEO. If it be love indeed, tell me how much.
> ANT. There's beggary in the love that can be reckoned.
> CLEO. I'll set a bourne how far to be beloved.
> ANT. Then must thou needs find out new heaven, new
> earth.

And directly after, when he is provoked by reminders of the news from Rome :

> Let Rome in Tiber melt, and the wide arch
> Of the ranged empire fall ! Here is my space.
> Kingdoms are clay : our dungy earth alike
> Feeds beast as man : the nobleness of life
> Is to do thus.

Here is the tragic excess, but with it the tragic greatness, the capacity of finding in something the infinite, and of pursuing it into the jaws of death.

The two aspects are shown here with the exaggeration proper in dramatic characters. Neither the phrase ' a strumpet's fool,' nor the assertion ' the nobleness of life is to do thus,' answers to the total effect of the play. But the truths they exaggerate are equally essential ; and the commoner mistake in criticism is to understate the second. It is plain that the love of Antony and Cleopatra is destructive ; that in some way it clashes with the nature of things ; that, while they are sitting in their paradise like gods, its walls move inward and crush them at last to death. This is no invention of moralising critics ; it is in the play ; and any one familiar with Shakespeare would expect beforehand to find it there. But then to forget because of it the other side, to deny the name of love to this ruinous passion, to speak as though the lovers had utterly missed the good of life, is to mutilate the tragedy and to ignore a great part of its effect upon us. For we sympathise with them in their passion ; we feel in it the infinity there is in man ; even while we acquiesce in their defeat we are exulting in their victory; and when they have vanished we say,

> the odds is gone,
> And there is nothing left remarkable
> Beneath the visiting moon.

Though we hear nothing from Shakespeare of the cruelty of Plutarch's Antony, or of the misery caused by his boundless profusion, we do not feel the hero of the tragedy to be a man of the noblest type, like Brutus, Hamlet, or Othello. He seeks power merely for himself, and uses it for his own pleasure. He is in some respects unscrupulous; and, while it would be unjust to regard his marriage exactly as if it were one in private life, we resent his treatment of Octavia, whose character Shakespeare was obliged to leave a mere sketch, lest our feeling for the hero and heroine should be too much chilled. Yet, for all this, we sympathise warmly with Antony, are greatly drawn to him, and are inclined to regard him as a noble nature half spoiled by his time.

It is a large, open, generous, expansive nature, quite free from envy, capable of great magnanimity, even of entire devotion. Antony is unreserved, naturally straightforward, we may almost say simple. He can admit faults, accept advice and even reproof, take a jest against himself with good-humour. He is courteous (to Lepidus, for example, whom Octavius treats with cold contempt); and, though he can be exceedingly dignified, he seems to prefer a blunt though sympathetic plainness, which is one cause of the attachment of his soldiers. He has none of the faults of the brooder, the sentimentalist, or the man of principle; his nature tends to splendid action and lusty enjoyment. But he is neither a mere soldier nor a mere sensualist. He has imagination, the temper of an artist who revels in abundant and rejoicing appetites, feasts his senses on the glow and richness of life, flings himself into its mirth and revelry, yet feels the poetry in all this,

and is able also to put it by and be more than
content with the hardships of adventure. Such a
man could never have sought a crown by a murder
like Macbeth's, or, like Brutus, have killed on principle the man who loved him, or have lost the world
or a Cressida.

Beside this strain of poetry he has a keen intellect,
a swift perception of the lie of things, and much
quickness in shaping a course to suit them. In
Julius Cæsar he shows this after the assassination,
when he appears as a dexterous politician as well as
a warm-hearted friend. He admires what is fine,
and can fully appreciate the nobility of Brutus ; but
he is sure that Brutus's ideas are moonshine, that
(as he says in our play) Brutus is mad ; and, since
his mighty friend, who was incomparably the finest
thing in the world, has perished, he sees no reason
why the inheritance should not be his own. Full of
sorrow, he yet uses his sorrow like an artist to work
on others, and greets his success with the glee of a
successful adventurer. In the earlier play he proves
himself a master of eloquence, and especially of
pathos ; and he does so again in the later. With a
few words about his fall he draws tears from his
followers and even from the caustic humorist
Enobarbus. Like Richard II., he sees his own fall
with the eyes of a poet, but a poet much greater
than the young Shakespeare, who could never have
written Antony's marvellous speech about the sunset
clouds. But we listen to Antony, as we do not to
Richard, with entire sympathy, partly because he is
never unmanly, partly because he himself is sympathetic and longs for sympathy.

The first of living soldiers, an able politician, a
most persuasive orator, Antony nevertheless was
not born to rule the world. He enjoys being a
great man, but he has not the love of rule for rule's
sake. Power for him is chiefly a means to pleasure.
The pleasure he wants is so huge that he needs a

huge power; but half the world, even a third of it, would suffice. He will not pocket wrongs, but he shows not the slightest wish to get rid of his fellow Triumvirs and reign alone. He never minded being subordinate to Julius Cæsar. By women he is not only attracted but governed; from the effect of Cleopatra's taunts we can see that he had been governed by Fulvia. Nor has he either the patience or the steadfastness of a born ruler. He contends fitfully, and is prone to take the step that is easiest at the moment. This is the reason why he consents to marry Octavia. It seems the shortest way out of an awkward situation. He does not intend even to try to be true to her. He will not think of the distant consequences.

A man who loved power as much as thousands of insignificant people love it, would have made a sterner struggle than Antony's against his enchantment. He can hardly be said to struggle at all. He brings himself to leave Cleopatra only because he knows he will return. In every moment of his absence, whether he wake or sleep, a siren music in his blood is singing him back to her; and to this music, however he may be occupied, the soul within his soul leans and listens. The joy of life had always culminated for him in the love of women: he could say 'no' to none of them: of Octavia herself he speaks like a poet. When he meets Cleopatra he finds his Absolute. She satisfies, nay glorifies, his whole being. She intoxicates his senses. Her wiles, her taunts, her furies and meltings, her laughter and tears, bewitch him all alike. She loves what he loves, and she surpasses him. She can drink him to his bed, out-jest his practical jokes, out-act the best actress who ever amused him, out-dazzle his own magnificence. She is his play-fellow, and yet a great queen. Angling in the river, playing billiards, flourishing the sword he used at Philippi, hopping forty paces in a public

street, she remains an enchantress. Her spirit is
made of wind and flame, and the poet in him
worships her no less than the man. He is under
no illusion about her, knows all her faults, sees
through her wiles, believes her capable of betraying
him. It makes no difference. She is his heart's
desire made perfect. To love her is what he was
born for. What have the gods in heaven to say
against it? To imagine heaven is to imagine her;
to die is to rejoin her. To deny that this is love is
the madness of morality. He gives her every atom
of his heart.

She destroys him. Shakespeare, availing himself of the historic fact, portrays, on Antony's return
to her, the suddenness and the depth of his descent.
In spite of his own knowledge, the protests of his
captains, the entreaties even of a private soldier,
he fights by sea simply and solely because she
wishes it. Then in mid-battle, when she flies, he
deserts navy and army and his faithful thousands
and follows her. 'I never saw an action of such
shame,' cries Scarus; and we feel the dishonour of
the hero keenly. Then Shakespeare begins to
raise him again. First, his own overwhelming sense
of shame redeems him. Next, we watch the rage
of the dying lion. Then the mere sally before the
final defeat—a sally dismissed by Plutarch in three
lines—is magnified into a battle, in which Antony
displays to us, and himself feels for the last time,
the glory of his soldiership. And, throughout, the
magnanimity and gentleness which shine through his
desperation endear him to us. How beautiful is
his affection for his followers and even for his servants, and the devotion they return! How noble
his reception of the news that Enobarbus has deserted
him! How touchingly significant the refusal of Eros
either to kill him or survive him! How pathetic
and even sublime the completeness of his love for
Cleopatra! His anger is born and dies in an hour.

One tear, one kiss, outweighs his ruin.   He believes
she has sold him to his enemy, yet he kills himself
because he hears that she is dead.   When, dying,
he learns that she has deceived him once more, no
thought of reproach crosses his mind : he simply
asks to be carried to her.   He knows well that she
is not capable of dying because he dies, but that
does not sting him ; when, in his last agony, he calls
for wine that he may gain a moment's strength to
speak, it is to advise her for the days to come.
Shakespeare borrowed from Plutarch the final
speech of Antony.   It is fine, but it is not miraculous.   The miraculous speeches belong only to his
own hero :

> I am dying, Egypt, dying ; only
> I here importune death awhile, until
> Of many thousand kisses the poor last
> I lay upon thy lips ;

or the first words he utters when he hears of Cleo·
patra's death :

> Unarm, Eros : the long day's task is done,
> And we must sleep.

If he meant the task of statesman and warrior, that
is not what his words mean to us.   They remind us
of words more familiar and less great—

> No rest but the grave for the pilgrim of love.

And he is more than love's pilgrim ; he is love's
martyr.

4.

To reserve a fragment of an hour for Cleopatra,
if it were not palpably absurd, would seem an insult.
If only one could hear her own remarks upon it!
But I had to choose between this absurdity and the
plan of giving her the whole hour ; and to that plan
there was one fatal objection.   She has been described (by Ten Brink) as a courtesan of genius.
So brief a description must needs be incomplete,
and Cleopatra never forgets, nor, if we read aright,

do we forget, that she is a great queen. Still the
phrase is excellent; only a public lecture is no
occasion for the full analysis and illustration of the
character it describes.

Shakespeare has paid Cleopatra a unique compliment. The hero dies in the fourth Act, and the
whole of the fifth is devoted to the heroine.[1] In
that Act she becomes unquestionably a tragic character, but, it appears to me, not till then. This, no
doubt, is a heresy; but as I cannot help holding it,
and as it is connected with the remarks already
made on the first half of the play, I will state it
more fully. Cleopatra stands in a group with
Hamlet and Falstaff. We might join with them
Iago if he were not decidedly their inferior in one
particular quality. They are inexhaustible. You
feel that, if they were alive and you spent your
whole life with them, their infinite variety could
never be staled by custom; they would continue
every day to surprise, perplex, and delight you.
Shakespeare has bestowed on each of them, though
they differ so much, his own originality, his genius.
He has given it most fully to Hamlet, to whom
none of the chambers of experience is shut, and
perhaps more of it to Cleopatra than to Falstaff.
Nevertheless, if we ask whether Cleopatra, in the
first four Acts, is a tragic figure like Hamlet, we
surely cannot answer 'yes.' Naturally it does not
follow that she is a comic figure like Falstaff. This
would be absurd; for, even if she were ridiculous
like Falstaff, she is not ridiculous to herself; she is
no humorist. And yet there is a certain likeness.
She shares a weakness with Falstaff—vanity; and
when she displays it, as she does quite naïvely
(for instance, in the second interview with the
Messenger), she does become comic. Again,
though like Falstaff she is irresistible and carries

---

[1] The point of this remark is unaffected by the fact that the play is
not divided into acts and scenes in the folios

us away no less than the people around her, we are
secretly aware, in the midst of our delight, that her
empire is built on sand.   And finally, as his love for
the Prince gives dignity and pathos to Falstaff in
his overthrow, so what raises Cleopatra at last into
pure tragedy is, in part, that which some critics
have denied her, her love for Antony.

Many unpleasant things can be said of Cleopatra;
and the more that are said the more wonderful she
appears.   The exercise of sexual attraction is the
element of her life ; and she has developed nature
into a consummate art.   When she cannot exert it
on the present lover she imagines its effects on him
in absence.   Longing for the living, she remembers
with pride and joy the dead ; and the past which
the furious Antony holds up to her as a picture of
shame is, for her, glory.   She cannot see an am-
bassador, scarcely even a messenger, without desiring
to bewitch him.   Her mind is saturated with this
element.   If she is dark, it is because the sun himself has been amorous of her.   Even when death is
close at hand she imagines his touch as a lover's.
She embraces him that she may overtake Iras and
gain Antony's first kiss in the other world.

She lives for feeling.   Her feelings are, so to
speak, sacred, and pain must not come near her.
She has tried numberless experiments to discover
the easiest way to die.   Her body is exquisitely
sensitive, and her emotions marvellously swift.
They are really so ; but she exaggerates them so
much, and exhibits them so continually for effect,
that some readers fancy them merely feigned.   They
are all-important, and everybody must attend to
them.   She announces to her women that she is
pale, or sick and sullen ; they must lead her to her
chamber but must not speak to her.   She is as
strong and supple as a leopard, can drink down a
master of revelry, can raise her lover's helpless heavy
body from the ground into her tower with the aid

only of two women; yet, when he is sitting apart
sunk in shame, she must be supported into his
presence, she cannot stand, her head droops, she
will die (it is the opinion of Eros) unless he comforts
her. When she hears of his marriage and has dis-
charged her rage, she bids her women bear her
away; she faints; at least she would faint, but that
she remembers various questions she wants put to
the Messenger about Octavia. Enobarbus has seen
her die twenty times upon far poorer moment than
the news that Antony is going to Rome.

Some of her feelings are violent, and, unless for a
purpose, she does not dream of restraining them;
her sighs and tears are winds and waters, storms
and tempests. At times, as when she threatens to
give Charmian bloody teeth, or hales the luckless
Messenger up and down by the hair, strikes him
and draws her knife on him, she resembles (if I dare
say it) Doll Tearsheet sublimated. She is a mother;
but the threat of Octavius to destroy her children if
she takes her own life passes by her like the wind
(a point where Shakespeare contradicts Plutarch).
She ruins a great man, but shows no sense of the
tragedy of his ruin. The anguish of spirit that
appears in his language to his servants is beyond
her; she has to ask Enobarbus what he means.
Can we feel sure that she would not have sacrificed
him if she could have saved herself by doing so?
It is not even certain that she did not attempt it.
Antony himself believes that she did—that the fleet
went over to Octavius by her orders. That she
and her people deny the charge proves nothing.
The best we can say is that, if it were true, Shakespeare would have made that clear. She is willing
also to survive her lover. Her first thought, to
follow him after the high Roman fashion, is too
great for her. She would live on if she could, and
would cheat her victor too of the best part of her
fortune. The thing that drives her to die is the

certainty that she will be carried to Rome to grace his triumph. That alone decides her.[1]

The marvellous thing is that the knowledge of all this makes hardly more difference to us than it did to Antony. It seems to us perfectly natural, nay, in a sense perfectly right, that her lover should be her slave ; that her women should adore her and die with her ; that Enobarbus, who foresaw what must happen, and who opposes her wishes and braves her anger, should talk of her with rapture and feel no bitterness against her ; that Dolabella, after a minute's conversation, should betray to her his master's intention and enable her to frustrate it. And when Octavius shows himself proof against her fascination, instead of admiring him we turn from him with disgust and think him a disgrace to his species. Why ? It is not that we consider him bound to fall in love with her. Enobarbus did not ; Dolabella did not ; we ourselves do not. The feeling she inspires was felt then, and is felt now, by women no less than men, and would have been shared by Octavia herself. Doubtless she wrought magic on the senses, but she had not extraordinary beauty, like Helen's, such beauty as seems divine.[2] Plutarch says so. The man who wrote the sonnets to the dark lady would have known it for himself. He goes out of his way to add to her age, and tells us of her wrinkles and the waning of her lip. But Enobarbus, in his very mockery, calls her a wonderful piece of work. Dolabella interrupts her with the cry, 'Most sovereign creature,' and we echo it. And yet Octavius, face to face with her and listening to her voice, can think only how best to trap her and drag her to public dishonour in the streets of Rome. We forgive him only for his words when he sees her dead :

> She looks like sleep,
> As she would catch another Antony
> In her strong toil of grace.

[1] See Note C.   [2] See Note D.

And the words, I confess, sound to me more like Shakespeare's than his.

That which makes her wonderful and sovereign laughs at definition, but she herself came nearest naming it when, in the final speech (a passage surpassed in poetry, if at all, only by the final speech of Othello), she cries,

> I am fire and air ; my other elements
> I give to baser life.

The fire and air which at death break from union with those other elements, transfigured them during her life, and still convert into engines of enchantment the very things for which she is condemned. I can refer only to one. She loves Antony. We should marvel at her less and love her more if she loved him more—loved him well enough to follow him at once to death ; but it is to blunder strangely to doubt that she loved him, or that her glorious description of him (though it was also meant to work on Dolabella) came from her heart. Only the spirit of fire and air within her refuses to be trammelled or extinguished ; burns its way through the obstacles of fortune and even through the resistance of her love and grief ; and would lead her undaunted to fresh life and the conquest of new worlds. It is this which makes her 'strong toil of grace' unbreakable ; speaks in her brows' bent and every tone and movement ; glorifies the arts and the rages which in another would merely disgust or amuse us ; and, in the final scenes of her life, flames into such brilliance that we watch her entranced as she struggles for freedom, and thrilled with triumph as, conquered, she puts her conqueror to scorn and goes to meet her lover in the splendour that crowned and robed her long ago, when her barge burnt on the water like a burnished throne, and she floated to Cydnus on the enamoured stream to take him captive for ever.[1]

[1] Of the 'good' heroines, Imogen is the one who has most of this

Why is it that, although we close the book in a triumph which is more than reconciliation, this is mingled, as we look back on the story, with a sadness so peculiar, almost the sadness of dis- enchantment? Is it that, when the glow has faded, Cleopatra's ecstasy comes to appear, I would not say factitious, but an effort strained and prodigious as well as glorious, not, like Othello's last speech, the final expression of character, of thoughts and emotions which have dominated a whole life? Perhaps this is so, but there is something more, something that sounds paradoxical : we are saddened by the very fact that the catastrophe saddens us so little ; it pains us that we should feel so much triumph and pleasure. In *Romeo and Juliet, Hamlet, Othello,* though in a sense we accept the deaths of hero and heroine, we feel a keen sorrow. We look back, think how noble or beautiful they were, wish that fate had opposed to them a weaker enemy, dream possibly of the life they might then have led. Here we can hardly do this. With all our admiration and sympathy for the lovers we do not wish them to gain the world. It is better for the world's sake, and not less for their own, that they should fail and die. At the very first they came before us, unlike those others, unlike Coriolanus and even Macbeth, in a glory already tarnished, half-ruined by their past. Indeed one source of strange and most un- usual effect in their story is that this marvellous passion comes to adepts in the experience and art of passion, who might be expected to have worn its charm away. Its splendour dazzles us ; but, when the splendour vanishes, we do not mourn, as we mourn for the love of Romeo or Othello, that a thing so bright and good should die. And the fact that we mourn so little saddens us.

spirit of fire and air ; and this (in union, of course, with other qualities) is perhaps the ultimate reason why for so many readers she is, what Mr. Swinburne calls her, ' the woman above all Shakespeare's women.'

A comparison of Shakespearean tragedies seems to prove that the tragic emotions are stirred in the fullest possible measure only when such beauty or nobility of character is displayed as commands unreserved admiration or love; or when, in default of this, the forces which move the agents, and the conflict which results from these forces, attain a terrifying and overwhelming power. The four most famous tragedies satisfy one or both of these conditions; *Antony and Cleopatra*, though a great tragedy, satisfies neither of them completely. But to say this is not to criticise it. It does not attempt to satisfy these conditions, and then fail in the attempt. It attempts something different, and succeeds as triumphantly as *Othello* itself. In doing so it gives us what no other tragedy can give, and it leaves us, no less than any other, lost in astonishment at the powers which created it.

1905

NOTE A

We are to understand, surely, that Enobarbus dies of 'thought' (melancholy or grief), and has no need to seek a 'swifter mean.' Cf. IV. vi. 34 *seq.*, with the death-scene and his address there to the moon as the 'sovereign mistress of true melancholy' (IV. ix.). Cf. also III. xiii., where, to Cleopatra's question after Actium, 'What shall we do, Enobarbus?' he answers, 'Think, and die.'

The character of Enobarbus is practically an invention of Shakespeare's. The death-scene, I may add, is one of the many passages which prove that he often wrote what pleased his imagination but would lose half its effect in the theatre. The darkness and moonlight could not be represented on a public stage in his time.

NOTE B

The scene is the first of the third Act. Here Ventidius says:

> Cæsar and Antony have ever won
> More in their officer than person : Sossius,
> One of my place in Syria, his lieutenant,
> For quick accumulation of renown,
> Which he achieved by the minute, lost his favour.

Plutarch (North, sec. 19) says that 'Sossius, one of Antonius' lieutenants in Syria, did notable good service,' but I cannot find in him the further statement that Sossius lost Antony's favour. I presume it is Shakespeare's invention, but I call attention to it on the bare chance that it may be found elsewhere than in Plutarch, when it would point to Shakespeare's use of a second authority.

NOTE C

Since this lecture was published (*Quarterly Review*, April, 1906) two notable editions of *Antony and Cleopatra* have been produced. Nothing recently written on Shakespeare, I venture to say, shows more thorough scholarship or better judgment than Mr. Case's edition in the Arden series; and Dr. Furness has added to the immense debt which students of Shakespeare owe to him, and (if that is possible) to the admiration and respect with which they regard him, by the appearance of *Antony and Cleopatra* in his New Variorum edition.

On one question about Cleopatra both editors, Mr. Case more tentatively and Dr. Furness very decidedly, dissent from the interpretation given in the last pages of my lecture. The question is how we are to understand the fact that, although on Antony's death Cleopatra expresses her intention of following him, she does not carry out this intention until she has satisfied herself that Octavius means to carry her to Rome to grace his triumph. Though I do not profess to feel certain that my interpretation is right, it still seems to me a good deal the most probable, and therefore I have not altered what I wrote. But my object here is not to defend my view or to criticise other views, but merely to call attention to the discussion of the subject in Mr. Case's Introduction and Dr. Furness's Preface.

NOTE D

Shakespeare, it seems clear, imagined Cleopatra as a gipsy. And this, I would suggest, may be the explanation of a word which has caused much difficulty. Antony, when 'all is lost,' exclaims (IV. x. 38):

> O this false soul of Egypt! this grave charm,—
> Whose eye beck'd forth my wars, and call'd them home,
> Whose bosom was my crownet, my chief end,—
> Like a right gipsy, hath, at fast and loose,
> Beguil'd me to the very heart of loss.

Pope changed 'grave' in the first line into 'gay.' Others conjecture 'great' and 'grand.' Steevens says that 'grave' means 'deadly,' and that the word 'is often used by Chapman' thus; and one of his two quotations supports his statement; but certainly in Shakespeare the word does not elsewhere bear this sense. It could mean 'majestic,' as Johnson takes it here. But why should it not have its usual meaning? Cleopatra, we know, was a being of 'infinite variety,' and her eyes may sometimes have had, like those of some gipsies, a mysterious gravity or solemnity which would exert a spell more potent than her gaiety. Their colour, presumably, was what is called 'black'; but surely they were not, like those of Tennyson's Cleopatra, '*bold* black eyes.' Readers interested in seeing what criticism is capable of may like to know that it has been proposed to read, for the first line of the quotation above, 'O this false fowl of Egypt! haggard charmer.' [Though I have not cancelled this note I have modified some phrases in it, as I have not much confidence in my suggestion. and am inclined to think that Steevens was right.]

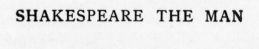

SHAKESPEARE THE MAN

SHAKESPEARE THE MAN

SUCH phrases as 'Shakespeare the man' or 'Shake speare's personality' are, no doubt, open to objection. They seem to suggest that, if we could subtract from Shakespeare the mind that produced his works, the residue would be the man himself; and that his mind was some pure impersonal essence un-affected by the accidents of physique, temperament, and character. If this were so, one could but echo Tennyson's thanksgiving that we know so little of Shakespeare. But as it is assuredly not so, and as 'Shakespeare the man' really means the one indivisible Shakespeare, regarded for the time from a particular point of view, the natural desire to know whatever can be known of him is not to be repressed merely because there are people so foolish as to be careless about his works and yet curious about his private life. For my own part I confess that, though I should care nothing about the man if he had not written the works, yet, since we possess them, I would rather see and hear him for five minutes in his proper person than discover a new one. And though we may be content to die without knowing his income or even the surname of Mr. W. H., we cannot so easily resign the wish to find the man in his writings, and to form some idea of the disposition, the likes and dislikes, the character and the attitude towards life, of the human being who seems to us to have understood best our common human nature.

The answer of course will be that our biographical knowledge of Shakespeare is so small, and his writings are so completely dramatic, that this wish, however natural, is idle. But I cannot think so. Doubtless, in trying to form an idea of Shakespeare, we soon reach the limits of reasonable certainty; and it is also true that the idea we can form without exceeding them is far from being as individual as we could desire. But it is more distinct than is often supposed, and it *is* reasonably certain; and although we can add to its distinctness only by more or less probable conjectures, they are not mere guesses, they really have probability in various degrees. On this whole subject there is a tendency at the present time to an extreme scepticism, which appears to me to be justified neither by the circumstances of the particular case nor by our knowledge of human nature in general.

This scepticism is due in part to the interest excited by Mr. Lee's discussion of the Sonnets in his *Life* of Shakespeare, and to the importance rightly attached to that discussion. The Sonnets are lyrical poems of friendship and love. In them the poet ostensibly speaks in his own person and expresses his own feelings. Many critics, no doubt, had denied that he really did so; but they had not Mr. Lee's knowledge, nor had they examined the matter so narrowly as he; and therefore they had not much weakened the general belief that the Sonnets, however conventional or exaggerated their language may sometimes be, do tell us a good deal about their author. Mr. Lee, however, showed far more fully than any previous writer that many of the themes, many even of the ideas, of these poems are commonplaces of Renaissance sonnet-writing; and he came to the conclusion that in the Sonnets Shakespeare 'unlocked,' not 'his heart,' but a very

different kind of armoury, and that the sole biographical inference deducible from them is that 'at
one time in his career Shakespeare disdained no
weapon of flattery in an endeavour to monopolise
the bountiful patronage of a young man of rank.'
Now, if that inference is correct, it certainly tells
us something about Shakespeare the man ; but it
also forbids us to take seriously what the Sonnets
profess to tell us of his passionate affection, with its
hopes and fears, its pain and joy ; of his pride and
his humility, his self-reproach and self-defence, his
weariness of life and his consciousness of immortal
genius. And as, according to Mr. Lee's statement,
the Sonnets alone of Shakespeare's works 'can be
held to throw any illumination on a personal trait,'
it seems to follow that, so far as the works are
concerned (for Mr. Lee is not specially sceptical as to
the external testimony), the only idea we can form
of the man is contained in that single inference.

Now, I venture to surmise that Mr. Lee's words
go rather beyond his meaning. But that is not our
business here, nor could a brief discussion do justice
to a theory to which those who disagree with it
are still greatly indebted. What I wish to deny
is the presupposition which seems to be frequently
accepted as an obvious truth. Even if Mr. Lee's
view of the Sonnets were indisputably correct, nay,
if even, to go much further, the persons and the
story in the Sonnets were as purely fictitious as
those of *Twelfth Night*, they might and would still
tell us something of the personality of their author.
For however free a poet may be from the emotions
which he simulates, and however little involved in
the conditions which he imagines, he cannot (unless
he is a mere copyist) write a hundred and fifty
lyrics expressive of those simulated emotions without disclosing something of himself, something of
the way in which he in particular *would* feel and
behave under the imagined conditions. And the

same thing holds in principle of the dramas. Is it really conceivable that a man can write some five and thirty dramas, and portray in them an enormous amount and variety of human nature, without betraying anything whatever of his own disposition and preferences? I do not believe that he could do this, even if he deliberately set himself to the task. The only question is how much of himself he would betray.

One is entitled to say this, I think, on general grounds; but we may appeal further to specific experience. Of many poets and novelists we know a good deal from external sources. And in these cases we find that the man so known to us appears also in his works, and that these by themselves would have left on us a personal impression which, though imperfect and perhaps in this or that point even false, would have been broadly true. Of course this holds of some writers much more fully than of others; but, except where the work is very scanty in amount, it seems to hold in some degree of all.[1] If so, there is an antecedent probability that it will apply to Shakespeare too. After all, he was human. We may exclaim in our astonishment that he was as universal and impartial as nature herself; but this is the language of religious rapture. If we assume that he was six times as universal as Sir Walter Scott, which is praise enough for a mortal, we may hope to form an idea of him from his plays only six times as dim as the idea of Scott that we should derive from the Waverley Novels.

And this is not all. As a matter of fact, the great majority of Shakespeare's readers—lovers of poetry

[1] Unquestionably it holds in a considerable degree of Browning, who in *At the Mermaid* and *House* wrote as though he imagined that neither his own work nor Shakespeare's betrayed anything of the inner man. But if we are to criticise those two poems as arguments, we must say that they involve two hopelessly false assumptions, that we have to choose between a self-revelation like Byron's and no self-revelation at all, and that the relation between a poet and his work is like that between the inside and the outside of a house.

untroubled by theories and questions—do form from
the plays some idea of the man. Knowingly or
not, they possess such an idea; and up to a certain
point the idea is the same. Ask such a man
whether he thinks Shakespeare was at all like
Shelley, or Wordsworth, or Milton, and it will not
occur to him to answer 'I have not the faintest
notion'; he will answer unhesitatingly No. Ask
him whether he supposes that Shakespeare was at
all like Fielding or Scott, and he will probably be
found to imagine that, while differing greatly from
both, he did belong to the same type or class. And
such answers unquestionably imply an idea which,
however deficient in detail, is definite.

Again, to go a little further in the same direction,
take this fact. After I had put together my notes
for the present lecture, I re-read Bagehot's essay
on Shakespeare the Man, and I read a book by
Goldwin Smith and an essay by Leslie Stephen
(who, I found, had anticipated a good deal that I
meant to say).[1] These three writers, with all their
variety, have still substantially the same idea of
Shakespeare; and it is the idea of the competent
'general reader' more fully developed. Nor is the
value of their agreement in the least diminished by
the fact that they make no claim to be Shakespeare
scholars. They show themselves much abler than
most scholars, and if they lack the scholar's
knowledge they are free from his defects. When
they wrote their essays they had not wearied
themselves with rival hypotheses, or pored over

[1] Almost all Shakespearean criticism, of course, contains something
bearing on our subject; but I have a practical reason for mentioning
in particular Mr. Frank Harris's articles in the *Saturday Review* for
1898. A good many of Mr. Harris's views I cannot share, and I had
arrived at almost all the ideas expressed in the lecture (except some
on the Sonnets question) before reading his papers. But I found in
them also valuable ideas which were quite new to me and would
probably be so to many readers. It is a great pity that the articles are
not collected and published in a book. [Mr. Harris has published, in
The Man Shakespeare, the substance of the articles, and also matter
which, in my judgment, has much less value.]

minutiae until they lost the broad and deep impressions which vivid reading leaves. Ultra-scepticism in this matter does not arise merely or mainly from the humility which every man of sense must feel as he creeps to and fro in Shakespeare's prodigious mind. It belongs either to the clever faddist who can see nothing straight, or it proceeds from those dangers and infirmities which the expert in any subject knows too well.

The remarks I am going to make can have an interest only for those who share the position I have tried to indicate ; who believe that the most dramatic of writers must reveal in his writings something of himself, but who recognise that in Shakespeare's case we can expect a reasonable certainty only within narrow limits, while beyond them we have to trust to impressions, the value of which must depend on familiarity with his writings, on freedom from prejudice and the desire to reach any particular result, and on the amount of perception we may happen to possess. I offer my own impressions, insecure and utterly unprovable as I know them to be, simply because those of other readers have an interest for me ; and I offer them for the most part without argument, because even where argument might be useful it requires more time than a lecture can afford. For the same reason I shall assume, without attempting to define it further, and without dilating on its implications, the truth of that general feeling about Shakespeare and Fielding and Scott.

But, before we come to impressions at all, we must look at the scanty store of external evidence : for we may lay down at once the canon that impressions derived from the works must supplement and not contradict this evidence, so far as it appears trustworthy. It is scanty, but it yields a decided outline.

> This figure that thou here seest put,
> It was for gentle Shakespeare cut :

—so Jonson writes of the portrait in the Folio, and the same adjective 'gentle' is used elsewhere of Shakespeare. It had not in Elizabethan English so confined a meaning as it has now ; but it meant something, and I do not remember that their contemporaries called Marlowe or Jonson or Marston 'gentle.' Next, in the earliest extant reference that we have to Shakespeare, the writer says that he himself has seen his 'demeanour' to be 'civil.'[1] It is not saying much ; but it is not the first remark an acquaintance would probably have made about Ben Jonson or Samuel Johnson. The same witness adds about Shakespeare that 'divers of worship have reported his uprightness of dealing which argues his honesty.' 'Honesty' and 'honest' in an Elizabethan passage like this mean more than they would now ; they answer rather to our 'honourable' or 'honour.' Lastly we have the witness borne by Jonson in the words : 'I loved the man, and do honour his memory, on this side idolatry, as much as any. He was, indeed, honest, and of an open and free nature.' With this notable phrase, to which I shall have to return, we come to an end of the testimony of eye-witnesses to Shakespeare the Man (for we have nothing to do with references to the mere actor or author). It is scanty, and insufficient to discriminate him from other persons who were gentle, civil, upright in their dealings, honourable, open, and free : but I submit that there have been not a few writers to whom all these qualities could not be truly ascribed, and that the testimony therefore does tell us something definite. To which must be added that we have absolutely

[1] He is apologising for an attack made on Shakespeare in a pamphlet of which he was the publisher and Greene the writer.

no evidence which conflicts with it. Whatever Greene in his jealous embitterment might have said would carry little weight, but in fact, apart from general abuse of actors, he only says that the upstart had an over-weening opinion of his own capacities.

There remain certain traditions and certain facts; and without discussing them I will mention what seems to me to have a more or less probable significance. Stratford stories of drinking bouts may go for nothing, but not the consensus of tradition to the effect that Shakespeare was a pleasant and convivial person, 'very good company, and of a very ready and pleasant smooth wit.'[1] That after his retirement to Stratford he spent at the rate of £1000 a year is incredible, but that he spent freely seems likely enough. The tradition that as a young man he got into trouble with Sir Thomas Lucy for deer-stealing (which would probably be an escapade rather than an essay in serious poaching) is supported by his unsavoury jest about the 'luces' in Sir Robert Shallow's coat. The more general statement that in youth he was wild does not sound improbable; and, obscure as the matter is, I cannot regard as comfortable the little we know of the circumstances of his very early marriage. A contemporary story of an amorous adventure in London may well be pure invention, but we have no reason to reject it peremptorily as we should any similar gossip about Milton. Lastly, certain inferences may safely be drawn from the facts that, once securely started in London, Shakespeare soon began to prosper, and acquired, for an actor and playwright, considerable wealth; that he bought property in his native town, and was consulted sometimes by fellow-townsmen

---

[1] It was said of him, indeed, in his lifetime that, had he not played some kingly parts in sport (*i.e.* on the stage), he would have been a companion for a king.

on matters of business ; that he enforced the pay-
ment of certain debts ; and that he took the trouble
to get a coat of arms.   But what cannot with any
logic or any safety be inferred is that he, any more
than Scott, was impelled to write simply and solely
by the desire to make money and improve his social
position ; and the comparative abundance of business
records will mislead only those who are thoughtless
enough to forget that, if they buy a house or sue a
debtor, the fact will be handed down, while their
kind or generous deeds may be recorded, if at all,
only in the statement that they were 'of an open
and free nature.'

That Shakespeare was a good and perhaps keen
man of business, or that he set store by a coat of
arms, we could not have inferred from his writings.
But we could have judged from them that he worked
hard, and have guessed with some probability that
he would rather have been a 'gentleman' than an
actor.   And most of the other characteristics that
appear from the external evidence would, I think,
have seemed probable from a study of the works.
This should encourage us to hope that we may be
right in other impressions which we receive from
them.   And we may begin with one on which the
external evidence has a certain bearing.

Readers of Shakespeare, I believe, imagine him
to have been not only sweet-tempered but modest
and unassuming.   I do not doubt that they are
right; and, vague as the Folio portrait and the
Stratford bust are, it would be difficult to believe
that their subject was an irritable, boastful, or push-
ing person.   But if we confine ourselves to the
works, it is not easy to give reasons for the idea that
their author was modest and unassuming ; and a
man is not necessarily so because he is open, free,
and very good company.   Perhaps we feel that a
man who was not so would have allowed much

more of himself to appear in his works than Shake-speare does.   Perhaps again we think that anything like presumption or self-importance was incompat-ible with Shakespeare's sense of the ridiculous, his sublime common-sense, and his feeling of man's insignificance.   And, lastly, it seems to us clear that the playwright admires and likes people who are modest, unassuming, and plain ; while it may perhaps safely be said that those who lack these qualities rarely admire them in others and not seldom despise them.   But, however we may justify our impres-sion that Shakespeare possessed them, we certainly receive it; and assuming it to be as correct as the similar impression left by the Waverley Novels indubitably is, I go on to observe that the possession of them does not of necessity imply a want of spirit, or of proper self-assertion or insistence on rights.[1] It did not in Scott, and we have ground for saying that it did not in Shakespeare.   If it had, he could not, being of an open and free nature, have prospered as he prospered.   He took offence at Greene's attack on him, and showed that he took it.   He was 'gentle,' but he liked his debts to be paid.   However his attitude as to the enclosure at Welcombe may be construed, it is clear that he had to be reckoned with.   It appears probable that he held himself wronged by Sir Thomas Lucy, and, pocketing up the injury because he could not resent it, gave him tit for tat after some fifteen years.   The man in the Sonnets forgives his friend easily, but it is not from humility ; and towards the world he is very far from humble.   Of the dedication of *The Rape of Lucrece* we cannot judge, for we do not know Shakespeare's relations with Lord Southampton at that date; but, as for the dedication of *Venus and Adonis*, could modesty and dignity be better mingled in a letter from a young poet to a great noble than they are there?

[1] Nor, *vice versa*, does the possession of these latter qualities at all imply, as some writers seem to assume, the absence of the former or of gentleness.

Some of Shakespeare's writings point to a strain of deep reflection and of quasi-metaphysical imagination in his nature; and a few of them seem to reveal a melancholy, at times merely sad, at times embittered or profound, if never hopeless. It is on this side mainly that we feel a decided difference between him and Fielding, and even between him and Scott. Yet nothing in the contemporary allusions or in the traditions would suggest that he was notably thoughtful or serious, and much less that he was melancholy. And although we could lay no stress on this fact if it stood alone, it is probably significant. Shakespeare's writings, on the whole, leave a strong impression that his native disposition was much more gay than grave. They seem always to have made this impression. Fuller tells us that 'though his genius generally was jocular and inclining him to festivity, yet he could, when so disposed, be solemn and serious, as appears by his tragedies.' [1] Johnson agreed with Rymer that his 'natural disposition' led him to comedy; and, although Johnson after his manner distorts a true idea by wilful exaggeration and by perverting distinctions into antitheses, there is truth in his development of Rymer's remark. It would be easy to quote nineteenth century critics to the same effect; and the study of Shakespeare's early works leads to a similar result. It has been truly said that we feel ourselves in much closer contact with his personality in the early comedies and in *Romeo and Juliet* than in *Henry VI.* and *Richard III.* and *Titus Andronicus*. In the latter, so far as we suppose them to be his own, he seems on the whole to be following, and then improving on, an existing style, and to be dealing with subjects which engage him as a play-

[1] Fuller may be handing down a tradition, but it is not safe to assume this. His comparison, on the other hand, of Shakespeare and Jonson, in their wit-combats, to an English man-of-war and a Spanish great galleon, reads as if his own happy fancy were operating on the reports, direct or indirect, of eye-witnesses.

wright without much appealing to him personally. With *Romeo and Juliet*, on the other hand, and with *Richard II.* (which seems clearly to be his first attempt to write historical tragedy in a manner entirely his own), it is different, and we feel the presence of the whole man. The stories are tragic, but it is not precisely the *tragic* aspect of them that attracts him most; and even Johnson's statement, grotesquely false of the later tragedies, that 'in tragedy he is always struggling after some occasion to be comic,' is no more than an exaggeration in respect to *Romeo and Juliet*.[1] From these tragedies, as from *Love's Labour's Lost* and the other early comedies, we should guess that the author was a young man, happy, alert, light-hearted, full of romance and poetry, but full also of fun; blessed with a keen enjoyment of absurdities, but, for all his intellectual subtlety and power, not markedly reflective, and certainly not particularly grave or much inclined to dejection. One might even suspect, I venture to think, that with such a flow of spirits and such exceeding alacrity of mind he might at present be a trifle wanting in feeling and disposed to levity. In any case, if our general impression is correct, we shall not find it hard to believe that the author of these plays and the creator of Falstaff was 'very good company' and a convivial good-fellow; and it might easily happen that he was tempted at times to 'go here and there' in society, and 'make himself a motley to the view' in a fashion that left some qualms behind.[2]

---

[1] See, for example, Act IV. Sc. v., to which I know no parallel in the later tragedies.

[2] I allude to Sonnet 110, Mr. Beeching's note on which seems to be unquestionably right : 'There is no reference to the poet's profession of player. The sonnet gives the confession of a favourite of society.' This applies, I think, to the whole group of sonnets (it begins with 107) in which the poet excuses his neglect of his friend, though there are *also* references to his profession and its effect on his nature and his reputation. (By a slip Mr. Beeching makes the neglect last for three years.)

There is a tradition that Shakespeare was 'a hand-
some well-shaped man.' If the Stratford monument
does not lie, he was not in later life a meagre man.
And if our notion of his temperament has any truth,
he can hardly have been physically feeble, bloodless,
or inactive. Most readers probably imagine him the
reverse. Even sceptical critics tell us that he was
fond of field-sports; and of his familiar knowledge
of them there can be no question. Yet—I can but
record the impression without trying to justify it—
his writings do not at all suggest to me that he was
a splendidly powerful creature like Fielding, or that
he greatly enjoyed bodily exertion, or was not easily
tired. He says much of horses, but he does not
make one think, as Scott does, that a gallop was a
great delight to him. Nor again do I feel after
reading him that he had a strong natural love of
adventurous deeds, or longed to be an explorer or a
soldier. The island of his boyish dreams—if he
heard much of voyages as a boy—was, I fancy, the
haunt of marmosets and hedgehogs, quaint moon-
calves and flitting sprites, lovely colours, sounds
and sweet airs that give delight and hurt not,
less like Treasure Island than the Coral Island of
Ballantyne in the original illustrations, and more
full of wonders than of dangers. He would have
liked the Arabian Nights better than Dumas.
Of course he admired men of action, understood
them, and could express their feelings; but we do
not feel particularly close to his personality as we
read the warrior speeches of Hotspur, Henry,
Othello, Coriolanus, as we do when we read of
Romeo or Hamlet, or when we feel the attraction
of Henry's modesty. In the same way, I suppose
nobody feels Shakespeare's personal presence in the
ambition of Macbeth or the pride of Coriolanus;
many feel it in Macbeth's imaginative terrors, and in
the disgust of Coriolanus at the idea of recounting
his exploits in order to win votes. When we seem

to hear Shakespeare's voice—and we hear it from
many mouths besides Romeo's or Hamlet's—it is the
voice of a man with a happy, enjoying, but still
contemplative and even dreamy nature, not of a
man richly endowed with the impulses and feelings
either of strenuous action or of self-assertion. If he
had drawn a Satan, we should not have felt his
personality, as we do Milton's, in Satan's pride and
indomitable courage and intolerance of rule.

We know how often Shakespeare uses the antithesis of blood or passion, and judgment or reason ;
how he praises the due commingling of the two, or
the control of the first by the second; how frequently it is the want of such control that exposes
his heroes to the attack of Fortune or Fate. What,
then, were the passions or the 'affections of the
blood' most dangerous to himself? Not, if we have
been right, those of pride or ambition ; nor yet those
of envy, hatred, or revenge ; and still less that of
avarice. But, in the first place, let us remember
Jonson's words, ' he was honest and of an open and
free nature,' and let me repeat an observation, made
elsewhere in passing, that these words are true also
of the great majority of Shakespeare's heroes, and
not least of his tragic heroes. Jonson almost quotes
Iago :

> The Moor is of a free and open nature,
> That thinks men honest that but seem to be so.

The king says that Hamlet,

> being remiss,
> Most generous, and free from all contrivings,
> Will not peruse the foils.

The words 'open and free' apply no less eminently
to Brutus, Lear, and Timon. Antony and Coriolanus are men naturally frank, liberal, and large.
Prospero lost his dukedom through his trustfulness.
Romeo and Troilus and Orlando, and many slighter
characters, are so far of the same type. Now such

a free and open nature, obviously, is specially exposed to the risks of deception, perfidy, and ingratitude. If it is also a nature sensitive and intense, but not particularly active or (if the word may be excused) volitional, such experiences will tempt it to melancholy, embitterment, anger, possibly even misanthropy. If it *is* thus active or volitional, it may become the prey of violent and destructive passion, such as that of Othello and of Coriolanus, and such as Lear's would be if he were not so old. These affections, passions, and sufferings of free and open natures are Shakespeare's favourite tragic subject; and his favouritism, surely, goes so far as to constitute a decided peculiarity, not found thus in other tragic poets. Here he painted most, one cannot but think, what his own nature was most inclined to feel. But it would rather be melancholy, embitterment, an inactive rage or misanthropy, than any destructive passion ; and it would be a further question whether, and how far, he may at any time have experienced what he depicts. I am speaking here only of his disposition.[1]

That Shakespeare was as much inclined to be a lover as most poets we may perhaps safely assume ; but can we conjecture anything further on this subject? I will confine myself to two points. He treats of love romantically, and tragically, and humorously. In the earlier plays especially the humorous aspect of the matter, the aspect so prominent in the *Midsummer-Night's Dream*, the changefulness, brevity, irrationality, of the feeling, is at least as much dwelt on as the romantic, and with at least as much relish :

Lord ! what fools these mortals be !

[1] It is perhaps most especially in his rendering of the shock and the effects of *disillusionment* in open natures that we seem to feel Shakespeare's personality. The nature of this shock is expressed in Henry's words to Lord Scroop :

I will weep for thee :
For this revolt of thine, methinks, is like
Another fall of man.

Now, if there is anything peculiar in the pictures here, it is, perhaps, the special interest that Shakespeare seems to take in what we may call the unreality of the feeling of love in an imaginative nature. Romeo as he first appears, and, in a later play, Orsino, are examples of this. They are perfectly sincere, of course, but neither of them is really in love with a woman; each is in love with the state of being in love. This state is able to attach itself to a particular object, but it is not induced by the particular qualities of that object; it is more a dream than a passion, and can melt away without carrying any of the lover's heart with it; and in that sense it is unreal. This weakness, no doubt, is not confined to imaginative natures, but they may well be specially disposed to it (as Shelley was), and Shakespeare may have drawn it from his own experience. The suspicion is strengthened when we think of *Richard II.* In Richard this imaginative weakness is exhibited again, though not in relation to love. He luxuriates in images of his royal majesty, of the angels who guard his divine right, and of his own pathetic and almost sacred sufferings. The images are not insincere, and yet they are like dreams, for they refuse to touch earth and to connect themselves either with his past misdeeds or with the actions he ought now to perform. A strain of a similar weakness appears again in Hamlet, though only as one strain in a much more deep and complex nature. But this is not a common theme in poetry, much less in dramatic poetry.[1]

---

[1] There is nothing of this semi-reality, of course, in the *passion* of love as portrayed, for example, in men so different as Orlando, Othello, Antony, Troilus, whose love for Cressida resembles that of Romeo for Juliet. What I have said of Romeo's 'love' for Rosaline corresponds roughly with Coleridge's view; and, without subscribing to all of Coleridge's remarks, I believe he was right in finding an intentional contrast between this feeling and the passion that displaces it (though it does not follow that the feeling would not have become a genuine passion if Rosaline had been kind). Nor do I understand the notion

To come to our second question. When Shakespeare painted Cressida or described her through
the mouth of Ulysses ('O these encounterers,' etc.),
or, again, when he portrayed the love of Antony for
Cleopatra, was he using his personal experience?
To answer that he *must* have done so would be as
ridiculous as to argue that Iago must be a portrait
of himself; and the two plays contain nothing
which, by itself, would justify us even in thinking
that he probably did so. But we have the series
of sonnets about the dark lady; and if we accept
the sonnets to the friend as to some considerable
extent based on fact and expressive of personal
feelings, how can we refuse to take the others
on the same footing? Even if the stories of the
two series were not intertwined, we should have
no ground for treating the two in different ways,
unless we could say that external evidence, or the
general impression we derive from Shakespeare's
works, forbids us to believe that he could ever have
been entangled in an intrigue like that implied in
the second series, or have felt and thought in the
manner there portrayed. Being unable to say this,
I am compelled, most regretfully, to hold it probable
that this series is, in the main, based on personal
experience. And I say 'most regretfully,' not merely
because one would regret to think that Shakespeare
was the victim of a Cressida or even the lover of
a Cleopatra, but because the story implied in these

---

that Coleridge's view is refuted and even rendered ridiculous by the
mere fact that Shakespeare found the Rosaline story in Brooke
(Halliwell-Phillipps, *Outlines*, 7th ed., illustrative note 2). Was he
compelled then to use whatever he found? Was it his practice to
do so? The question is always *why* he used what he found, and
how. Coleridge's view of this matter, it need hardly be said, is far
from indisputable; but it must be judged by our knowledge of
Shakespeare's mind and not of his material alone. I may add, as I
have referred to Halliwell-Phillipps, that Shakespeare made changes
in the story he found; that it is arbitrary to assume (not that it
matters) that Coleridge, who read Steevens, was unaware of Shakespeare's use of Brooke; and that Brooke was by no means a
'wretched poetaster.'

sonnets is of quite another kind. They leave, on the whole, a very disagreeable impression. We cannot compare it with the impressions produced, for example, by the 'heathen' spirit of Goethe's *Roman Elegies*, or by the passion of Shakespeare's Antony. In these two cases, widely dissimilar of course, we may speak of 'immorality,' but we are not discomfited, much less disgusted. The feeling and the attitude are poetic, whole-hearted, and in one case passionate in the extreme. But the state of mind expressed in the sonnets about the dark lady is half-hearted, often prosaic, and never worthy of the name of passion. It is uneasy, dissatisfied, distempered, the state of mind of a man who despises his 'passion' and its object and himself, but, standing intellectually far above it, still has not resolution to end it, and only pains us by his gross and joyless jests. In *Troilus and Cressida*—not at all in the portrayal of Troilus's love, but in the atmosphere of the drama—we seem to trace a similar mood of dissatisfaction, and of intellectual but practically impotent contempt.

In this connection it is natural to think of the 'unhappy period' which has so often been surmised in Shakespeare's life. There is not time here to expand the summary remarks made elsewhere on this subject; but I may refer a little more fully to a persistent impression left on my mind by writings which we have reason to assign to the years 1602-6.[1] There is surely something unusual in their tone regarding certain 'vices of the blood,' regarding drunkenness and sexual corruption. It does not lie in Shakespeare's *view* of these vices, but in an undertone of disgust. Read Hamlet's language about the habitual drunkenness of his uncle, or even

---

[1] *Hamlet, Measure for Measure, Othello, Troilus and Cressida, King Lear, Timon of Athens.* See *Shakespearean Tragedy*, pp. 79-85, 275-6. I should like to insist on the view there taken that the tragedies subsequent to *Lear* and *Timon* do not show the pressure of painful feelings.

Cassio's words about his casual excess; then think of the tone of *Henry IV.* or *Twelfth Night* or the *Tempest*; and ask if the difference is not striking. And if you are inclined to ascribe it wholly to the fact that *Hamlet* and *Othello* are tragedies, compare the passages in them with the scene on Pompey's galley in *Antony and Cleopatra.* The intent of that scene is terrible enough, but in the tone there is no more trace of disgust than in *Twelfth Night.* As to the other matter, what I refer to is not the transgression of lovers like Claudio and Juliet, nor even light-hearted irregularities like those of Cassio : here Shakespeare's speech has its habitual tone. But, when he is dealing with lechery and corruption, the undercurrent of disgust seems to become audible. Is it not true that in the plays from *Hamlet* to *Timon* that subject, in one shape or another, is continually before us ; that the intensity of loathing in Hamlet's language about his mother's lust is unexampled in Shakespeare ; that the treatment of the subject in *Measure for Measure*, though occasionally purely humorous, is on the whole quite unlike the treatment in *Henry IV.* or even in the brothel scenes of *Pericles* ;[1] that while *Troilus and Cressida* is full of disgust and contempt, there is not a trace of either in *Antony and Cleopatra*, though some of the jesting there is obscene enough ; that this same tone is as plainly heard in the unquestioned parts of *Timon* ; and that, while it is natural in Timon to inveigh against female lechery when he speaks to Alcibiades and his harlots, there is no apparent reason why Lear in his exalted madness should choose this subject for similar invectives ? ' Pah ! give me an ounce of civet, good apothecary, to sweeten my imagination '—it is a fainter echo of this exclamation that one seems to hear in the plays of those years. Of course I am not suggesting that it is

---

[1] It is not implied that these scenes are certainly Shakespeare's ; but I see no sufficient ground for decisively rejecting them.

mainly due, or as regards drunkenness due in the least, to any private experience of Shakespeare's. It may have no connection whatever with that experience. It might well be connected with it only in so far as a man frequently wearied and depressed might be unusually sensitive to the ugly aspects of life. But, if we do not take the second series of sonnets to be purely fanciful, we shall think it probable that to some undefined extent it owed its origin to the experience depicted in them.[1]

There remain the sonnets addressed to the friend. Even if it were possible to discuss the general question about them here, it would be needless; for I accept almost wholly, and in some points am greatly indebted to, the views put forward by Mr. Beeching in his admirable edition, to which I may therefore refer my hearers.[2] I intend only to state the main reason why I believe the sonnets to be, substantially, what they purport to be, and then to touch upon one or two of the points where they seem to throw light on Shakespeare's personality.

The sonnets to the friend are, so far as we know, unique in Renaissance sonnet literature in being a prolonged and varied record of the intense affection of an older friend for a younger, and of other feelings arising from their relations. They have no real parallel in any series imitative of Virgil's second Eclogue, or in occasional sonnets to patrons or patron-friends couched in the high-flown language of the time. The intensity of the feelings expressed, however, ought not, by itself, to convince us that

---

[1] That experience, certainly in part and probably wholly, belongs to an earlier time, since sonnets 138 and 144 were printed in the *Passionate Pilgrim*. But I see no difficulty in that. What bears little fruit in a normal condition of spirits may bear abundant fruit later, in moods of discouragement and exasperation induced largely by other causes.

[2] *The Sonnets of Shakespeare with an Introduction and Notes*. Ginn & Co., 1904.

they are personal. The author of the plays could, I make no doubt, have written the most intimate of these poems to a mere creature of his imagination and without ever having felt them except in imagination. Nor is there any but an aesthetic reason why he should not have done so if he had wished. But an aesthetic reason there is ; and this is the decisive point. No capable poet, much less a Shakespeare, intending to produce a merely 'dramatic' series of poems, would dream of inventing a story like that of these sonnets, or, even if he did, of treating it as they treat it. The story is very odd and unattractive. Such capacities as it has are but slightly developed. It is left obscure, and some of the poems are unintelligible to us because they contain allusions of which we can make nothing. Now all this is perfectly natural if the story is substantially a real story of Shakespeare himself and of certain other persons ; if the sonnets were written from time to time as the relations of the persons changed, and sometimes in reference to particular incidents ; and if they were written *for* one or more of these persons (far the greater number for only one), and perhaps in a few cases for other friends,—written, that is to say, for people who knew the details and incidents of which we are ignorant. But it is all unnatural, well-nigh incredibly unnatural, if, with the most sceptical critics, we regard the sonnets as a free product of mere imagination.[1]

Assuming, then, that the persons of the story, with their relations, are real, I would add only two remarks about the friend. In the first place, Mr. Beeching seems to me right in denying that there is sufficient evidence of his standing to Shakespeare and the 'rival' poet or poets in the position of a literary patron ; while, even if he did, it appears to

[1] I find that Mr. Beeching, in the Stratford Town edition of Shakespeare (1907), has also urged these considerations.

me quite impossible to take the language of many
of the sonnets as that of interested flattery. And in
the second place I should be inclined to push even
further Mr. Beeching's view on another point. It
is clear that the young man was considerably
superior to the actor-dramatist in social position; but
any gentleman would be so, and there is nothing to
prove that he was more than a gentleman of some
note, more than plain 'Mr. W. H.' (for these, on
the obvious though not compulsory interpretation of
the dedication, seem to have been his initials). It
is remarkable besides that, while the earlier sonnets
show much deference, the later show very little, so
little that, when the writer, finding that he has
pained his young friend by neglecting him, begs to
be forgiven, he writes almost, if not quite, as an
equal. Read, for example, sonnets 109, 110, 120,
and ask whether it is probable that Shakespeare is
addressing here a great nobleman. It seems therefore most likely (though the question is not of much
importance) that the sonnets are, to quote Meres's
phrase,[1] his 'sonnets among his private friends.'

If then there is, as it appears, no obstacle of any
magnitude to our taking the sonnets as substantially
what they purport to be, we may naturally look in
them for personal traits (and, indeed, to repeat a
remark made earlier, we might still expect to find
such traits even if we knew the sonnets to be purely
dramatic). But in drawing inferences we have to
bear in mind what is implied by the qualification
'substantially.' We have to remember that *some*
of these poems may be mere exercises of art; that
all of them are poems, and not letters, much less
affidavits; that they are Elizabethan poems; that
the Elizabethan language of deference, and also of
affection, is to our minds habitually extravagant and

[1] I do not mean to imply that Meres necessarily refers to the
sonnets we possess, or that all of these are likely to have been written
by 1598.

fantastic ;[1] and that in Elizabethan plays friends openly express their love for one another as Englishmen now rarely do. Allowance being made, however, on account of these facts, the sonnets will still leave two strong impressions—that the poet was exceedingly sensitive to the charm of beauty, and that his love for his friend was, at least at one time, a feeling amounting almost to adoration, and so intense as to be absorbing. Those who are surprised by the first of these traits must have read Shakespeare's dramas with very inactive minds, and I must add that they seem to be somewhat ignorant of human nature. We do not necessarily love best those of our relatives, friends, and acquaintances who please our eyes most ; and we should look askance on anyone who regulated his behaviour chiefly by the standard of beauty ; but most of us, I suppose, love any human being, of either sex and of any age, the better for being beautiful, and are not the least ashamed of the fact. It is further the case that men who are beginning, like the writer of the sonnets, to feel tired and old, are apt to feel an increased and special pleasure in the beauty of the young.[2] If we remember, in addition, what some critics appear constantly to forget, that Shakespeare was a particularly poetical being, we shall hardly be surprised that the beginning of this friendship seems to have been something like a falling in love ; and, if we must needs praise and blame, we should also remember that it became a 'marriage of true minds.'[3] And as to the intensity of the feeling expressed in the sonnets, we can easily believe it to be characteristic

[1] A fact to be remembered in regard to references to the social position of the friend.

[2] Mr. Beeching's illustration of the friendship of the sonnets from the friendship of Gray and Bonstetten is worth pages of argument.

[3] In 125 the poet repudiates the accusation that his friendship is too much based on beauty.

of the man who made Valentine and Proteus, Brutus
and Cassius, Horatio and Hamlet; who painted
that strangely moving portrait of Antonio, middle-
aged, sad, and almost indifferent between life and
death, but devoted to the young, brilliant spend-
thrift Bassanio ; and who portrayed the sudden
compelling enchantment exercised by the young
Sebastian over the Antonio of *Twelfth Night.* ' If
you will not murder me for your love, let me be
your servant.' Antonio is accused of piracy : he
may lose his life if he is identified :

> I have many enemies in Orsino's court,
> But, come what may, I do adore thee so
> That danger shall seem sport, and I will go.

The adoration, the ' prostration,' of the writer of the
sonnets is of one kind with this.

I do not remember what critic uses the word
' prostration.' It applies to Shakespeare's attitude
only in some of the sonnets, but there it does apply,
unless it is taken to suggest humiliation. *That* is
the term used by Hallam, but chiefly in view of a
particular point, namely the failure of the poet to
' resent,' though he ' felt and bewailed,' the injury
done him in ' the seduction of his mistress.' Though
I think we should substitute ' resent more strongly '
for the mere ' resent,' I do not deny that the poet's
attitude in this matter strikes us at first as surprising as well as unpleasant to contemplate. But
Hallam's explanation of it as perhaps due to the
exalted position of the friend, would make it much
more than unpleasant; and his language seems to
show that he, like many critics, did not fully imagine
the situation. It is not easy to speak of it in public
with the requisite frankness ; but it is necessary
to realise that, whatever the friend's rank might
be, he and the poet were intimate friends ; that,
manifestly, it was rather the mistress who seduced
the friend than the friend the mistress ; and that she

was apparently a woman not merely of no reputation, but of such a nature that she might readily be
expected to be mistress to two men at one and the
same time. Anyone who realises this may call the
situation 'humiliating' in one sense, and I cannot
quarrel with him ; but he will not call it 'humiliating'
in respect of Shakespeare's relation to his friend ;
nor will he wonder much that the poet felt more
pain than resentment at his friend's treatment of
him. There is something infinitely stranger in a
play of Shakespeare's, and it may be symptomatic.
Ten Brink called attention to it. Proteus actually
offers violence to Sylvia, a spotless lady and the true
love of his friend Valentine ; and Valentine not only
forgives him at once when he professes repentance,
but offers to resign Sylvia to him! The incident
is to us so utterly preposterous that we find it hard
to imagine how the audience stood it ; but, even if
we conjecture that Shakespeare adopted it from
the story he was using, we can hardly suppose that
it was so absurd to him as it is to us.[1] And it is
not the Sonnets alone which lead us to surmise
that forgiveness was particularly attractive to him,
and the forgiveness of a friend much easier than
resentment. From the Sonnets we gather—and
there is nothing in the plays or elsewhere to
contradict the impression—that he would not be
slow to resent the criticisms, slanders, or injuries of
strangers or the world, and that he bore himself
towards them with a proud, if silent, self-sufficiency.
But, we surmise, for anyone whom he loved

> He carried anger as a flint bears fire ;
> Who, much enforced, shows a hasty spark
> And straight is cold again ;

and towards anyone so fondly loved as the friend of
the Sonnets he was probably incapable of fierce or
prolonged resentment.

[1] This does not imply that the Sonnets are as early as the *Two
Gentlemen of Verona*, and much less that they are earlier.

The Sonnets must not occupy us further; and I will not dwell on the indications they afford that Shakespeare sometimes felt bitterly both the social inferiority of his position as an actor,[1] and its influence on his own character; or that (as we have already conjectured) he may sometimes have played the fool in society, sometimes felt weary of life, and often was over-tired by work. It is time to pass on to a few hesitating conjectures about what may be called his tastes.

Some passages of his about music have become household words. It is not downright impossible that, like Bottom, having only a reasonable good ear, he liked best the tongs and the bones; that he wondered, with Benedick, how sheeps-guts should hale souls out of men's bodies; and that he wrote the famous lines in the *Merchant of Venice* and in *Twelfth Night* from mere observation and imagination. But it is futile to deal with scepticism run well-nigh mad, and certainly inaccessible to argument from the cases of poets whose tastes are matter of knowledge. Assuming therefore that Shakespeare was fond of music, I may draw attention to two points. Almost always he speaks of music as having a softening, tranquillising, or pensive influence. It lulls killing care and grief of heart to sleep. It soothes the sick and weary, and even makes them drowsy. Hamlet calls for it in his hysterical excitement after the success of the play scene. When it is hoped that Lear's long sleep will have carried his madness away, music is played as he awakes, apparently to increase the desired 'temperance.' It harmonises with the still and moonlit night, and the dreamy happiness of newly-

---

[1] This seems to be referred to in lines by John Davies of Hereford, reprinted in Ingleby's *Shakespeare's Centurie of Prayse*, second edition, pp. 58, 84, 94. In the first of these passages, dated 1603 (and perhaps in the second, 1609), there are signs that Davies had read Sonnet 111, a fact to be noted with regard to the question of the chronology of the Sonnets.

wedded lovers. Almost all the rare allusions to lively or exciting music, apart from dancing, refer, I believe, to 'the lofty instruments of *war*.' These facts would almost certainly have a personal significance if Shakespeare were a more modern poet. Whether they have any, or have much, in an Elizabethan I do not venture to judge.

The second point is diminutive, but it may be connected with the first. The Duke in *Measure for Measure* observes that music often has

a charm
To make bad good and good provoke to harm.

If we ask how it should provoke good to harm, we may recall what was said (p. 326) of the weaknesses of some poetic natures, and that no one speaks more feelingly of music than Orsino; further, how he refers to music as 'the food of love,' and who it is that almost repeats the phrase.

Give me some music: music, moody food
Of us that trade in love:

—the words are Cleopatra's.[1] Did Shakespeare as he wrote them remember, I wonder, the dark lady to whose music he had listened (Sonnet 128)?

We should be greatly surprised to find in Shakespeare signs of the nineteenth century feeling for mountain scenery, but we can no more doubt that within certain limits he was sensitive to the beauty of nature than that he was fond of music.[2] The only

[1]'Mistress Tearsheet' too 'would fain hear some music,' and 'Sneak's noise' had to be sent for (2 *Henry IV.*, II. iv. 12).

[2] It is tempting, though not safe, to infer from the *Tempest* and the great passage in *Pericles* that Shakespeare must have been in a storm at sea ; but that he felt the poetry of a sea-storm is beyond all doubt. Few moments in the reading of his works are more overwhelming than that in which, after listening not without difficulty to the writer of the first two Acts of *Pericles*, suddenly, as the third opens, one hears the authentic voice :

Thou god of this great vast, rebuke these surges
That wash both heaven and hell. . . . The seaman's whistle
Is as a whisper in the ears of death,
Unheard.

Knowing that this is coming, I cannot stop to read the Prologue to

question is whether we can guess at any preferences here. It is probably inevitable that the flowers most often mentioned should be the rose and the lily ;[1] but hardly that the violet should come next and not far behind, and that the fragrance of the violet should be spoken of more often even than that of the rose, and, it seems, with special affection. This may be a fancy, and it will be thought a sentimental fancy too ; but poets, like other people, may have favourite flowers ; that of Keats, we happen to know, was the violet.

Again, if we may draw any conclusion from the frequency and the character of the allusions, the lark held for Shakespeare the place of honour among birds ; and the lines,

> Hark ! hark ! the lark at heaven's gate sings,
> And Phœbus gins arise,

may suggest one reason for this. The lark, as several other collocations show, was to him the bird of joy that welcomes the sun ; and it can hardly be doubted that dawn and early morning was the time of day that most appealed to him. That he felt the beauty of night and of moonlight is obvious; but we find very little to match the lines in *Richard II.*,

> The setting sun, and music at the close,
> As the last taste of sweets, is sweetest last ;

and still less to prove that he felt the magic of

Act III., though I believe Shakespeare wrote it. How it can be imagined that he did more than touch up Acts I. and II. passes my comprehension.

I may call attention to another point. Unless I mistake, there is nothing in Shakespeare's authorities, as known to us, which corresponds with the feeling of Timon's last speech, beginning,

> Come not to me again : but say to Athens,
> Timon hath made his everlasting mansion
> Upon the beached verge of the salt flood :

a feeling made more explicit in the final speech of Alcibiades.

[1] The lily seems to be in almost all cases the Madonna lily. It is very doubtful whether the lily of the valley is referred to at all

evening twilight, the 'heavenliest hour' of a famous
passage in *Don Juan*.   There is a wonderful line in
Sonnet 132,

> And that full star that ushers in the even,

but I remember little else of the same kind.   Shakespeare, as it happens, uses the word 'twilight' only
once, and in an unforgetable passage :

> In me thou see'st the twilight of such day
> As after sunset fadeth in the west :
> Which by and by black night doth take away,
> Death's second self that seals up all in rest.

And this feeling, though not often so solemn, is on
the whole the prevailing sentiment in the references
to sunset and evening twilight.   It corresponds with
the analogy between the times of the day and the
periods of human life.   The sun sets from the
weariness of age ; but he rises in the strength and
freshness of youth, firing the proud tops of the
eastern pines, and turning the hills and the sea into
burnished gold, while jocund day stands tiptoe on
the misty mountain tops, and the lark sings at the
gate of heaven.   In almost all the familiar lines
about dawn one seems to catch that 'indescribable
gusto' which Keats heard in Kean's delivery of the
words :

> Stir with the lark to-morrow, gentle Norfolk.

Two suggestions may be ventured as to Shakespeare's feelings towards four-footed animals.   The
first must be very tentative.   We do not expect in
a writer of that age the sympathy with animals
which is so beautiful a trait in much of the poetry
of the last hundred and fifty years.   And I can
remember in Shakespeare scarcely any sign of *fondness* for an animal,—not even for a horse, though he
wrote so often of horses.   But there are rather
frequent, if casual, expressions of pity, in references,
for example, to the hunted hare or stag, or to the

spurred horse :[1] and it may be questioned whether
the passage in *As You Like It* about the wounded
deer is quite devoid of personal significance. No
doubt Shakespeare thought the tears of Jaques
sentimental; but he put a piece of himself into
Jaques. And, besides, it is not Jaques alone who
dislikes the killing of the deer, but the Duke; and
we may surely hear some tone of Shakespeare's
voice in the Duke's speech about the life in the
forest. Perhaps we may surmise that, while he
enjoyed field-sports, he felt them at times to be out
of tune with the harmony of nature.

On the second point, I regret to say, I can feel
no doubt. Shakespeare did not care for dogs, as
Homer did; he even disliked them, as Goethe did.
Of course he can write eloquently about the points
of hounds and the music of their voices in the
chase, and humorously about Launce's love for his
cur and even about the cur himself; but this is no
more significant on the one side than is his conventional use of 'dog' as a term of abuse on the
other. What is significant is the absence of allusion, or (to be perfectly accurate) of sympathetic
allusion, to the characteristic virtues of dogs, and
the abundance of allusions of an insulting kind.
Shakespeare has observed and recorded, in some
instances profusely, every vice that I can think of
in an ill-conditioned dog. He fawns and cringes
and flatters, and then bites the hand that caressed
him; he is a coward who attacks you from behind,
and barks at you the more the farther off you
go; he knows neither charity, humanity, nor gratitude; as he flatters power and wealth, so he takes

---

[1] But there is something disappointing, and even estranging, in
Sonnet 50, which, promising to show a real sympathy, cheats us in
the end. I may observe, without implying that the fact has any
personal significance, that the words about 'the poor beetle that
we tread upon' are given to a woman (Isabella), and that it is Marina
who says :

I trod upon a worm against my will,
But I wept for it.

part against the poor and unfashionable, and if fortune turns against you so does he.[1] The plays swarm with these charges. Whately's exclamation —uttered after a College meeting or a meeting of Chapter, I forget which—'The more I see of men, the more I like dogs,' would never have been echoed by Shakespeare. The things he most loathed in men he found in dogs too. And yet all this might go for nothing if we could set anything of weight against it. But what can we set? Nothing whatever, so far as I remember, except a recognition of courage in bear-baiting, bull-baiting mastiffs. For I cannot quote as favourable to the spaniel the appeal of Helena :

> I am your spaniel; and, Demetrius,
> The more you beat me I will fawn on you :
> Use me but as your spaniel, spurn me, strike me,
> Neglect me, lose me ; only give me leave,
> Unworthy as I am, to follow you.

This may show that Shakespeare was alive to the baseness of a spaniel-owner, but not that he appreciated that self-less affection which he describes. It is more probable that it irritated him, as it does many men still ; and, as for its implying fidelity, there is no reference, I believe, to the fidelity of the dog in the whole of his works, and he chooses the spaniel himself as a symbol of flattery and ingratitude : his Cæsar talks of

> Knee-crooked court'sies and base spaniel-fawning ;

his Antony exclaims :

> the hearts
> That spaniel'd me at heels, to whom I gave
> Their wishes, do discandy, melt their sweets
> On blossoming Cæsar.

To all that he loved most in men he was blind in dogs. And then we call him universal!

---

[1] Three times in one drama Shakespeare refers to this detestable trait. See *Shakespearean Tragedy*, p. 268, where I should like to qualify still further the sentence containing the qualification 'on the whole.' Good judges, at least, assure me that I have admitted too much against the dog.

This line of research into Shakespeare's tastes
might be pursued a good deal further, but we must
return to weightier matters. We saw that he could
sympathise with anyone who erred and suffered
from impulse, affections of the blood, or even such
passions as were probably no danger to himself,—
ambition, for instance, and pride. Can we learn
anything more about him by observing virtues or
types of character with which he appears to feel
little sympathy, though he may approve them? He
certainly does not show this imperfect sympathy
towards self-control ; we seem to feel even a special
liking for Brutus, and again for Horatio, who has
suffered much, is quietly patient, and has mastered
both himself and fortune. But, not to speak of
coldly selfish natures, he seems averse to bloodless
people, those who lack, or those who have deadened,
the natural desires for joy and sympathy, and those
who tend to be precise.[1] Nor does he appear to
be drawn to men who, as we say, try to live or to
act on principle ; nor to those who aim habitually
at self-improvement ; nor yet to the saintly type of
character. I mean, not that he *could* not sympathise
with them, but that they did not attract him.
Isabella, in *Measure for Measure*, is drawn, of
course, with understanding, but, it seems to me,
with little sympathy. Her readiness to abandon her
pleading for Claudio, out of horror at his sin and
a sense of the justice of Angelo's reasons for refusing his pardon, is doubtless in character ; but if
Shakespeare had sympathised more with her at this
point, so should we ; while, as it is, we are tempted
to exclaim,

> She loves him not, she wants the natural touch ;

and perhaps if Shakespeare had liked her better and
had not regarded her with some irony, he would

---

[1] Nor can I recall any sign of liking, or even approval, of that
'prudent, *cautious*, self-control' which, according to a passage in
Burns, is 'wisdom's root.'

not have allowed himself, for mere convenience,
to degrade her by marrying her to the Duke.
Brutus and Cordelia, on the other hand, are drawn
with the fullest imaginative sympathy, and they, it
may be said, are characters of principle; but then
(even if Cordelia could be truly so described) they
are also intensely affectionate, and by no means
inhumanly self-controlled.

The mention of Brutus may carry us somewhat
farther. Shakespeare's Brutus kills Cæsar, not
because Cæsar aims at absolute power, but because
Brutus fears that absolute power may make him
cruel. That is not Plutarch's idea, it is Shakespeare's. He could fully sympathise with the
gentleness of Brutus, with his entire superiority to
private aims and almost entire freedom from personal susceptibilities, and even with his resolution
to sacrifice his friend; but he could not so sympathise with mere horror of monarchy or absolute
power. And now extend this a little. Can you
imagine Shakespeare an enthusiast for an 'idea'; a
devotee of divine right, or the rights of Parliament,
or any particular form of government in Church or
State; a Fifth Monarchy man, or a Quaker, or a
thick-and-thin adherent of any compact, exclusive,
abstract creed, even if it were as rational and noble
as Mazzini's? This type of mind, even at its best,
is alien from his. Scott is said, rightly or wrongly,
to have portrayed the Covenanters without any deep
understanding of them; it would have been the
same with Shakespeare. I am not praising him,
or at least not merely praising him. One may even
suggest that on this side he was limited. In any
age he would have been safe against fanaticism and
one-sided ideas; but perhaps in no age would he
have been the man to insist with the necessary
emphasis on those one-sided ideas which the moment
may need, or even to give his whole heart to men
who join a forlorn hope or are martyred for a faith.

And though it is rash to suggest that anything in the way of imagination was beyond his reach, perhaps the legend of Faust, with his longings for infinite power and knowledge and enjoyment of beauty, would have suited him less well than Marlowe; and if he had written on the subject that Cervantes took, his Don Quixote would have been at least as laughable as the hero we know, but would he have been a soul so ideally noble and a figure so profoundly pathetic?

This would be the natural place to discuss Shakespeare's politics if we were to discuss them at all. But even if the question whether he shows any interest in the political differences of his time, or any sympathies or antipathies in regard to them, admits of an answer, it could be answered only by an examination of details; and I must pass it by, and offer only the briefest remarks on a wider question. Shakespeare, as we might expect, shows no sign of believing in what is sometimes called a political 'principle.' The main ideas which, consciously or unconsciously, seem to govern or emerge from his presentation of state affairs, might perhaps be put thus. National welfare is the end of politics, and the criterion by which political actions are to be judged. It implies of necessity 'degree'; that is, differences of position and function in the members of the body politic.[1] And the first requisites of national welfare are the observance of this degree, and the concordant performance of these functions in the general interest. But there appear to be no further absolute principles than these: beyond them all is relative to the particular case and its particular conditions. We find no hint, for example, in *Julius Cæsar* that Shakespeare regarded a monarchical form of government as intrinsically better than a republican, or *vice versa*; no trace in *Richard II.* that the author shares the king's belief in his

[1] The *locus classicus*, of course, is *Troilus and Cressida*, I. iii. 75 ff.

inviolable right, or regards Bolingbroke's usurpation
as justifiable. We perceive, again, pretty clearly
in several plays a dislike and contempt of dema-
gogues, and an opinion that mobs are foolish, fickle,
and ungrateful. But these are sentiments which the
most determined of believers in democracy, if he has
sense, may share ; and if he thinks that the attitude
of aristocrats like Volumnia and Coriolanus is
inhuman and as inexcusable as that of the mob, and
that a mob is as easily led right as wrong and has
plenty of good nature in it, he has abundant ground
for holding that Shakespeare thought so too. That
Shakespeare greatly liked and admired the typical
qualities of the best kind of aristocrat seems highly
probable ; but then this taste has always been compatible with a great variety of political opinions.
It is interesting but useless to wonder what his own
opinions would have been at various periods of
English history : perhaps the only thing we can be
pretty sure of in regard to them is that they would
never have been extreme, and that he would never
have supposed his opponents to be entirely wrong.

We have tried to conjecture the impulses,
passions, and errors with which Shakespeare could
easily sympathise, and the virtues and types of
character which he may have approved without
much sympathy. It remains to ask whether we can
notice tendencies and vices to which he felt any
special antipathy ; and it is obvious and safe to
point to those most alien to a gentle, open, and
free nature, the vices of a cold and hard disposition.
self-centred and incapable of fusion with others.
Passing over, again, the plainly hideous forms or
extremes of such vice, as we see them in characters
like Richard III., Iago, Goneril and Regan, or the
Queen in *Cymbeline*, we seem to detect a particular
aversion to certain vices which have the common
mark of baseness ; for instance, servility and flattery

(especially when deliberate and practised with a view to self-advancement), feigning in friendship, and ingratitude. Shakespeare's *animus* against the dog arises from the attribution of these vices to him, and against them in men are directed the invectives which seem to have a personal ring. There appears to be traceable also a feeling of a special, though less painful, kind against unmercifulness. I do not mean, of course, cruelty, but unforgivingness, and even the tendency to prefer justice to mercy. From no other dramatic author, probably, could there be collected such prolonged and heart-felt praises of mercy as from Shakespeare. He had not at all strongly, I think, that instinct and love of justice and retribution which in many men are so powerful ; but Prospero's words,

> they being penitent,
> The sole drift of my purpose doth extend
> Not a jot further,

came from his heart. He perceived with extreme clearness the connection of acts with their consequences ; but his belief that in this sense 'the gods are just' was accompanied by the strongest feeling that forgiveness ought to follow repentance, and (if I may so put it) his favourite petition was the one that begins 'Forgive us our trespasses.' To conclude, I have fancied that he shows an unusual degree of disgust at slander and dislike of censoriousness ; and where he speaks in the Sonnets of those who censured him he betrays an exceptionally decided feeling that a man's offences are his own affair and not the world's.[1]

Some of the vices which seem to have been particularly odious to Shakespeare have, we may notice, a special connection with prosperity and power. Men feign and creep and flatter to please

---

[1] Of all the evils inflicted by man on man those chosen for mention in the dirge in *Cymbeline*, one of the last plays, are the frown o' the great, the tyrant's stroke, slander, censure rash.

the powerful and to win their own way to ease or
power; and they envy and censure and slander
their competitors in the race; and when they
succeed, they are ungrateful to their friends and
helpers and patrons; and they become hard and
unmerciful, and despise and bully those who are
now below them. So, perhaps, Shakespeare said
to himself in those years when, as we imagine,
melancholy and embitterment often overclouded his
sky, though they did not obscure his faith in goodness and much less his intellectual vision. And
prosperity and power, he may have added, come
less frequently by merit than by those base arts
or by mere fortune. The divorce of goodness and
power was, to Shelley, the 'woe of the world';
if we substitute for 'goodness' the wider word
'merit,' we may say that this divorce, with the evil
bred by power, is to Shakespeare also the root of
bitterness. This fact, presented in its extreme form
of the appalling cruelty of the prosperous, and the
heartrending suffering of the defenceless, forms
the problem of his most tremendous drama. We
have no reason to surmise that his own sufferings
were calamitous; and the period which seems to
be marked by melancholy and embitterment was
one of outward, or at least financial, prosperity; but
nevertheless we can hardly doubt that he felt on
the small scale of his own life the influence of that
divorce of power and merit. His complaint against
Fortune, who had so ill provided for his life, runs
through the Sonnets. Even if we could regard as
purely conventional the declarations that his verses
would make his friend immortal, it is totally impossible that he can have been unaware of the gulf
between his own gifts and those of others, or can
have failed to feel the disproportion between his position and his mind. Hamlet had never experienced

> the spurns
> That patient merit of the unworthy takes,

and that make the patient soul weary of life; the
man who had experienced them was the writer of
Sonnet 66, who cried for death because he was tired
with beholding

> desert a beggar born,
> And needy nothing trimmed in jollity,

—a beggarly soul flaunting in brave array. Neither
had Hamlet felt in his own person 'the insolence of
office'; but the actor had doubtless felt it often
enough, and we can hardly err in hearing his own
voice in dramatic expressions of wonder and contempt at the stupid pride of mere authority and at
men's slavish respect for it. Two examples will
suffice. 'Thou hast seen a farmer's dog bark at a
beggar, and the creature run from the cur? There
thou mightst behold the great image of authority.
A dog's obeyed in office': so says Lear, when
madness has cleared his vision, and indignation
makes the Timon-like verses that follow. The
other example is almost too famous for quotation
but I have a reason for quoting it:

> man, proud man,
> Drest in a little brief authority,
> Most ignorant of what he's most assured,
> His glassy essence, like an angry ape,
> Plays such fantastic tricks before high heaven
> As makes the angels weep; who, with our spleens,
> Would all themselves laugh mortal.

It is Isabella who says that; but it is scarcely in
character; Shakespeare himself is speaking.[1]

It is with great hesitation that I hazard a few
words on Shakespeare's religion. Any attempt to
penetrate his reserve on this subject may appear a
crowning impertinence; and, since his dramas are
almost exclusively secular, any impressions we

---

[1] Having written these paragraphs, I should like to disclaim the
belief that Shakespeare was habitually deeply discontented with his
position in life.

may form must here be even more speculative than
usual.   Yet it is scarcely possible to read him much
without such speculations ; and there are at least
some theories which may confidently be dismissed.
It cannot be called absolutely impossible that Shakespeare was indifferent to music and to the beauty of
Nature, and yet the idea is absurd ; and in the same
way it is barely possible, and yet it is preposterous,
to suppose that he was an ardent and devoted
atheist or Brownist or Roman Catholic, and that
all the indications to the contrary are due to his
artfulness and determination not to get into trouble.
There is no absurdity, on the other hand, nor of
necessity anything hopeless, in the question whether
there are signs that he belonged to this or that
church, and was inclined to one mode of thought
within it rather than to another.   Only the question
is scarcely worth asking for our present purpose,
unless there is some reason to believe that he took
a keen interest in these matters.   Suppose, for
example, that we had ground to accept a tradition
that he 'died a papist,' this would not tell us much
about him unless we had also ground to think that
he lived a papist, and that his faith went far into
his personality.   But in fact we receive from his
writings, it appears to me, a rather strong impression that he concerned himself little, if at all, with
differences of doctrine or church government.[1]   And
we may go further.   Have we not reason to surmise
that he was not, in the distinctive sense of the
word, a religious man—a man, that is to say, whose
feelings and actions are constantly and strongly
influenced by thoughts of his relation to an object of
worship ?   If Shakespeare had been such a man, is
it credible that we should find nothing in tradition
or in his works to indicate the fact ; and is it likely

[1] Allusions to puritans show at most what we take almost for
granted, that he did not like precisians or people hostile to the
stage.

that we should find in his works some things that we do find there?[1]

Venturing with much doubt a little farther I will put together certain facts and impressions without at once drawing any conclusion from them. Almost all the speeches that can be called pronouncedly religious and Christian in phraseology and spirit are placed in the mouths of persons to whom they are obviously appropriate, either from their position (*e.g.* bishops, friars, nuns), or from what Shakespeare found in histories (*e.g.* Henry IV., V., and VI.), or for some other plain reason. We cannot build, therefore, on these speeches in the least. On the other hand (except, of course, where they are hypocritical or politic), we perceive in Shakespeare's tone in regard to them not the faintest trace of dislike or contempt; nor can we find a trace anywhere of such feelings, or of irreverence, towards Christian ideas, institutions, or customs (mere humorous irreverence is not relevant here); and in the case of 'sympathetic' characters, living in Christian times but not in any decided sense religious, no disposition is visible to suppress or ignore their belief in, and use of, religious ideas. Some characters, again, Christian or heathen, who appear to be drawn with rather marked sympathy, have strong, if simple, religious convictions (*e.g.* Horatio, Edgar, Hermione); and in others, of whom so much can hardly be said, but who strike many readers, rightly or wrongly, as having a good deal of Shakespeare in

---

[1] In the Sonnets, for example, there is an almost entire absence of definitely religious thought or feeling. The nearest approach to it is in Sonnet 146 ('Poor soul, the centre of my sinful earth'), where, however, there is no allusion to a divine law or judge. According to Sonnet 129, lust in action is

The expense of spirit in a waste of shame;

but no word shows that it is also felt as alienation from God. It must be added that in 108 and 110 there are references to the Lord's Prayer and, perhaps, to the First Commandment, from which a decidedly religious Christian would perhaps have shrunk. Of course I am not saying that we can draw any *necessary* inference from these facts.

them (*e.g.* Romeo and Hamlet), we observe a quiet but deep sense that they and other men are neither their own masters nor responsible only to themselves and other men, but are in the hands of 'Providence' or guiding powers 'above.'[1]

To this I will add two remarks. To every one, I suppose, certain speeches sound peculiarly personal. Perhaps others may share my feeling about Hamlet's words :

> There's a divinity that shapes our ends,
> Rough-hew them how we will ;

and about those other words of his :

> There are more things in heaven and earth, Horatio,
> Than are dreamt of in your philosophy ;

and about the speech of Prospero ending, 'We are such stuff as dreams are made on.'[2] On the other hand, we observe that Hamlet seems to have arrived at that conviction as to the 'divinity' after reflection, and that, while he usually speaks as one who accepts the received Christian ideas, yet, when meditating

[1] It is only this 'quiet but deep sense' that is significant. No inference can be drawn from the fact that the mere belief in powers above seems to be taken as a matter of course in practically all the characters, good and bad alike. On the other hand there may well be something symptomatic in the apparent absence of interest in theoretical disbelief in such powers and in the immortality of the soul. I have observed elsewhere that the atheism of Aaron does not increase the probability that the conception of the character is Shakespeare's.

[2] With the first compare, what to me has, though more faintly, the same ring, Hermione's
> If powers divine
> Behold our human actions, as they do :

with the second, Helena's
> It is not so with Him that all things knows
> As 'tis with us that square our guess by shows ;
> But most it is presumption in us when
> The help of heaven we count the act of men :

followed soon after by Lafeu's remark :

They say miracles are past ; and we have our philosophical persons to make modern and familiar things supernatural and causeless. Hence it is that we make trifles of terrors, ensconcing ourselves into seeming knowledge, when we should submit ourselves to an unknown fear.

profoundly, he appears to ignore them.[1] In the same way the Duke in *Measure for Measure* is for the most part, and necessarily, a Christian ; yet nobody would guess it from the great speech, 'Be absolute for death,' addressed by a supposed friar to a youth under sentence to die, yet containing not a syllable about a future life.[2]

Without adducing more of the endless but baffling material for a conclusion, I will offer the result left on my mind, and, merely for the sake of brevity, will state it with hardly any of the qualifications it doubtless needs. Shakespeare, I imagine, was not, in the sense assigned to the word some minutes ago, a religious man. Nor was it natural to him to regard good and evil, better and worse, habitually from a theological point of view. But (this appears certain) he had a lively and serious sense of 'conscience,' of the pain of self-reproach and self-condemnation, and of the torment to which this pain might rise.[3] He was not in the least disposed to regard conscience as somehow illusory or a human invention, but on the contrary thought of it (I use the most non-committal phrase I can find) as connected with the power that rules the world and is not escapable by man. He realised very fully and felt very keenly, after his youth was past

[1] It is worth noting that the reference, which appears in the First Quarto version of 'To be or not to be,' to 'an everlasting judge,' disappears in the revised versions.

[2] The suggested inference, of course, is that this speech, thus out of character, and Hamlet's 'To be or not to be' (though that is in character), show us Shakespeare's own mind. It has force, I think, but not compulsory force. The topics of these speeches are, in the old sense of the word, commonplaces. Shakespeare may have felt, Here is my chance to show what I can do with certain feelings and thoughts of supreme interest to men of all times and places and modes of belief. It would not follow from this that they are not 'personal,' but any inference to a non-acceptance of received religious ideas would be much weakened. ('All the world's a stage' is a patent example of the suggested elaboration of a commonplace.)

[3] What actions in particular *his* conscience approved and disapproved is another question and one not relevant here.

and at certain times of stress, the sufferings and wrongs of men, the strength of evil, the hideousness of certain forms of it, and its apparent incurability in certain cases. And he must sometimes have felt all this as a terrible problem. But, however he may have been tempted, and may have yielded, to exasperation and even despair, he never doubted that it is best to be good; felt more and more that one must be patient and must forgive;[1] and probably maintained unbroken a conviction, practical if not formulated, that to be good is to be at peace with that unescapable power. But it is unlikely that he attempted to theorise further on the nature of the power. All was for him, in the end, mystery; and, while we have no reason whatever to attribute to him a belief in the ghosts and oracles he used in his dramas, he had no inclination to play the spy on God or to limit his power by our notions of it. That he had dreams and ponderings about the mystery such as he never put into the mouths of actors I do not doubt; but I imagine they were no more than dreams and ponderings and movings about in worlds unrealised.

Whether to this 'religion' he joined a more or less conventional acceptance of some or all of the usual Christian ideas, it is impossible to tell. There is no great improbability to me in the idea that he did not, but it is more probable to me that he did,— that, in fact, though he was never so tormented as Hamlet, his position in this matter was, at least in middle life (and he never reached old age), much like Hamlet's. If this were so it might naturally happen that, as he grew older and wearier of labour, and perhaps of the tumult of pleasure and thought and pain, his more personal religion, the natural piety which seems to gain in weight and serenity in the latest plays, came to be more closely joined with

---

[1] This does not at all imply to Shakespeare, so far as we see, that evil is never to be forcibly resisted.

Christian ideas. But I can find no clear indications that this did happen; and though some have believed that they discovered these ideas displayed in full, though not explicitly, in the *Tempest*, I am not able to hear there more than the stream of Shakespeare's own 'religion' moving with its fullest volume and making its deepest and most harmonious music.[1]

This lecture must end, though its subject is endless, and I will touch on only one point more,—one that may to some extent recall and connect the scattered suggestions I have offered.

If we were obliged to answer the question which of Shakespeare's plays contains, not indeed the fullest picture of his mind, but the truest expression of his nature and habitual temper, unaffected by special causes of exhilaration or gloom, I should be disposed to choose *As You Like It*. It wants, to go no further, the addition of a touch of Sir Toby or Falstaff, and the ejection of its miraculous conversions of ill-disposed characters. But the misbehaviour of Fortune, and the hardness and ingratitude of men, form the basis of its plot, and are a frequent topic of complaint. And, on the other hand, he who is reading it has a smooth brow and smiling lips, and a heart that murmurs,

> Happy is your grace,
> That can translate the stubbornness of fortune
> Into so quiet and so sweet a style.

[1] I do not mean to reject the idea that in some passages in the *Tempest* Shakespeare, while he wrote them with a dramatic purpose, also thought of himself. It seems to me likely. And if so, there *may* have been such a thought in the words,

> And thence retire me to my Milan, where
> Every third thought shall be my grave;

and also in those lines about prayer and pardon which close the Epilogue, and to my ear come with a sudden effect of great seriousness, contrasting most strangely with their context. If they *had* a grave and personal under-meaning it cannot have been intended for the audience, which would take the prayer as addressed to itself.

And it is full not only of sweetness, but of romance,
fun, humour of various kinds, delight in the oddities
of human nature, love of modesty and fidelity and
high spirit and patience, dislike of scandal and censure, contemplative curiosity, the feeling that in the
end we are all merely players, together with a touch
of the feeling that

> Then is there mirth in heaven
> When earthly things made even
> Atone together.

And, finally, it breathes the serene holiday mood of
escape from the toil, competition, and corruption of
city and court into the sun and shadow and peace
of the country, where one can be idle and dream
and meditate and sing, and pursue or watch the deer
as the fancy takes one, and make love or smile at
lovers according to one's age.[1]

If, again, the question were put to us, which of
Shakespeare's characters reveals most of his personality, the majority of those who consented to
give an answer would answer 'Hamlet.' This
impression may be fanciful, but it is difficult to
think it wholly so, and, speaking for those who share
it, I will try to trace some of its sources. There is
a good deal of Shakespeare that is not in Hamlet.
But Hamlet, we think, is the only character in
Shakespeare who could possibly have composed his
plays (though it appears unlikely, from his verses to
Ophelia, that he could have written the best songs).
Into Hamlet's mouth are put what are evidently
Shakespeare's own views on drama and acting.
Hamlet alone, among the great serious characters,
can be called a humorist. When in some trait of
another character we seem to touch Shakespeare's

---

[1] It may be added that *As You Like It*, though idyllic, is not so
falsely idyllic as some critics would make it. It is based, we may
roughly say, on a contrast between court and country ; but those who
inhale virtue from the woodland are courtiers who bring virtue with
them, and the country has its churlish masters and unkind or uncouth
maidens.

personality, we are frequently reminded of Hamlet.[1] When in a profound reflective speech we hear Shakespeare's voice, we usually hear Hamlet's too, and his peculiar humour and turns of phrase appear unexpectedly in persons otherwise unlike him and unlike one another. The most melancholy group of Sonnets (71-74) recalls Hamlet at once, here and there recalls even his words ; and he and the writer of Sonnet 66 both recount in a list the ills that make men long for death. And then Hamlet ' was indeed honest and of an open and free nature' ; sweet-tempered and modest, yet not slow to resent calumny or injury; of a serious but not a melancholy disposition ; and the lover of his friend. And, with these traits, we remember his poet ecstasy at the glory of earth and sky and the marvellous endowments of man ; his eager affectionate response to everything noble or sweet in human nature; his tendency to dream and to live in the world of his own mind ; his liability to sudden vehement emotion, and his admiration for men whose blood and judgment are better commingled; the overwhelming effect of disillusionment upon him ; his sadness, fierceness, bitterness and cynicism. All this, and more : his sensitiveness to the call of duty ; his longing to answer to it, and his anguish over his strange delay ; the conviction gathering in his tortured soul that man's purposes and failures are divinely shaped to ends beyond his vision ; his incessant meditation, and his sense that there are mysteries which no meditation can fathom ; nay, even little traits like his recourse to music to calm his excitement, or his feeling on the one hand that the peasant should not tread on the courtier's heels, and on the other that the mere courtier is spacious in the possession of dirt—all this, I say, corresponds with our impression of Shakespeare, or rather of characteristic traits in Shakespeare, probably here

[1] This has been strongly urged and fully illustrated by Mr. Harris.

and there a good deal heightened, and mingled with others not characteristic of Shakespeare at all. And if this is more than fancy, it may explain to us why Hamlet is the most fascinating character, and the most inexhaustible, in all imaginative literature. What else should he be, if the world's greatest poet, who was able to give almost the reality of nature to creations totally unlike himself, put his own soul straight into this creation, and when he wrote Hamlet's speeches wrote down his own heart?[1]

1904.

[1] It may be suggested that, in the catalogue above, I should have mentioned that imaginative 'unreality' in love referred to on p. 326. But I do not see in Hamlet either this, or any sign that he took Ophelia for an Imogen or even a Juliet, though naturally he was less clearly aware of her deficiencies than Shakespeare.

I may add, however, another item to the catalogue. We do not feel that the problems presented to most of the tragic heroes could have been fatal to Shakespeare himself. The immense breadth and clearness of his intellect would have saved him from the fate of Othello, Troilus, or Antony. But we do feel, I think, and he himself may have felt, that he could not have coped with Hamlet's problem ; and there is no improbability in the idea that he may have experienced in some degree the melancholia of his hero.

SHAKESPEARE'S THEATRE AND AUDIENCE.

SHAKESPEARE'S THEATRE AND AUDIENCE.

WHY should we concern ourselves with Shakespeare's theatre and audience? The vast majority of his readers since the Restoration have known nothing about them, and have enjoyed his plays enormously. And if they have enjoyed without fully understanding, it was for want of imagination and of knowledge of human nature, and not from ignorance of the conditions under which his plays were produced. At any rate, such ignorance does not exclude us from the *soul* of Shakespearean drama, any more than from the soul of Homeric epic or Athenian tragedy; and it is the soul that counts and endures. For the rest, we all know that Shakespeare's time was rough, indecorous, and inexpert in regard to machinery; and so we are prepared for coarse speech and primitive stage-arrangements, and we make allowance for them without thinking about the matter. Antiquarians may naturally wish to know more; but what more is needed for intelligent enjoyment of the plays?

I have begun with these questions because I sympathise with their spirit. Everything I am going to speak of in this lecture is comparatively unimportant for the appreciation of that which is most vital in Shakespeare; and if I were allowed my choice between an hour's inspection of a performance at the Globe and a glimpse straight into his mind when he was planning the *Tempest*, I should not hesitate which to choose. Nevertheless, to say nothing of the intrinsic interest of antiquarian knowledge, we cannot make a clear division between the soul and body, or the eternal and the perishable, in works of art. Nor can we lay the finger on a line which separates that which has poetic interest from that which has none. Nor yet can we assume that any knowledge of Shakespeare's theatre and audience, however trivial it may appear, may not help us to appreciate, or save us from misapprehending, the 'soul' of a play or a scene. If our own souls were capacious and vivid enough, every atom of information on these subjects, or again on the material he used in composing, would so assist us. The danger of devotion to such knowledge lies merely in our weakness. Research, though toilsome, is easy ; imaginative vision, though delightful, is difficult; and we may be tempted to prefer the first. Or we note that in a given passage Shakespeare has used what he found in his authority ; and we excuse ourselves from asking why he used it and what he made of it. Or we see that he has done something that would please his audience ; and we dismiss it as accounted for, forgetting that perhaps it also pleased *him*, and that we have to account for *that*. Or knowledge of his stage shows us the stage-convenience of a scene ; and we say that the scene was due to stage-convenience, as if the cause of a thing must needs be single and simple. Such errors provoke the man who reads his Shakespeare poetically, and make him blaspheme our knowledge. But we ought not to fall into them ; and we cannot reject any knowledge that may help us into Shakespeare's mind because of the danger it brings.

I cannot attempt to describe Shakespeare's theatre and audience, and much less to discuss the evidence on which a description must be based, or the difficult problems it raises. I must confine myself for the

most part to a few points which are not always fully
realised, or on which there is a risk of misapprehension.

I.

Shakespeare, we know, was a popular playwright.
I mean not only that many of his plays were
favourites in his day, but that he wrote, mainly at
least, for the more popular kind of audience, and
that, within certain limits, he conformed to its tastes.
He was not, to our knowledge, the author of
masques composed for performance at Court or in a
great mansion, or of dramas intended for a University or one of the Inns of Court; and though his
company for some time played at the Blackfriars, we
may safely assume that the great majority of his
works were meant primarily for a common or 'public'
theatre like the Globe. The broad distinction between a 'private' and a 'public' theatre is familiar,
and I need only remind you that at the former,
which was smaller, provided seats even in the area,
and was nowhere open to the weather, the audience
was more select. Accordingly, dramatists who express their contempt for the audience, and their
disapproval of those who consult its tastes, often
discriminate between the audiences at the private
and public theatres, and reserve their unmeasured
language for the latter. It was for the latter that
Shakespeare mainly wrote; and it is pretty clear
that Jonson, who greatly admired and loved him,
was still of opinion that he condescended to his
audience.[1]

So far we seem to be on safe ground; and yet
even here there is some risk of mistake. We are
not to imagine that the audience at a private theatre
(say the Blackfriars) accepted Jonson's dramatic

---

[1] This, one may suspect, was also the position of Webster, who praises
Shakespeare, but groups him with Dekker and Heywood, and mentions
him after Chapman, Jonson, and Beaumont and Fletcher (Preface to
the *White Devil*).

theories, while the audience at the Globe rejected them; or that the one was composed chiefly of cultured and 'judicious' gentlemen, and the other of riotous and malodorous plebeians; and still less that Shakespeare tried to please the latter section in preference to the former, and was beloved by the one more than by the other. The two audiences must have had the same general character, differing only in degree. Neither of them accepted Jonson's theories, nor were the 'judicious' of one mind on that subject. The same play was frequently offered to both. Both were very mixed. The tastes to which objection was taken cannot have been confined to the mob. From our knowledge of human nature generally, and of the Elizabethan nobility and gentry in particular, we may be sure of this; and Jonson himself implies it. Nor is it credible that an appreciation of the best things was denied to the mob, which doubtless loved what we should despise, but appears also to have admired what we admire, and to have tolerated more poetry than most of us can stomach. Neither can these groundlings have formed the majority of the 'public' audience or have been omnipotent in their theatre, when it was possible for dramatists (Shakespeare included) to say such rude things of them to their faces. We must not delude ourselves as to these matters; and in particular we must realise that the mass of the audience in both kinds of theatre must have been indifferent to the unities of time and place, and more or less so to improbabilities and to decorum (at least as we conceive it) both in manners and in speech; and that it must have liked excitement, the open exhibition of violent and bloody deeds, and the intermixture of seriousness and mirth. What distinguished the more popular audience, and the more popular section in it, was a higher degree of this indifference and this liking, and in addition a special fondness for certain sources of inartistic joy.

The most prominent of these, perhaps, were noise; rant; mere bawdry; 'shews'; irrelevant songs, ballads, jokes, dances, and clownage in general; and, lastly, target-fighting and battles.[1]

We may describe Shakespeare's practice in broad and general terms by saying that he neither resisted the wishes of his audience nor gratified them without reserve. He accepted the type of drama that he found, and developed it without altering its fundamental character. And in the same way, in particular matters, he gave the audience what it wanted, but in doing so gave it what it never dreamed of. It liked tragedy to be relieved by rough mirth, and it got the Grave-diggers in *Hamlet* and the old countryman in *Antony and Cleopatra*. It liked a 'drum and trumpet' history, and it got *Henry V*. It liked clowns or fools, and it got Feste and the Fool in *King Lear*. Shakespeare's practice was by no means always on this level, but this was its tendency; and I imagine that (unless perhaps in early days) he knew clearly what he was doing, did it deliberately, and, when he gave the audience poor stuff, would not seriously have defended himself. Jonson, it would seem, did not understand this position. A fool was a fool to him; and if a play could be called a drum and trumpet history it was at once condemned in his eyes. One can hardly doubt that he was alluding to the *Tempest* and the *Winter's Tale* when, a few years after the probable date of their appearance, he spoke of writers who 'make nature afraid in their plays,' begetting 'tales, tempests, and such like drolleries,' and bringing in 'a servant-monster' or 'a nest of antiques.' Caliban was a 'monster,' and the London public loved to gape at monsters; and so, it appears, that wonderful creation was to Jonson something like the fat woman, or the calf with five legs, that we pay a

[1] I am obliged to speak summarily. Some of these things declined in popularity as time went on.

penny to see at a fair.   In fact (how could he fail to take the warning?) he saw Caliban with the eyes of Trinculo and Stephano.   'A strange fish!' says Trinculo: 'were I in England now, as once I was, and had but this fish painted, not a holiday fool there but would give a piece of silver.'   'If I can recover him,' says Stephano, 'and keep him tame and get to Naples with him, he's a present for any emperor that ever trod on neat's-leather.'   Shakespeare understood his monster otherwise; but, I fancy, when Jonson fulminated at the Mermaid against Caliban, he smiled and said nothing.

But my present subject is rather the tastes of the audience than Shakespeare's way of meeting them.[1]

[1] The examples just cited show his method at its best, and it would be easy to mention others far less satisfactory.   Nor do I doubt that his plays would be much more free from blemishes of various kinds if his audience had added to their virtues greater cultivation.   On the other hand the question whether, or how far, he knowingly 'wrote down to' his audience, in the sense of giving it what he despised, seems to me very difficult, if not impossible, to answer: and I may mention some causes of this difficulty.

(1) There is no general presumption against interpolations in an Elizabethan drama published piratically or after the author's death. We have, further, positive grounds of the strongest kind for believing that 'Shakespeare's plays' contain a good deal that Shakespeare never wrote.   We cannot therefore simply take it for granted that he wrote every silly or offensive thing that we find in the volume; and least of all should we do this when the passage is more or less irrelevant and particularly easy to excise.   I do not say that these considerations have great importance here, but they have some; and readers of Shakespeare, and even some scholars, constantly tend to forget them, and to regard the texts as if they had been published by himself, or by scrupulously careful men of letters immediately after his death.

(2) We must never take for granted that what seems to us feeble or bad seemed so to Shakespeare.   Evidently he was amused by puns and quips and verbal ingenuities in which most of us find little entertainment.   Gross jokes, scarcely redeemed in our eyes by their humour, may have diverted him.   He sometimes writes, and clearly in good faith, what seems to us bombastic or 'conceited.'   So far as this was the case he was not writing down to his audience.   He shared its tastes, or the tastes of some section of it.   So it may have been, again, with such a blot as the blinding of Gloucester on the open stage.

(3) Jonson defied his audience, yet he wrote a good deal that we think bad.   In the same way certain of Shakespeare's faults *cannot* be due to condescension to his audience: *e.g.* the obscurities and distortions of language not infrequent in his later plays.   And this may be

Let me give two illustrations of them which may have some novelty. His public, in the first place, dearly loved to see soldiers, combats, and battles on the stage. They swarm in some of the dramas a little earlier than Shakespeare's time, and the cultured dramatists speak very contemptuously of these productions, if not of Shakespeare's historical plays. We may take as an example the First Part of *Henry VI.*, a feeble piece, to which Shakespeare probably contributed touches throughout, and perhaps one or two complete scenes. It appears from the stage directions (which may be defective, but cannot well be redundant) that in this one play there were represented a pitched battle of two armies, an attack on a city wall with scaling-ladders, two street-scuffles, four single combats, four skirmishes, and seven excursions. No genuine play of Shakespeare's, I suppose, is so military from beginning to end; and we know how in *Henry V.* he laments that he must disgrace the name of Agincourt by showing four or five men with vile and ragged foils

> Right ill-disposed in brawl ridiculous.

Still he does show them; and his serious dramas contain such a profusion of combats and battles as no playwright now would dream of exhibiting. We

so with some faults which have the appearance of arising from that condescension.

(4) Other defects again he might have deliberately defended; *e.g.* the highly improbable conclusions and the distressing mis-marriages of some of the comedies. 'It is of the essence of romantic comedy,' he might have said, 'to treat such things with indifference. There is a convention that you should take the characters with some degree of seriousness while they are in difficulties, and should cease to do so when they are to be delivered from them.' Do not we ourselves adopt this point of view to some extent when we go to the theatre now?

I added this note after reading Mr. Bridges's very interesting and original contribution to the Stratford Town edition of Shakespeare (vol. x.). I disagree with some of Mr. Bridges's remarks, and am not always repelled by things that he dislikes. But this brief note is not, of course, meant for an answer to his paper; it merely suggests reasons for at least diminishing the proportion of defect attributable to a conscious sacrifice of art to the tastes of the audience.

expect these things perhaps in the English history-plays, and we find them in abundance there : but not there alone. The last Act in *Julius Cæsar, Troilus and Cressida, King Lear, Macbeth,* and *Cymbeline* ; the fourth Act of *Antony and Cleopatra* ; the opening Acts of *Coriolanus,*—these are all full of battle-scenes. If battle cannot be shown, it can be described. If it cannot be described, still soldiers can be shown, and twice in *Hamlet* Fortinbras and his army march upon the stage.[1] At worst there can be street-brawls and single fights, as in *Romeo and Juliet.* In reading Shakespeare we scarcely realise how much of this kind is exhibited. In seeing him acted we do not fully realise it, for much of it is omitted. But beyond doubt it helped to make him the most popular dramatist of his time.

If we examine Shakespeare's battles we shall observe a certain peculiarity, which is connected with the nature of his theatre and also explains the treatment of them in ours. In most cases he does not give a picture of two whole armies engaged, but makes a pair of combatants rush upon the stage, fight, and rush off again ; and this pair is succeeded by a second, and perhaps by a third. This hurried series of single combats admitted of speech-making ; perhaps it also gave some impression of the changes and confusion of a battle. Our tendency, on the other hand, is to contrive one spectacle with scenic effects, or even to exhibit one magnificent tableau in which nobody says a word. And this plan, though it has the advantage of getting rid of Shakespeare's poetry, is not exactly dramatic. It is adopted chiefly because the taste of our public is, or is supposed to be, less dramatic than spectacular, and because, unlike the Elizabethans, we are able to gratify such a taste. But there is another fact to be remembered

---

[1] To us their first appearance is of interest chiefly because it intro-duces the soliloquy 'How all occasions.' But, it is amusing to notice, the Folio, which probably represents the acting version in 1623, omits the soliloquy but retains the marching soldiers.

here. Few playgoers now can appreciate a fencing-match, and much fewer a broad-sword and target fight. But the Elizabethan public went to see performances of this kind as we go to see cricket or football matches. They might watch them in the very building which at other times was used as a playhouse.[1] They could judge of the merit of the exhibition when Hotspur and Prince Henry fought, when Macduff 'laid on,' or when Tybalt and Mercutio used their rapiers. And this was probably another reason why Shakespeare's battles so often consist of single combats, and why these scenes were beloved by the simpler folk among his audience.

Our second illustration concerns the popular appetite for musical and other sounds. The introduction of songs and dances[2] was censured as a corrupt gratification of this appetite. And so it was when the songs and dances were excessive in number, irrelevant, or out of keeping with the scene. I do not remember that in Shakespeare's plays this is ever the case; but, in respect of songs, we may perhaps take Marston's *Antonio and Mellida* as an instance of abuse. For in each of the two Parts of that play there are directions for five songs; and, since not even the first lines of these songs are printed, we must suppose that the leader of the band, or the singing actor in the company, introduced whatever he chose. In addition to songs and dances, the musicians, at least in some plays, performed between the Acts; and the practice of accompanying certain speeches by low music—a practice which in some performances of Shakespeare now has become a pest—has the sanction of several Elizabethan playwrights, and (to a slight extent) of Shakespeare. It seems

[1] I do not refer to the Globe.

[2] The latter, no doubt, accompanied by the band, except when the clown played the tabor while he danced alone.

clear, for example, that in *Twelfth Night* low
music was played while the lovely opening lines
('That strain again') were being spoken, and also
during a part of the dialogue preceding the song
'Come away, come away, death.' Some lines, too,
of Lorenzo's famous speech about music in the
Merchant of Venice were probably accompanied;
and there is a still more conspicuous instance in
the scene where Lear wakes from his long sleep
and sees Cordelia standing by his side.

But, beyond all this, if we attend to the stage-
directions we shall realise that in the serious plays
of Shakespeare other musical sounds were of frequent occurrence. Almost always the ceremonial
entrance of a royal person is marked by a 'flourish'
or a 'sennet' on trumpets, cornets, or hautboys;
and wherever we have armies and battles we find
directions for drums, or for particular series of notes
of trumpets or cornets appropriate to particular
military movements. In the First Part of *Henry VI.*,
to take that early play again, we must imagine a
dead march, two other marches, three retreats, three
sennets, seven flourishes, eighteen alarums; and
there are besides five directions for drums, one for a
horn, and five for soundings, of a kind not specified,
by trumpets. In the last three scenes of the first
Act in *Coriolanus*—scenes containing less than three
hundred and fifty lines—there are directions for a
parley, a retreat, five flourishes, and eight alarums,
with three, less specific, for trumpets, and four for
drums. We find about twenty such directions in
King Lear, and about twenty-five in *Macbeth*,
a short play in which hautboys seem to have
been unusually favoured.[1] It is evident that the
audience loved these sounds, which, from their
prevalence in passages of special kinds, seem to
have been intended chiefly to stimulate excitement,

[1] This may possibly be one of the signs that *Macbeth* was altered
after Shakespeare's retirement or death.

and sometimes to heighten impressions of grandeur or of awe.

But this is not all. Such purposes were also served by noises not musical. Four times in *Macbeth*, when the Witches appear, thunder is heard. It thunders and lightens at intervals through the storm-scenes in *King Lear*. Casca and Cassius, dark thoughts within them, walk the streets of Rome in a terrific thunderstorm. That loud insistent knocking which appalled Macbeth is repeated thrice at intervals while Lady Macbeth in vain endeavours to calm him, and five times while the Porter fumbles with his keys. The gate has hardly been opened and the murder discovered when the castle-bell begins its hideous alarum. The alarm-bell is used for the same purpose of intensifying excitement in the brawl that ruins Cassio, and its effect is manifest in Othello's immediate order, 'Silence that dreadful bell.' I will add but one instance more. In the days of my youth, before the melodrama audience dreamed of seeing chariot-races, railway accidents, or the infernal regions, on the stage, it loved few things better than the explosion of fire-arms; and its favourite weapon was the pistol. The Elizabethans had the same fancy for fire-arms, only they preferred cannon. Shakespeare's theatre was burnt down in 1613 at a performance of *Henry VIII.*, not, I suppose, as Prynne imagined, by a Providence which shared his opinion of the drama, but because the wadding of a cannon fired during the play flew to the thatch of the roof and set it ablaze. In *Hamlet* Shakespeare gave the public plenty that they could not understand, but he made it up to them in explosions. While Hamlet, Horatio, and Marcellus are waiting for the Ghost, a flourish is heard, and then the roar of cannon. It is the custom to fire them when the King drinks a pledge; and this King drinks many. In the fencing-scene at the end he proposes to drink one for every

hit scored by his beloved nephew ; and the first hit
is duly honoured by the cannon. Unexpected events
prevented the celebration of the second, but the
audience lost nothing by that. While Hamlet lies
dying, a sudden explosion is heard. Fortinbras is
coming with his army. And, as if that were not
enough, the very last words of the play are, ' Go,
bid the soldiers shoot,' and the very last sound of
the performance is a peal of ordnance. Into this
most mysterious and inward of his works, it would
seem, the poet flung, as if in derision of his cultured
critics, well-nigh every stimulant of popular excitement he could collect: 'carnal, bloody, and unnatural
acts '; five deaths on the open stage, three appearances of a ghost, two of a mad woman, a dumb-
show, two men raving and fighting in a grave at a
funeral, the skulls and bones of the dead, a clown
bandying jests with a prince, songs at once indecent
and pathetic, marching soldiers, a fencing-match,
then a litter of corpses, and explosions in the first
Act and explosions in the last.   And yet out of this
sensational material—not in spite of it, but out of
it—he made the most mysterious and inward of his
dramas, which leaves us haunted by thoughts beyond
the reaches of our souls ; and he knew that the very
audience that rejoiced in ghosts and explosions
would listen, even while it was waiting for the
ghost, to that which the explosion had suggested,—
a general disquisition, twenty-five lines long, on the
manner in which one defect may spoil a noble
reputation.   In this strange harmony of discords,
surely unexampled before or since, we may see at
a glance the essence of Elizabethan drama, of its
poet, and of its audience.

2.

We have been occupied so far with characteristics
of the drama which reflect the more distinctively
popular tastes objected to by critics like Jonson.

We may now pass on to arrangements common to all public theatres, whether the play performed were Jonson's or Shakespeare's; and in the first instance to a characteristic common to the public and private theatres alike.

As everyone knows, the female parts in stage-plays were taken by boys, youths, or men (a mask being sometimes worn in the last case).   The inde-corous Elizabethans regarded this custom almost entirely from the point of view of decorum and morality.   And as to morality, no one, I believe, who examines the evidence, especially as it concerns the state of things that followed the introduction of actresses at the Restoration, will be very ready to dissent from their opinion.   But it is often assumed as a matter beyond dispute that, on the side of dramatic effect, the Elizabethan practice was ex-tremely unfortunate, if not downright absurd.   This idea appears to me, to say the least, exaggerated. Our practice may be the better; for a few Shake-spearean parts it *ought* to be much better; but that, on the whole, it is decidedly so, or that the old custom had anything absurd about it, there seems no reason to believe.   In the first place, experience in private and semi-private performances shows that female parts may be excellently acted by youths or men, and that the most obvious drawback, that of the adult male voice, is not felt to be nearly so serious as we might anticipate.   For a minute or two it may call for a slight exertion of imagination in the audience; but there is no more radical error than to suppose that an audience finds this irksome, or to forget that the use of imagination at one point quickens it at other points, and so is a positive gain. And we have further to remember that the Eliza-bethan actor of female parts was no amateur, but a professional as carefully trained as an actress now; while dramatically he had this advantage over the actress, that he was regarded simply as a player, and not also as a woman with an attractive or unattractive person.[1]

In the second place, if the current ideas on this subject were true, there would be, it seems to me, more evidence of their truth. We should find, for example, that when first the new fashion came in, it was hailed by good judges as a very great improvement on the old. But the traces of such an opinion appear very scanty and doubtful, while it is certain that one of the few actors who after the Restoration still played female parts maintained a high reputation and won great applause. Again, if these parts in Shakespeare's day were very inadequately performed, would not the effect of that fact be distinctly visible in the plays themselves? The rôles in question would be less important in Shakespeare's dramas, for example, than in dramas of later times: but I do not see that they are. Besides, in the Shakespearean play itself the female parts would be much less important than the male: but on the whole they are not. In the tragedies and histories, it is true, the impelling forces of the action usually belong in larger measure to men than to women. But that is because the action in such plays is laid in the sphere of public life; and in cases where, in spite of this, the heroine is as prominent as the hero, her part—the part of Juliet, Cleopatra, Lady Macbeth—certainly requires as good acting as his. As to the comedies, if we ask ourselves who are the central or the most interesting figures in them, we shall find that we pronounce a woman's name at least as often as a man's. I understate the case. Of Shakespeare's mature comedies the *Merchant of Venice*, I believe, is the only one where this name would unquestionably be a man's, and in three of the last five it would almost certainly be a woman's—

[1] Surely every company that plays Shakespeare should include a boy. There would then be no excuse for giving to a woman such parts as Ariel and Brutus's boy Lucius.

Isabella's, Imogen's, Hermione's. How shall we reconcile with these facts the idea that in his day the female parts were, on the whole, much less adequately played than the male? And finally, if the dramatists themselves believed this, why do we not find frequent indications of the belief in their prologues, epilogues, prefaces, and plays?[1]

We must conclude, it would seem, that the absence of actresses from the Elizabethan theatre, though at first it may appear to us highly important, made no great difference to the dramas themselves.

3.

That certainly cannot be said of the construction and arrangements of the stage. On this subject a great deal has been written of late years, and as regards many details there is still much difference of opinion.[2] But fortunately all that is of great moment for our present purpose is tolerably certain. In trying to bring it out, I will begin by reminding you of our present stage. For it is the stage, and not the rest of the theatre, that is of special interest here; and no serious harm will be done if, for the rest, we imagine Shakespeare's theatre with boxes, circles, and galleries like our own, though in the shape of a more elongated horse-shoe than ours. We must imagine, of course, an area too; but there, as we shall see, an important difference comes in.

[1] This question will not be answered by the citation of one famous speech of Cleopatra's—a speech, too, which is strictly in character. But, as to this matter and the other considerations put forward above, I must add that, while my impression is that what has been said of Shakespeare holds of most of the contemporary dramatists, I have not verified it by a research. A student looking for a subject for his thesis might well undertake such a research.

[2] When the lecture was given (in 1902) I went more fully into details, having arrived at certain conclusions mainly by an examination of Elizabethan dramas. I suppress them here because I have been unable to study all that has since been written on the Elizabethan stage. The reader who is interested in the subject should refer in the first instance to an excellent article by Mr. Archer in the *Quarterly Review* for April, 1908.

Our present stage may be called a box with one of its sides knocked out. Through this opening, which has an ornamental frame, we look into the box. Its three upright sides (for we may ignore the bottom and the top) are composed of movable painted scenes, which are changed from time to time during the course of the play. Before the play and after it the opening is blocked by a curtain, dropped from the top of the frame ; and this is also dropped at intervals during the performance, that the scenes may be changed.

In all these respects the Elizabethan arrangement was quite different. The stage came forward to about the middle of the area ; so that a line bisecting the house would have coincided with the line of footlights, if there had been such things. The stage was therefore a platform viewed from both sides and not only from the front ; and along its sides, as well as in front of it, stood the people who paid least, the groundlings, sometimes punningly derided by dramatists as 'the men of understanding.' Obviously, the sides of this platform were open; nor were there movable scenes even at the back of it ; nor was there any front curtain. It was overshadowed by a projecting roof; but the area, or 'yard,' where the groundlings stood, was open to the weather, and accordingly the theatre could not be darkened. It will be seen that, when the actors were on the forward part of the stage, they were (to exaggerate a little) in the middle of the audience, like the performers in a circus now. And on this forward naked part of the stage most of a Shakespearean drama was played. We may call it the main or front stage.[1]

If now we look towards the rear of this stage, what do we find ? In the first place, while the back

---

[1] This is a description of a public theatre. A private one, it will be remembered, had seats in the area (there called the pit), was completely roofed, and could be darkened.

of our present-day box consists of a movable scene,
that of the Elizabethan stage was formed by the
'tiring-house,' or dressing-room, of the actors. In
its wall were two doors, by which entrances and
exits were made. But it was not merely a tiring-
house. In the play it might represent a room, a
house, a castle, the wall of a town; and the doors
played their parts accordingly. Again, when a
person speaks 'from within,' that doubtless means
that he is in the tiring-house, opens one of the doors
a little, and speaks through the chink. So apparently did the prompter.

Secondly, on the top of the tiring-house was the
'upper stage' or 'balcony,' which looked down on
the platform stage. It is hardly possible to make
brief statements about it that would be secure. For
our purposes it may be imagined as a balcony
jutting forward a little from the line of the tiring-
house; and it will suffice to add that, though the
whole or part of it was on some occasions, or in
some theatres, occupied by spectators, the whole or
part of it was sometimes used by the actors and was
indispensably requisite to the performance of the
play. 'Enter above' or 'enter aloft' means that
the actor was to appear on this upper stage or
balcony. Usually, no doubt, he reached it by a
ladder or stair inside the tiring-house; but on
occasions there were ascents or descents directly
from, or to, the main stage, as we see from 'climbs
the tree and is received above' or 'the citizens leap
from the walls.' The reader of Shakespeare will at
once remember many scenes where the balcony was
used. On it, as the city wall, appeared the Governor
and citizens of Harfleur, while King Henry and his
train stood before the gates below. From it Arthur
made his fatal leap. It was Cleopatra's monument,
into which she and her women drew up the dying
Antony. Juliet talked to Romeo from it; and from
it Romeo ('one kiss and I'll descend') 'goeth down'

to the main stage. Richard appeared there between
the two bishops ; and there the spectators imagined
Duncan murdered in his sleep.[1] But they could not
look into his chamber. The balcony could be concealed by curtains, running, like all Elizabethan
stage curtains, on a rod.

In the third place, there was, towards the back of
the main stage, a part that could be curtained off,
and so separated from the front part of that stage.
Let us call it the back stage. It is the matter about
which there is most difficulty and controversy ; but
the general description just given would be accepted
by almost all scholars and will suffice for us. Here
was the curtain (more strictly, the curtains) through
which the actors peeped at the audience before the
play began, and at which the groundlings hurled
apples and other missiles to hasten their coming or
signify disapproval of them. And this 'back stage'
was essential to many performances, and was used in
a variety of ways. It was the room where Henry IV.
lay dying ; the cave of Timon or of Belarius ; probably the tent in which Richmond slept before the
battle of Bosworth ; the cell of Prospero, who draws
the curtains apart and shows Ferdinand and Miranda
playing at chess within ; and here, I imagine, and
not on the balcony, Juliet, after drinking the potion,
'falls upon her bed within the curtains.'[2] Finally, the
back stage accounts for those passages where, at the
close of a death-scene, there is no indication that
the corpse was carried off the stage. If the death
took place on the open stage, as it usually did, this
of course was necessary, since there was no front
curtain to drop ; and so we usually find in the

---

[1] 'The doors are open, and the surfeited grooms Do mock their
charge with snores,' says Lady Macbeth on the stage below ; and no
doubt the tiring-house doors *were* open.

[2] This view, into the grounds of which I cannot go, implies that
Juliet's bedroom was, in one scene, the upper stage, and, in another,
the back stage ; but the Elizabethans, I believe, would make no difficulty about that.

dialogue words like 'Take up the bodies' (*Hamlet*), or 'Bear them from hence' (*King Lear*). But Desdemona was murdered in her bed on the back stage; and there died also Othello and Emilia; so that Lodovico orders the bodies to be 'hid,' not carried off. The curtains were drawn together, and the dead actors withdrew into the tiring-house unseen,[1] while the living went off openly.

This triple stage is the primary thing to remember about Shakespeare's theatre: a platform coming well forward into the yard, completely open in the larger front part, but having further back a part that could be curtained off, and overlooked by an upper stage or balcony above the tiring-house. Only a few further details need be mentioned. Though scenery was unknown, there were plenty of properties, as may be gathered from the dramas and, more quickly, from the accounts of Henslowe, the manager of the Rose. Chairs, benches, and tables are a matter of course. Kent sat in the stocks. The witches had a caldron. Imogen slept in a bed, and Iachimo crept out of his trunk in her room. Falstaff was carried off the stage in a clothes-basket. I have quoted the direction 'climb the tree.' A 'banquet' figures in Henslowe's list, and in the *Tempest* 'several strange shapes' bring one in. He mentions a 'tomb,' and it is possible, though not likely, that the tomb of the Capulets was a property; and he mentions a 'moss-bank,' doubtless such as that where the wild thyme was blowing for Titania. Her lover, you remember, wore an ass's head, and the Falstaff of the *Merry Wives* a buck's. There were whole animals, too. 'A great horse with his legs'

---

[1] Perhaps. It seems necessary to suppose that the sides of the back-stage, as well as its front, could be open; otherwise many of the spectators could not have seen what took place there. But it is not *necessary*, so far as I remember, to suppose that the sides could be closed by curtains. The Elizabethans probably would not have been troubled by seeing dead bodies get up and go into the tiring-house when a play or even a scene was over.

is in Henslowe's list; and in a play not by Shakespeare Jonah is cast out of the whale's belly on to the stage. Besides these properties there was a contrivance with ropes and pulleys, by which a heavenly being could descend from the stage-roof (the 'heaven'), as in *Cymbeline* Jupiter descends upon his eagle. When his speech is over we find the direction 'ascends.' Soon after comes another direction: 'vanish.' This is addressed not to Jupiter but to various ghosts who are present. For there was a hollow space under the stage, and a trap-door into it. Through this ghosts usually made their entrances and exits; and 'vanish' seems commonly to mean an exit that way. Through it, too, arose and sank the witches' caldron and the apparitions shown to Macbeth. A person could speak from under the stage, as the Ghost does when Hamlet calls him 'old mole'; and the musicians could go and play there, as they do in the scene where Antony's soldiers hear strange music on the night before the battle; 'Musicke of the Hoboyes is under the Stage' the direction runs ('Hoboyes' were used also in the witch-scene just mentioned).

4.

We have now to observe certain ways in which this stage with its arrangements influenced the dramas themselves; and we shall find that the majority of these influences are connected with the absence of scenery. In this, to begin with, lies the main, though not the whole, explanation of the shortness of the performance. In our Shakespeare revivals the drama is always considerably cut down; and yet, even where no excessive prominence is given to scenic display, the time occupied is seldom less than three hours, and often a good deal more. In Shakespeare's day, as we gather from various sources (*e.g.* from the Prologues to *Romeo and Juliet* and *Henry VIII.*), the customary time taken by the un-shortened play was about two hours. And the chief reason of this great difference obviously is that the time which we spend in setting and changing scenes his company spent in acting the piece. At a given signal certain characters appeared. Unless a placard announced the place where they were supposed to be,[1] the audience gathered this from their conversation, or in the absence of such indications asked no questions on the subject. They talked for a time and went away ; and at once another set appeared. The intervals between the acts (if intervals there were, and however they were occupied) had no purpose connected with scene-changing, and must have been short ; and the introduction and removal of a few properties would take next to no time from the performance.[2] We may safely assume that not less than a hundred of the hundred and twenty minutes were given to the play itself.

The absence of scenery, however, will not wholly account for the difference in question. If you take a Shakespearean play of average length and read it at about the pace usual in our revivals, you will find, I think, that you have occupied considerably more than a hundred or a hundred and twenty minutes.[3] The Elizabethan actor can hardly have spoken so slowly. Probably the position of the stage, and especially of the front part of it where most of the action took place, was of advantage to him in this respect. Standing almost in the middle of his audience, and at no great distance from any section

[1] Where this contrivance was used at all it probably only announced the general place of the action throughout the play : *e.g. Denmark*, or, a little more fully, *Verona, Mantua.*

[2] It is possibly significant that *Macbeth* and the *Tempest*, plays containing more 'shews' than most, are exceptionally short.

[3] It suffices for this rough experiment to read a column in an edition like the Globe, and then to multiply the time taken by the number of columns in the play.

of it, he could with safety deliver his lines much
faster than an actor can now.   He could speak even
a 'passionate' speech 'trippingly on the tongue.'
Hamlet bids him do so, warns him not to mouth,
and, when the time for his speech comes, calls im-
patiently to him to leave his damnable faces and
begin ; and this is not the only passage in Elizabethan literature which suggests that good judges
objected to a slow and over-emphatic delivery.
We have some actors not inferior in elocution, we
must presume, to Burbage or Taylor, but even Mr.
Vezin or Mr. Forbes Robertson may find it difficult
to deliver blank verse intelligibly, musically, and
rapidly out of our stage-box.[1]

I return to the absence of scenery, which even in
this matter must be more important than the position
of the stage or the preference for rapid speech.   It
explains, secondly, the great difference between
Elizabethan and more modern plays in the number
of the scenes.[2] This number, with Shakespeare,
averages somewhere about twenty : it reaches forty-
two in *Antony and Cleopatra*, and sinks to nine
in *Love's Labour's Lost*, the *Midsummer-Night's
Dream*, and the *Tempest*.   In the fourth act of the
first of these plays there are thirteen scenes, no one
of them in the same place as the next.   The average
number in Schiller's plays seems to be about eight.
In plays written now it corresponds not unfrequently
with the number of acts.[3]   The primary cause of
this difference, though not the only one, is, I presume, that we expect to see appropriate surroundings,

[1] I do not know whether the average size of our theatres differs much
from that of the Elizabethan.   The diameter of the area at the *Fortune*
and the *Globe* seems to have been fifty feet.

[2] I mean by a scene a section of a play before and after which the
stage is unoccupied.   Most editions of Shakespeare are faulty in the
division of scenes (see *Shakespearean Tragedy*, p. 451).

[3] So it very nearly does in some Restoration comedies.   In the *Way
of the World* the scenery is changed only twice in the five acts, though
there are more than five scenes.

at the least, for every part of the story. Such
surroundings mean more or less elaborate scenery,
which, besides being expensive, takes a long time to
set and change. For a dramatist accordingly who
is a dramatist and wishes to hold his audience by
the play itself, it is an advantage to have as few
scenes as may be. And so the absence of scenery
in Shakespeare's day, and its presence in ours,
result in two totally different systems, not merely
of theatrical effect, but of dramatic construction.

In certain ways it was clearly an advantage to a
playwright to be able to produce a large number of
scenes, varying in length according to his pleasure,
and separated by almost inappreciable intervals. Nor
could there be any disadvantage in this freedom, if
he had a strong feeling for dramatic construction,
and a gift for it, and a determination to construct
as well as he could. But, as a matter of fact, many,
perhaps the majority, of the pre-Shakespearean
dramas are put together very loosely ; scene follows
scene in the manner of a casual narrative rather
than a play ; and a good deal is admitted for the
sake of its immediate attraction and not because it
is essential to the plot. The freedom which we are
considering, though it could not necessitate these
defects, gave the widest scope for them ; the majority of the audience probably was, and continued to
be, well-nigh indifferent to them ; and a large proportion of the plays of Shakespeare's time exhibits
them in some degree. The average drama of that
day has great merits of a strictly dramatic kind,
but it is not well-built, it is not what we mean by
'a good play'; and if we look at it from the
restricted point of view implied by that phrase we
shall be inclined, I think, to believe that it would
have been a better play if its author had been
compelled by the stage-arrangements to halve the
number of the scenes. These remarks will hold of
Shakespeare himself. Some of his most delightful

dramas, indeed,—for instance, the two Parts of
Henry IV.—make little or no pretence to be well-
constructed wholes ; and even in those which fully
deserve that title a certain amount of matter not
indispensable to the plot is usually to be found.   In
point of construction *Othello* is the best of his
tragedies, *Julius Cæsar* better than *King Lear*, and
Antony and Cleopatra perhaps the faultiest.   To
say that this depends solely on the number of scenes
would be ridiculous, but still it is probably significant
that the numbers are, respectively, fifteen, eighteen,
twenty-one, and forty-two.

The average Elizabethan play could not, of
course, have been converted into a well-built fabric
by a *mere* reduction of the number of its scenes ;
and in some cases no amount of rearrangement
of the whole material employed could have produced
this result.   This means, however, on the other
hand, that the Elizabethans, partly from the very
simplicity of their theatrical conditions, were able to
handle with decided, though usually imperfect,
dramatic effect subjects which would present difficulties still greater, if not insuperable, to a playwright
now.   And in Shakespeare we can trace, in this
respect and in others, the advantages connected
with the absence of scenery.   He could carry his
audience freely from one country, town, house or
room, to another, or from this part of a battle-field
to that, because the audience imagined each place
and saw none.   I take an extreme example.   The
Third Act of *Antony and Cleopatra*, according to
modern editions, contains thirteen scenes, and these
are the localities assigned to them : (1) a plain in
Syria, (2) Rome, an ante-chamber in Cæsar's house,
(3) Alexandria, Cleopatra's palace, (4) Athens, a
room in Antony's house, (5) the same, another room,
(6) Rome, Cæsar's house, (7) near Actium, Antony's
camp, (8) a plain near Actium, (9) another part of
the plain, (10) another part of the plain, (11)

Alexandria, Cleopatra's palace, (12) Egypt, Cæsar's camp, (13) Alexandria, Cleopatra's palace. I wonder how long this Act would take on our stage, where each locality must be represented. Three hours perhaps, of which the performance might occupy one-eighth. But in Shakespeare's day there was no occasion for any stage-direction as to locality throughout the Act.

Again, Shakespeare's method of working a double plot depends largely on his ability to bring the persons belonging to the two plots on to the stage in alternate scenes of no great length until the threads are combined. This is easily seen in *King Lear*; and there we can observe, further, how he varies the pitch of feeling and provides relief by interposing short quiet scenes between longer exciting ones. By this means, as I have pointed out elsewhere, the Storm-scene on the heath, which if undivided would be intolerable, is broken into three, separated by very short duologues spoken within the Castle and in prose. Again, since scene follows scene without a pause, he could make one tell on another in the way either of intensification or of contrast. We catch the effect in reading, but in our theatres it is usually destroyed by the interval. Finally, however many scenes an Act may contain, Shakespeare can keep attention glued to the play throughout the Act, because there are no intervals. So can our playwrights, because they have but one or two scenes in the Act. But in our reproductions of Shakespeare, though the number of scenes is reduced, it can scarcely ever be reduced to that extent; so that several times during an Act, and many times during the play, we are withdrawn perforce from the dramatic atmosphere into that of everyday life, solitary impatience or ennui, distracting conversation, third-rate music, or, occasionally, good music half-drowned in a babble of voices.

If we consider the characteristics on which I have been dwelling, and bear in mind also the rapidity of speech which we have found to be probable, we shall realise that a performance in Shakespeare's day, though more of the play was performed, must have been something much more variegated and changeful, and much lighter in movement, than a revival now. And this difference will have been observed by those who have seen Shakespeare acted by the Elizabethan Stage Society, under the direction of Mr. Poel, who not only played scene after scene without intervals, but secured in a considerable degree that rapidity of speech.

A minor point remains. The Elizabethan stage, we have seen, had no front curtain. The front curtain and the use of scenery naturally came in together, for the second, so far as the front stage was concerned, was dependent on the first; and as we have already glanced at some effects of the absence of the second, that of the first will require but a few additional words. It was clearly in some ways a great disadvantage; for every situation at the front of the stage had to be begun and ended before the eyes of the audience. In our dramas the curtain may rise on a position which the actors then had to produce by movements not really belonging to the play; and, what is more important, the scene may advance to a striking climax, the effect of which would be greatly diminished and sometimes destroyed if the actors had to leave the stage instead of being suddenly hidden. In Elizabethan plays, accordingly, we seldom meet with this kind of effect, though it is not difficult to discover places where it would have been appropriate. But we shall not find them, I venture to think, in tragedies. This effect, in other words, appears properly to belong to comedy and to melodrama (if that species of play is to be considered here at all); and the Elizabethans lost nothing by their inability to misuse it in tragedy, and especially

at the close of a tragedy. Whether it can be artistic
to end any serious scene whatever at the point of
greatest tension seems doubtful, but surely it is little
short of barbarous to drop the curtain on the last
dying words, or, it may be, the last convulsion, of a
tragic hero. In tragedy the Elizabethan practice,
like the Greek, was to lower the pitch of emotion
from this point by a few quiet words, followed perhaps by sounds which, in intention at least, were
majestic or solemn, and so to restore the audience
to common life ' in calm of mind, all passion spent.'
Thus Shakespeare's tragedies always close ; and the
end of Marlowe's *Doctor Faustus* is not *Exeunt
Devils with Faustus*, but the speech beginning

> Cut is the branch that might have grown full straight,
> And burned is Apollo's laurel-bough,
> That sometime grew within this learned man.

In this particular case Marlowe, if he had not been a
poet, might have dispensed with the final descent.
or ascent, from the violent emotions attending the
catastrophe ; but in the immense majority of their
tragedies the Elizabethans, even if they had wished
to do as we too often do, were saved from the
temptation by the absence of a front curtain.[1]

---

[1] The 'back' stage, which had curtains, must, I suppose, have been
too small to accommodate the number of persons commonly present,
alive or dead, at the close of a tragedy. I do not know if any recent
writer has raised and discussed the questions how often the back stage
is used in the last scene of an Elizabethan play, and, again, whether it
is often employed at all in order to produce, by the closing of the
curtains, the kind of effect referred to in the paragraph above. Perhaps
the fact that the curtains had to be closed by an actor, within them or
without, made this effect impossible. Or perhaps it was not desired.
In Shakespeare's tragedies, if my memory serves me, the only sudden
or startling appeals of an outward kind (apart, of course, from actions)
are those produced by supernatural appearances and disappearances,
as in *Hamlet* and *Macbeth*. These, we have seen, were usually
managed by means of the trap-door, which, it would seem from some
passages, must have been rather large. These matters deserve in-
vestigation if they have not already received it.

5.

Hitherto we have not considered a Shakespearean performance on the side, I will not say of its spectacular, but of its pictorial effect. This must be our last subject. We have to bear in mind here three things : the fact that the stage was viewed from three sides, its illumination by daylight throughout the play, and the absence of scenery. It is obvious that the last two deprived the audience of many attractive or impressive pictures ; while, as to the first, it seems unlikely that actors who were watched from the sides as well as the front would study to group themselves as parts of a composition addressed to the eye. Indeed one may doubt whether, except in regard to costume, they seriously attended to the pictorial effect of a drama at all ; their tiny crowds and armies, for example, cannot have provided much of a show. And in any case it is clear that the audience had to dispense with many more or less beautiful sights that we may now enjoy. But the question whether their loss was, on the whole, a disadvantage is not so easy to answer ; for here again it freed them from a temptation—that of sacrificing dramatic to pictorial effect; and we cannot tell whether, or how far, they would have been proof against its influence. Let us try, however, to see the position clearly.

The essence of drama—and certainly of Shakespearean drama—lies in actions and words expressive of inward movements of human nature. Pictorial effects (if for convenience' sake the various matters under consideration may be signified by that phrase) are in themselves no more dramatic than songs, dances, military music, or the jests of a 'fool.' Like these other things, they may be made dramatic. They may be used and apprehended, that is to say, as elements fused with the essential elements of dramatic effect. And, so far as this is the case and

they thus contribute to that effect, they are, it seems
clear, an unmixed advantage. But a distinct and
separate attention to them is another matter; for,
the moment it sets in, attention begins to be withdrawn from the actions and words, and therefore
from the inward movements that these express. And
experience shows that, as soon as pictorial attractions exceed a certain limit, impossible to specify in
general terms, they at once influence the average
play-goer in this mischievous way. It is, further,
well-nigh inevitable that this should happen. However interesting the actions, words, and inward
movements may be, they call for some effort of
imagination and of other mental activities,[1] while
stage-pictures demand very little; and accordingly,
at the present time at any rate, the bulk of an
audience to which the latter are abundantly presented will begin to enjoy them for their own sakes,
or as parts of a panorama and not of a drama. No
one, I think, can honestly doubt this who watches
and listens to the people sitting near him at what
the newspapers too truly call 'an amazing Shakespearean spectacle.' If we are offered a pretty
picture of the changing colours of the sky at dawn,
or of a forest glade with deer miraculously moving
across its sunny grass, most of us cease for the time
to be an audience and become mere spectators; and
let Romeo and Juliet, or Rosalind and Orlando, talk
as like angels as they will, they will talk but half-
heeded. Our dramatists know this well enough.
Mr. Barrie and Mr. Pinero and Mr. Shaw, who

---

[1] I do not refer to such deliberate and sustained effort as a reader
may sometimes make. It is not commonly realised that continuous
attention to any imaginative or intellectual matter, however enjoyable,
involves considerable strain. If at a lecture or sermon a careless
person makes himself observable in arriving late or leaving early, the
eyes of half the audience will turn to him and follow him. And the
reason is not always that the speaker bores them; it is that involun-
tarily they seek relief from this strain. The same thing may be seen
in the concert-room or theatre, but very much less at a panorama,
because the mere use of the eyes, even when continuous, is comparatively easy.

want the audience to listen and understand, take good care not to divert its attention and deaden its imagination by scenic displays. And yet, with the heartiest admiration for their best work, one may say that Shakespeare's requires more attention and imagination than theirs.

Whether the Elizabethan companies, if they had had the power to use the attractions of scenery, would have abused it, and whether in that case the audience would have been as readily debauched as ours, it is useless to dispute. The audience was not composed mainly of groundlings; and even the groundlings in that age had drama in their blood. But I venture to disbelieve that the main fault in these matters lies, in any age, with the audience. It is like the populace in Shakespeare's plays, easy to lead wrong but just as easy to lead right. If you give people in the East End, or even in the Albert Hall, nothing but third-rate music, most of them will be content with it, and possibly may come to disrelish what is better. But if you have a little faith in great art and in human nature, and offer them, I do not say the Diabelli variations, but such music as the symphonies of Beethoven or even of Brahms, they will justify your faith. This is not theory, but fact; and I cannot think that it is otherwise with drama, or at least with the dramas of Shakespeare. Did they ever 'spell ruin to managers' if they were, through the whole cast, satisfactorily acted? What spells real ruin to managers and actors alike is what spells degradation to audiences.[1]

---

[1] I am not referring here, or elsewhere, to such a moderate use of scenery in Shakespearean performances as most of our actor-managers (e.g. Mr. Benson) now adopt. I regret it in so far as it involves a curtailing of the play; but I do not think it withdraws from the play any attention that is of value, and for some of the audience it probably heightens the dramatic effect. Still, in my belief, it would be desirable to decrease it, because the less there is of it, the more is good acting necessary, and the more of the play itself can be acted. Some use of scenery, with its consequences to the play, must unquestionably be accepted as the rule, but I would add that it ought always to be

But whether or no Shakespeare's audience could have been easily degraded by scenic pleasure, it had not the chance; and I will not raise the further question how far its disabilities were the cause of its virtues, but will end with a few words on two of the virtues themselves.   It possessed, first, a vivid imagination.   Shakespeare could address to it not in vain the injunction, ' Work, work your thoughts!' Probably in three scenes out of five the place and surroundings of the action were absolutely invisible to its eyes.   In a fourth it took the barest symbol for reality.   A couple of wretched trees made the Forest of Arden for it, five men with ragged foils the army that conquered at Agincourt : are we stronger than it, or weaker?   It heard Romeo say

> Look, love, what envious streaks
> Do lace the severing clouds in yonder east;

and to its mind's eye they were there.   It looked at a shabby old balcony, but as it listened it saw the swallows flitting round the sun-lit battlements of Macbeth's castle, and our pitiful sense of grotesque incongruity never troubled it.[1]   The simplest convention sufficed to set its imagination at work.   If Prospero entered wearing a particular robe, it knew that no one on the stage could see his solid shape ;[2] and if Banquo, rising through the trap-door, had his bloody face dusted over with meal, it recognised him for a ghost and thrilled with horror; and we, Heaven help us, should laugh.   Though the stage stood in broad daylight, again, Banquo, for it, was being murdered on a dark wet night, for he carried

possible for us to see performances, such as we owed to Mr. Poel, nearer to those of Shakespeare's time.

[1] When, in the time of Malone and Steevens, the question was debated whether Shakespeare's stage had scenery, it was argued that it must have had it, because otherwise the contrast between the words and the visible stage in the passage referred to would have been hopelessly ludicrous.

[2] ' Enter invisible' (a common stage-direction) means 'Enter in the dress which means to the audience that you are invisible.'

a torch and spoke of rain ; and the chaste stars were
shining for it outside Desdemona's chamber as the
awful figure entered and extinguished the lamp.
Consider how extraordinary is the fact I am about
to mention, and what a testimony it bears to the
imagination of the audience. In *Hamlet, Othello*,
and *Macbeth*, not one scene here and there but
actually the majority of the most impressive scenes
take place at night, and, to a reader, depend not
a little on the darkness for their effect. Yet the
Ghost-scenes, the play-scene, the sparing of the king
at prayer, that conversation of Hamlet with his
mother which is opened by the killing of Polonius
and interrupted by the appearance of the Ghost;
the murder of Duncan, the murder of Banquo, the
Banquet-scene, the Sleep-walking scene ; the whole
of the first Act of *Othello*, the scene of Cassio's
drunken revel and fight, and the whole of the terrible
last Act,—all of this was played in a theatre open to
the afternoon sun, and was written by a man who
knew that it was so to be played.   But he knew his
audience too.[1]

That audience had not only imagination, and the
power to sink its soul in the essence of drama.   It
had something else of scarcely less import for
Shakespeare, the love of poetry.   Ignorant, noisy,
malodorous, too fond of dances and songs and dirty
jokes, of soldiers and trumpets and cannon, the
groundling might be : but he liked poetry.   If he
had not liked it, he, with his brutal manners, would
have silenced it, and the Elizabethan drama could
never have been the thing it was.   The plays of
Shakespeare swarm with long speeches, almost all
of which are cut down or cut clean away for our
theatres.   They are never, of course, irrelevant;
sometimes they are indispensable to the full appre-

[1] Probably he never needed to think of the audience, but wrote what
pleased his own imagination, which, like theirs, was not only dramatic
but, in the best sense, theatrical

ciation of a character; but it is manifest that they were not written solely for a dramatic purpose, but also because the author and his audience loved poetry. A sign of this is the fact that they especially abound where, from the nature of the story, the dramatic structure is imperfect.[1] They abound in *Troilus and Cressida* and *Henry V.* more than in *Othello* or *Much Ado*. Remember, for a standard of size, that 'To be or not to be' is thirty-three lines in length, and then consider the following fact. *Henry V.* contains seventeen speeches longer than that soliloquy. Five of them are between forty and fifty lines long, two between fifty and sixty, and two exceed sixty. Yet if any play entirely by Shakespeare were open to the charge of being a 'drum and trumpet history' written to please the populace, it would be *Henry V.* Not only then the cultured section of the audience loved poetry; the whole audience loved it. How long would they have continued to relish this 'perpetual feast of nectared sweets' if their eyes had been feasted too? Or is it likely that, once habituated to spectacular stimulants, they would have welcomed 'the crystal clearness of the Muses' spring'?

1902.

---

[1] Their abundance in *Hamlet* results partly from the character of the hero. They helped, however, to make that play too long; and the omission of 'How all occasions' from the Folio doubtless means that the company cut this soliloquy (whether they did so in the author's life-time we cannot tell). It may be noticed that, where a play shows clear signs of revision by Shakespeare himself, we rarely find a disposition to shorten long poetical speeches.

[In

In some of these lectures[1]—for the duties and
pleasures that have fallen to me as Professor of
Poetry are now to end—I may have betrayed a
certain propensity to philosophise. But I should
ask pardon for this only if I believed it to intrude
where it has no place, in the imaginative perception
of poetry. Philosophy has long been at home in
this University ; in the remarkable development of
English philosophical thought during the last five-
and-thirty years Oxford has played a leading part ;
and I hope the time will never come when a son of
hers will need to apologise to his brethren for talking
philosophy. Besides, though I owe her gratitude
for many gifts, and most for the friendships she gave
me, her best intellectual gift was the conviction
that what imagination loved as poetry reason might
love as philosophy, and that in the end these are
two ways of saying the same thing. And, finally, I
hoped, by dwelling in these lectures (for instance,
with reference to the poets of Wordsworth's time)
on the connection of poetry with the wider life around
it, to correct an impression which my opening lecture
seems here and there to have left. Not that I can
withdraw or even modify the view put forward then.
So far as any single function of spiritual life can be
said to have an intrinsic value, poetry, it seems to
me, possesses it just as other functions do, and it is
in each case irreplaceable. And further, it seems to
me, poetry attains its own aim, and in doing so
makes its contribution to the whole, most surely and
fully when it seeks its own end without attempting

[1] As the order of the lectures has been changed for the purposes of
publication, I have been obliged to move these concluding sentences
from their original place at the end of the lecture on *The Long Poem
in the Age of Wordsworth.*

to reach those of co-ordinate functions, such as the attainment of philosophic truth or the furtherance of moral progress.   But then I believe this because I also believe that the unity of human nature in its diverse activities is so intimate and pervasive that no influence can affect any one of them alone, and that no one of them can operate or change without transmitting its influence to the rest.   If I may use the language of paradox I would say that the pursuit of poetry for its own sake is the pursuit both of truth and of goodness.   Devotion to it is devotion to ' the good cause of the world ' ; and wherever the imagination is satisfied, there, if we had a knowledge we have not, we should discover no idle fancy but the image of a truth.

PRINTED IN GREAT BRITAIN BY
MORRISON AND GIBB LTD., LONDON AND EDINBURGH